Mastering Linux - System Administration

A catalogue record for this book is available from the Hong Kong Public Libraries.

Published in Hong Kong by Samurai Media Limited.

Email: info@samuraimedia.org

ISBN 978-988-8406-17-3

Background Cover Image by https://www.flickr.com/people/webtreatsetc/

Table of Contents

List of Tables

Part I. process management

Table of Contents

Chapter 1. introduction to processes

1.1. terminology

1.1.1. process

A **process** is compiled source code that is currently running on the system.

1.1.2. PID

All processes have a **process id** or **PID**.

1.1.3. PPID

Every process has a parent process (with a **PPID**). The **child** process is often started by the **parent** process.

1.1.4. init

The **init** process always has process ID 1. The **init** process is started by the **kernel** itself so technically it does not have a parent process. **init** serves as a **foster parent** for **orphaned** processes.

1.1.5. kill

When a process stops running, the process dies, when you want a process to die, you **kill** it.

1.1.6. daemon

Processes that start at system startup and keep running forever are called **daemon** processes or **daemons**. These **daemons** never die.

1.1.7. zombie

When a process is killed, but it still shows up on the system, then the process is referred to as **zombie**. You cannot kill zombies, because they are already dead.

1.2. basic process management

1.2.1. $$ and $PPID

Some shell environment variables contain information about processes. The **$$** variable will hold your current **process ID**, and **$PPID** contains the **parent PID**. Actually **$$** is a shell parameter and not a variable, you cannot assign a value to it.

Below we use **echo** to display the values of **$$** and **$PPID**.

```
[paul@RHEL4b ~]$ echo $$ $PPID
4224 4223
```

1.2.2. pidof

You can find all process id's by name using the **pidof** command.

```
root@rhel53 ~# pidof mingetty
2819 2798 2797 2796 2795 2794
```

1.2.3. parent and child

Processes have a **parent-child** relationship. Every process has a parent process.

When starting a new **bash** you can use **echo** to verify that the **pid** from before is the **ppid** of the new shell. The **child** process from above is now the **parent** process.

```
[paul@RHEL4b ~]$ bash
[paul@RHEL4b ~]$ echo $$ $PPID
4812 4224
```

Typing **exit** will end the current process and brings us back to our original values for **$$** and **$PPID**.

```
[paul@RHEL4b ~]$ echo $$ $PPID
4812 4224
[paul@RHEL4b ~]$ exit
exit
[paul@RHEL4b ~]$ echo $$ $PPID
4224 4223
[paul@RHEL4b ~]$
```

1.2.4. fork and exec

A process starts another process in two phases. First the process creates a **fork** of itself, an identical copy. Then the forked process executes an **exec** to replace the forked process with the target child process.

```
[paul@RHEL4b ~]$ echo $$
4224
[paul@RHEL4b ~]$ bash
[paul@RHEL4b ~]$ echo $$ $PPID
5310 4224
[paul@RHEL4b ~]$
```

1.2.5. exec

With the **exec** command, you can execute a process without forking a new process. In the following screenshot a **Korn shell** (ksh) is started and is being replaced with a **bash shell** using the **exec** command. The **pid** of the **bash shell** is the same as the **pid** of the **Korn shell**. Exiting the child **bash shell** will get me back to the parent **bash**, not to the **Korn shell** (which does not exist anymore).

```
[paul@RHEL4b ~]$ echo $$
4224                                    # PID of bash
[paul@RHEL4b ~]$ ksh
$ echo $$ $PPID
5343 4224                               # PID of ksh and bash
$ exec bash
[paul@RHEL4b ~]$ echo $$ $PPID
5343 4224                               # PID of bash and bash
[paul@RHEL4b ~]$ exit
exit
[paul@RHEL4b ~]$ echo $$
4224
```

1.2.6. ps

One of the most common tools on Linux to look at processes is **ps**. The following screenshot shows the parent child relationship between three bash processes.

```
[paul@RHEL4b ~]$ echo $$ $PPID
4224 4223
[paul@RHEL4b ~]$ bash
[paul@RHEL4b ~]$ echo $$ $PPID
4866 4224
[paul@RHEL4b ~]$ bash
[paul@RHEL4b ~]$ echo $$ $PPID
4884 4866
[paul@RHEL4b ~]$ ps fx
  PID TTY      STAT   TIME COMMAND
 4223 ?        S      0:01 sshd: paul@pts/0
 4224 pts/0    Ss     0:00  \_ -bash
 4866 pts/0    S      0:00      \_ bash
 4884 pts/0    S      0:00          \_ bash
 4902 pts/0    R+     0:00              \_ ps fx
[paul@RHEL4b ~]$ exit
exit
[paul@RHEL4b ~]$ ps fx
  PID TTY      STAT   TIME COMMAND
 4223 ?        S      0:01 sshd: paul@pts/0
 4224 pts/0    Ss     0:00  \_ -bash
 4866 pts/0    S      0:00      \_ bash
 4903 pts/0    R+     0:00          \_ ps fx
[paul@RHEL4b ~]$ exit
exit
[paul@RHEL4b ~]$ ps fx
  PID TTY      STAT   TIME COMMAND
 4223 ?        S      0:01 sshd: paul@pts/0
 4224 pts/0    Ss     0:00  \_ -bash
 4904 pts/0    R+     0:00      \_ ps fx
[paul@RHEL4b ~]$
```

On Linux, **ps fax** is often used. On Solaris **ps -ef** (which also works on Linux) is common. Here is a partial output from **ps fax**.

```
[paul@RHEL4a ~]$ ps fax
PID TTY      STAT   TIME COMMAND
1 ?        S      0:00 init [5]

...

3713 ?        Ss     0:00 /usr/sbin/sshd
5042 ?        Ss     0:00  \_ sshd: paul [priv]
5044 ?        S      0:00      \_ sshd: paul@pts/1
5045 pts/1    Ss     0:00          \_ -bash
5077 pts/1    R+     0:00              \_ ps fax
```

1.2.7. pgrep

Similar to the **ps -C**, you can also use **pgrep** to search for a process by its command name.

```
[paul@RHEL5 ~]$ sleep 1000 &
[1] 32558
[paul@RHEL5 ~]$ pgrep sleep
32558
[paul@RHEL5 ~]$ ps -C sleep
  PID TTY          TIME CMD
32558 pts/3    00:00:00 sleep
```

You can also list the command name of the process with pgrep.

```
paul@laika:~$ pgrep -l sleep
9661 sleep
```

1.2.8. top

Another popular tool on Linux is **top**. The **top** tool can order processes according to **cpu usage** or other properties. You can also **kill** processes from within top. Press **h** inside **top** for help.

In case of trouble, top is often the first tool to fire up, since it also provides you memory and swap space information.

1.3. signalling processes

1.3.1. kill

The **kill** command will kill (or stop) a process. The screenshot shows how to use a standard **kill** to stop the process with **pid** 1942.

```
paul@ubuntu910:~$ kill 1942
paul@ubuntu910:~$
```

By using the **kill** we are sending a **signal** to the process.

1.3.2. list signals

Running processes can receive signals from each other or from the users. You can have a list of signals by typing **kill -l**, that is a letter **l**, not the number 1.

```
[paul@RHEL4a ~]$ kill -l
1) SIGHUP       2) SIGINT       3) SIGQUIT      4) SIGILL
5) SIGTRAP      6) SIGABRT      7) SIGBUS       8) SIGFPE
9) SIGKILL     10) SIGUSR1     11) SIGSEGV     12) SIGUSR2
13) SIGPIPE     14) SIGALRM     15) SIGTERM     17) SIGCHLD
18) SIGCONT     19) SIGSTOP     20) SIGTSTP     21) SIGTTIN
22) SIGTTOU     23) SIGURG      24) SIGXCPU     25) SIGXFSZ
26) SIGVTALRM   27) SIGPROF     28) SIGWINCH    29) SIGIO
30) SIGPWR      31) SIGSYS      34) SIGRTMIN    35) SIGRTMIN+1
36) SIGRTMIN+2  37) SIGRTMIN+3  38) SIGRTMIN+4  39) SIGRTMIN+5
40) SIGRTMIN+6  41) SIGRTMIN+7  42) SIGRTMIN+8  43) SIGRTMIN+9
44) SIGRTMIN+10 45) SIGRTMIN+11 46) SIGRTMIN+12 47) SIGRTMIN+13
48) SIGRTMIN+14 49) SIGRTMIN+15 50) SIGRTMAX-14 51) SIGRTMAX-13
52) SIGRTMAX-12 53) SIGRTMAX-11 54) SIGRTMAX-10 55) SIGRTMAX-9
56) SIGRTMAX-8  57) SIGRTMAX-7  58) SIGRTMAX-6  59) SIGRTMAX-5
60) SIGRTMAX-4  61) SIGRTMAX-3  62) SIGRTMAX-2  63) SIGRTMAX-1
64) SIGRTMAX
[paul@RHEL4a ~]$
```

1.3.3. kill -1 (SIGHUP)

It is common on Linux to use the first signal **SIGHUP** (or HUP or 1) to tell a process that it should re-read its configuration file. Thus, the **kill -1 1** command forces the **init** process (**init** always runs with **pid 1**) to re-read its configuration file.

```
root@deb503:~# kill -1 1
root@deb503:~#
```

It is up to the developer of the process to decide whether the process can do this running, or whether it needs to stop and start. It is up to the user to read the documentation of the program.

1.3.4. kill -15 (SIGTERM)

The **SIGTERM** signal is also called a **standard kill**. Whenever **kill** is executed without specifying the signal, a **kill -15** is assumed.

Both commands in the screenshot below are identical.

```
paul@ubuntu910:~$ kill 1942
paul@ubuntu910:~$ kill -15 1942
```

1.3.5. kill -9 (SIGKILL)

The **SIGKILL** is different from most other signals in that it is not being sent to the process, but to the **Linux kernel**. A **kill -9** is also called a **sure kill**. The **kernel** will shoot down the process. As a developer you have no means to intercept a **kill -9** signal.

```
root@rhel53 ~# kill -9 3342
```

1.3.6. SIGSTOP and SIGCONT

A running process can be **suspended** when it receives a **SIGSTOP** signal. This is the same as **kill -19** on Linux, but might have a different number in other Unix systems.

A **suspended** process does not use any **cpu cycles**, but it stays in memory and can be re-animated with a **SIGCONT** signal (**kill -18** on Linux).

Both signals will be used in the section about **background** processes.

1.3.7. pkill

You can use the **pkill** command to kill a process by its command name.

```
[paul@RHEL5 ~]$ sleep 1000 &
[1] 30203
[paul@RHEL5 ~]$ pkill sleep
[1]+  Terminated              sleep 1000
[paul@RHEL5 ~]$
```

1.3.8. killall

The **killall** command will send a **signal 15** to all processes with a certain name.

```
paul@rhel65:~$ sleep 8472 &
[1] 18780
paul@rhel65:~$ sleep 1201 &
[2] 18781
paul@rhel65:~$ jobs
[1]-  Running                 sleep 8472 &
[2]+  Running                 sleep 1201 &
paul@rhel65:~$ killall sleep
[1]-  Terminated              sleep 8472
[2]+  Terminated              sleep 1201
paul@rhel65:~$ jobs
paul@rhel65:~$
```

1.3.9. killall5

Its SysV counterpart **killall5** can by used when shutting down the system. This screenshot shows how Red Hat Enterprise Linux 5.3 uses **killall5** when halting the system.

```
root@rhel53 ~# grep killall /etc/init.d/halt
action $"Sending all processes the TERM signal..." /sbin/killall5 -15
action $"Sending all processes the KILL signal..."  /sbin/killall5 -9
```

1.3.10. top

Inside **top** the **k** key allows you to select a **signal** and **pid** to kill. Below is a partial screenshot of the line just below the summary in **top** after pressing **k**.

```
PID to kill: 1932

Kill PID 1932 with signal [15]: 9
```

1.4. practice : basic process management

1. Use **ps** to search for the **init** process by name.

2. What is the **process id** of the **init** process ?

3. Use the **who am i** command to determine your terminal name.

4. Using your terminal name from above, use **ps** to find all processes associated with your terminal.

5. What is the **process id** of your shell ?

6. What is the **parent process id** of your shell ?

7. Start two instances of the **sleep 3342** in background.

8. Locate the **process id** of all **sleep** commands.

9. Display only those two **sleep** processes in **top**. Then quit top.

10. Use a **standard kill** to kill one of the **sleep** processes.

11. Use one command to kill all **sleep** processes.

1.5. solution : basic process management

1. Use **ps** to search for the **init** process by name.

```
root@rhel53 ~# ps -C init
  PID TTY          TIME CMD
    1 ?        00:00:04 init
```

2. What is the **process id** of the **init** process ?

```
1
```

3. Use the **who am i** command to determine your terminal name.

```
root@rhel53 ~# who am i
paul     pts/0        2010-04-12 17:44 (192.168.1.38)
```

4. Using your terminal name from above, use **ps** to find all processes associated with your terminal.

```
oot@rhel53 ~# ps fax | grep pts/0
 2941 ?        S      0:00      \_ sshd: paul@pts/0
 2942 pts/0    Ss     0:00          \_ -bash
 2972 pts/0    S      0:00              \_ su -
 2973 pts/0    S      0:00                  \_ -bash
 3808 pts/0    R+     0:00                      \_ ps fax
 3809 pts/0    R+     0:00                      \_ grep pts/0
```

or also

```
root@rhel53 ~# ps -ef | grep pts/0
paul      2941  2939  0 17:44 ?        00:00:00 sshd: paul@pts/0
paul      2942  2941  0 17:44 pts/0    00:00:00 -bash
root      2972  2942  0 17:45 pts/0    00:00:00 su -
root      2973  2972  0 17:45 pts/0    00:00:00 -bash
root      3816  2973  0 21:25 pts/0    00:00:00 ps -ef
root      3817  2973  0 21:25 pts/0    00:00:00 grep pts/0
```

5. What is the **process id** of your shell ?

```
2973 in the screenshot above, probably different for you
```

echo $$ should display same number as the one you found

6. What is the **parent process id** of your shell ?

```
2972 in the screenshot above, probably different for you
```

in this example the PPID is from the **su -** command, but when inside gnome then for example gnome-terminal can be the parent process

7. Start two instances of the **sleep 3342** in background.

```
sleep 3342 &
sleep 3342 &
```

8. Locate the **process id** of all **sleep** commands.

```
pidof sleep
```

9. Display only those two **sleep** processes in **top**. Then quit top.

```
top -p pidx,pidy (replace pidx pidy with the actual numbers)
```

10. Use a **standard kill** to kill one of the **sleep** processes.

```
kill pidx
```

11. Use one command to kill all **sleep** processes.

```
pkill sleep
```

Chapter 2. process priorities

2.1. priority and nice values

2.1.1. introduction

All processes have a **priority** and a **nice** value. Higher priority processes will get more **cpu time** than lower priority processes. You can influence this with the **nice** and **renice** commands.

2.1.2. pipes (mkfifo)

Processes can communicate with each other via **pipes**. These **pipes** can be created with the **mkfifo** command.

The screenshots shows the creation of four distinct pipes (in a new directory).

```
paul@ubuntu910:~$ mkdir procs
paul@ubuntu910:~$ cd procs/
paul@ubuntu910:~/procs$ mkfifo pipe33a pipe33b pipe42a pipe42b
paul@ubuntu910:~/procs$ ls -l
total 0
prw-r--r-- 1 paul paul 0 2010-04-12 13:21 pipe33a
prw-r--r-- 1 paul paul 0 2010-04-12 13:21 pipe33b
prw-r--r-- 1 paul paul 0 2010-04-12 13:21 pipe42a
prw-r--r-- 1 paul paul 0 2010-04-12 13:21 pipe42b
paul@ubuntu910:~/procs$
```

2.1.3. some fun with cat

To demonstrate the use of the **top** and **renice** commands we will make the **cat** command use the previously created **pipes** to generate a full load on the **cpu**.

The **cat** is copied with a distinct name to the current directory. (This enables us to easily recognize the processes within **top**. You could do the same exercise without copying the cat command, but using different users. Or you could just look at the **pid** of each process.)

```
paul@ubuntu910:~/procs$ cp /bin/cat proj33
paul@ubuntu910:~/procs$ cp /bin/cat proj42
paul@ubuntu910:~/procs$ echo -n x | ./proj33 - pipe33a > pipe33b &
[1] 1670
paul@ubuntu910:~/procs$ ./proj33 <pipe33b >pipe33a &
[2] 1671
paul@ubuntu910:~/procs$ echo -n z | ./proj42 - pipe42a > pipe42b &
[3] 1673
paul@ubuntu910:~/procs$ ./proj42 <pipe42b >pipe42a &
[4] 1674
```

The commands you see above will create two **proj33** processes that use **cat** to bounce the x character between **pipe33a** and **pipe33b**. And ditto for the z character and **proj42**.

2.1.4. top

Just running **top** without options or arguments will display all processes and an overview of innformation. The top of the **top** screen might look something like this.

```
top - 13:59:29 up 48 min,  4 users,  load average: 1.06, 0.25, 0.14
Tasks: 139 total,   3 running, 136 sleeping,   0 stopped,   0 zombie
Cpu(s):  0.3%us, 99.7%sy, 0.0%ni, 0.0%id, 0.0%wa, 0.0%hi, 0.0%si, 0.0%st
Mem:    509352k total,   460040k used,    49312k free,    66752k buffers
Swap:   746980k total,         0k used,   746980k free,   247324k cached
```

Notice the **cpu idle time (0.0%id)** is zero. This is because our **cat** processes are consuming the whole **cpu**. Results can vary on systems with four or more **cpu cores**.

2.1.5. top -p

The **top -p 1670,1671,1673,1674** screenshot below shows four processes, all of then using approximately 25 percent of the **cpu**.

```
paul@ubuntu910:~$ top -p 1670,1671,1673,1674

  PID USER      PR  NI  VIRT  RES  SHR S %CPU %MEM    TIME+  COMMAND
 1674 paul      20   0  2972  616  524 S 26.6  0.1   0:11.92 proj42
 1670 paul      20   0  2972  616  524 R 25.0  0.1   0:23.16 proj33
 1671 paul      20   0  2972  616  524 S 24.6  0.1   0:23.07 proj33
 1673 paul      20   0  2972  620  524 R 23.0  0.1   0:11.48 proj42
```

All four processes have an equal **priority (PR)**, and are battling for **cpu time**. On some systems the **Linux kernel** might attribute slightly varying **priority values**, but the result will still be four processes fighting for **cpu time**.

2.1.6. renice

Since the processes are already running, we need to use the **renice** command to change their **nice value (NI)**.

The screenshot shows how to use **renice** on both the **proj33** processes.

```
paul@ubuntu910:~$ renice +8 1670
1670: old priority 0, new priority 8
paul@ubuntu910:~$ renice +8 1671
1671: old priority 0, new priority 8
```

Normal users can attribute a **nice value** from zero to 20 to processes they own. Only the **root** user can use negative nice values. Be very careful with negative nice values, since they can make it impossible to use the keyboard or ssh to a system.

2.1.7. impact of nice values

The impact of a nice value on running processes can vary. The screenshot below shows the result of our **renice +8** command. Look at the **%CPU** values.

```
  PID USER      PR  NI  VIRT  RES  SHR S %CPU %MEM    TIME+  COMMAND
 1674 paul      20   0  2972  616  524 S 46.6  0.1   0:22.37 proj42
 1673 paul      20   0  2972  620  524 R 42.6  0.1   0:21.65 proj42
 1671 paul      28   8  2972  616  524 S  5.7  0.1   0:29.65 proj33
 1670 paul      28   8  2972  616  524 R  4.7  0.1   0:29.82 proj33
```

Important to remember is to always make less important processes nice to more important processes. Using **negative nice values** can have a severe impact on a system's usability.

2.1.8. nice

The **nice** works identical to the **renice** but it is used when starting a command.

The screenshot shows how to start a script with a **nice** value of five.

```
paul@ubuntu910:~$ nice -5 ./backup.sh
```

2.2. practice : process priorities

1. Create a new directory and create six **pipes** in that directory.

2. Bounce a character between two **pipes**.

3. Use **top** and **ps** to display information (pid, ppid, priority, nice value, ...) about these two cat processes.

4. Bounce another character between two other pipes, but this time start the commands **nice**. Verify that all **cat** processes are battling for the cpu. (Feel free to fire up two more cats with the remaining pipes).

5. Use **ps** to verify that the two new **cat** processes have a **nice** value. Use the -o and -C options of **ps** for this.

6. Use **renice** te increase the nice value from 10 to 15. Notice the difference with the usual commands.

2.3. solution : process priorities

1. Create a new directory and create six **pipes** in that directory.

```
[paul@rhel53 ~]$ mkdir pipes ; cd pipes
[paul@rhel53 pipes]$ mkfifo p1 p2 p3 p4 p5 p6
[paul@rhel53 pipes]$ ls -l
total 0
prw-rw-r-- 1 paul paul 0 Apr 12 22:15 p1
prw-rw-r-- 1 paul paul 0 Apr 12 22:15 p2
prw-rw-r-- 1 paul paul 0 Apr 12 22:15 p3
prw-rw-r-- 1 paul paul 0 Apr 12 22:15 p4
prw-rw-r-- 1 paul paul 0 Apr 12 22:15 p5
prw-rw-r-- 1 paul paul 0 Apr 12 22:15 p6
```

2. Bounce a character between two **pipes**.

```
[paul@rhel53 pipes]$ echo -n x | cat - p1 > p2 &
[1] 4013
[paul@rhel53 pipes]$ cat <p2 >p1 &
[2] 4016
```

3. Use **top** and **ps** to display information (pid, ppid, priority, nice value, ...) about these two cat processes.

```
top (probably the top two lines)

[paul@rhel53 pipes]$ ps -C cat
  PID TTY          TIME CMD
 4013 pts/0    00:03:38 cat
 4016 pts/0    00:01:07 cat

[paul@rhel53 pipes]$ ps fax | grep cat
 4013 pts/0    R      4:00  |           \_ cat - p1
 4016 pts/0    S      1:13  |           \_ cat
 4044 pts/0    S+     0:00  |           \_ grep cat
```

4. Bounce another character between two other pipes, but this time start the commands **nice**. Verify that all **cat** processes are battling for the cpu. (Feel free to fire up two more cats with the remaining pipes).

```
echo -n y | nice cat - p3 > p4 &
nice cat <p4 >p3 &
```

5. Use **ps** to verify that the two new **cat** processes have a **nice** value. Use the -o and -C options of **ps** for this.

```
[paul@rhel53 pipes]$ ps -C cat -o pid,ppid,pri,ni,comm
  PID  PPID PRI  NI COMMAND
 4013  3947  14   0 cat
 4016  3947  21   0 cat
 4025  3947  13  10 cat
 4026  3947  13  10 cat
```

6. Use **renice** te increase the nice value from 10 to 15. Notice the difference with the usual commands.

```
[paul@rhel53 pipes]$ renice +15 4025
4025: old priority 10, new priority 15
[paul@rhel53 pipes]$ renice +15 4026
```

```
4026: old priority 10, new priority 15

[paul@rhel53 pipes]$ ps -C cat -o pid,ppid,pri,ni,comm
  PID  PPID PRI  NI COMMAND
 4013  3947  14   0 cat
 4016  3947  21   0 cat
 4025  3947   9  15 cat
 4026  3947   8  15 cat
```

Chapter 3. background jobs

3.1. background processes

3.1.1. jobs

Stuff that runs in background of your current shell can be displayed with the **jobs** command. By default you will not have any **jobs** running in background.

```
root@rhel53 ~# jobs
root@rhel53 ~#
```

This **jobs** command will be used several times in this section.

3.1.2. control-Z

Some processes can be **suspended** with the **Ctrl-Z** key combination. This sends a **SIGSTOP** signal to the **Linux kernel**, effectively freezing the operation of the process.

When doing this in **vi(m)**, then **vi(m)** goes to the background. The background **vi(m)** can be seen with the **jobs** command.

```
[paul@RHEL4a ~]$ vi procdemo.txt

[5]+  Stopped                   vim procdemo.txt
[paul@RHEL4a ~]$ jobs
[5]+  Stopped                   vim procdemo.txt
```

3.1.3. & ampersand

Processes that are started in background using the **&** character at the end of the command line are also visible with the **jobs** command.

```
[paul@RHEL4a ~]$ find / > allfiles.txt 2> /dev/null &
[6] 5230
[paul@RHEL4a ~]$ jobs
[5]+  Stopped                   vim procdemo.txt
[6]-  Running                   find / >allfiles.txt 2>/dev/null &
[paul@RHEL4a ~]$
```

3.1.4. jobs -p

An interesting option is **jobs -p** to see the **process id** of background processes.

```
[paul@RHEL4b ~]$ sleep 500 &
[1] 4902
[paul@RHEL4b ~]$ sleep 400 &
[2] 4903
[paul@RHEL4b ~]$ jobs -p
4902
4903
[paul@RHEL4b ~]$ ps `jobs -p`
```

```
  PID TTY         STAT   TIME COMMAND
 4902 pts/0       S      0:00 sleep 500
 4903 pts/0       S      0:00 sleep 400
[paul@RHEL4b ~]$
```

3.1.5. fg

Running the **fg** command will bring a background job to the foreground. The number of the background job to bring forward is the parameter of **fg**.

```
[paul@RHEL5 ~]$ jobs
[1]   Running                 sleep 1000 &
[2]-  Running                 sleep 1000 &
[3]+  Running                 sleep 2000 &
[paul@RHEL5 ~]$ fg 3
sleep 2000
```

3.1.6. bg

Jobs that are **suspended** in background can be started in background with **bg**. The **bg** will send a **SIGCONT** signal.

Below an example of the sleep command (suspended with **Ctrl-Z**) being reactivated in background with **bg**.

```
[paul@RHEL5 ~]$ jobs
[paul@RHEL5 ~]$ sleep 5000 &
[1] 6702
[paul@RHEL5 ~]$ sleep 3000

[2]+  Stopped                 sleep 3000
[paul@RHEL5 ~]$ jobs
[1]-  Running                 sleep 5000 &
[2]+  Stopped                 sleep 3000
[paul@RHEL5 ~]$ bg 2
[2]+ sleep 3000 &
[paul@RHEL5 ~]$ jobs
[1]-  Running                 sleep 5000 &
[2]+  Running                 sleep 3000 &
[paul@RHEL5 ~]$
```

3.2. practice : background processes

1. Use the **jobs** command to verify whether you have any processes running in background.

2. Use **vi** to create a little text file. Suspend **vi** in background.

3. Verify with **jobs** that **vi** is suspended in background.

4. Start **find / > allfiles.txt 2>/dev/null** in foreground. Suspend it in background before it finishes.

5. Start two long **sleep** processes in background.

6. Display all **jobs** in background.

7. Use the **kill** command to suspend the last **sleep** process.

8. Continue the **find** process in background (make sure it runs again).

9. Put one of the **sleep** commands back in foreground.

10. (if time permits, a general review question...) Explain in detail where the numbers come from in the next screenshot. When are the variables replaced by their value ? By which shell ?

```
[paul@RHEL4b ~]$ echo $$ $PPID
4224 4223
[paul@RHEL4b ~]$ bash -c "echo $$ $PPID"
4224 4223
[paul@RHEL4b ~]$ bash -c 'echo $$ $PPID'
5059 4224
[paul@RHEL4b ~]$ bash -c `echo $$ $PPID`
4223: 4224: command not found
```

3.3. solution : background processes

1. Use the **jobs** command to verify whether you have any processes running in background.

```
jobs (maybe the catfun is still running?)
```

2. Use **vi** to create a little text file. Suspend **vi** in background.

```
vi text.txt
(inside vi press ctrl-z)
```

3. Verify with **jobs** that **vi** is suspended in background.

```
[paul@rhel53 ~]$ jobs
[1]+  Stopped                 vim text.txt
```

4. Start **find / > allfiles.txt 2>/dev/null** in foreground. Suspend it in background before it finishes.

```
[paul@rhel53 ~]$ find / > allfiles.txt 2>/dev/null
   (press ctrl-z)
[2]+  Stopped                 find / > allfiles.txt 2> /dev/null
```

5. Start two long **sleep** processes in background.

```
sleep 4000 & ; sleep 5000 &
```

6. Display all **jobs** in background.

```
[paul@rhel53 ~]$ jobs
[1]-  Stopped                 vim text.txt
[2]+  Stopped                 find / > allfiles.txt 2> /dev/null
[3]   Running                 sleep 4000 &
[4]   Running                 sleep 5000 &
```

7. Use the **kill** command to suspend the last **sleep** process.

```
[paul@rhel53 ~]$ kill -SIGSTOP 4519
[paul@rhel53 ~]$ jobs
[1]   Stopped                 vim text.txt
[2]-  Stopped                 find / > allfiles.txt 2> /dev/null
[3]   Running                 sleep 4000 &
[4]+  Stopped                 sleep 5000
```

8. Continue the **find** process in background (make sure it runs again).

```
bg 2 (verify the job-id in your jobs list)
```

9. Put one of the **sleep** commands back in foreground.

```
fg 3 (again verify your job-id)
```

10. (if time permits, a general review question...) Explain in detail where the numbers come from in the next screenshot. When are the variables replaced by their value ? By which shell ?

```
[paul@RHEL4b ~]$ echo $$ $PPID
4224 4223
[paul@RHEL4b ~]$ bash -c "echo $$ $PPID"
```

```
4224 4223
[paul@RHEL4b ~]$ bash -c 'echo $$ $PPID'
5059 4224
[paul@RHEL4b ~]$ bash -c `echo $$ $PPID`
4223: 4224: command not found
```

The current bash shell will replace the $$ and $PPID while scanning the line, and before executing the echo command.

```
[paul@RHEL4b ~]$ echo $$ $PPID
4224 4223
```

The variables are now double quoted, but the current bash shell will replace $$ and $PPID while scanning the line, and before executing the bach -c command.

```
[paul@RHEL4b ~]$ bash -c "echo $$ $PPID"
4224 4223
```

The variables are now single quoted. The current bash shell will **not** replace the $$ and the $PPID. The bash -c command will be executed before the variables replaced with their value. This latter bash is the one replacing the $$ and $PPID with their value.

```
[paul@RHEL4b ~]$ bash -c 'echo $$ $PPID'
5059 4224
```

With backticks the shell will still replace both variable before the embedded echo is executed. The result of this echo is the two process id's. These are given as commands to bash -c. But two numbers are not commands!

```
[paul@RHEL4b ~]$ bash -c `echo $$ $PPID`
4223: 4224: command not found
```

Part II. disk management

Table of Contents

Chapter 4. disk devices

This chapter teaches you how to locate and recognise **hard disk devices**. This prepares you for the next chapter, where we put **partitions** on these devices.

4.1. terminology

4.1.1. platter, head, track, cylinder, sector

Data is commonly stored on magnetic or optical **disk platters**. The platters are rotated (at high speeds). Data is read by **heads**, which are very close to the surface of the platter, without touching it! The heads are mounted on an arm (sometimes called a comb or a fork).

Data is written in concentric circles called **tracks**. Track zero is (usually) on the outside. The time it takes to position the head over a certain track is called the **seek time**. Often the platters are stacked on top of each other, hence the set of tracks accessible at a certain position of the comb forms a **cylinder**. Tracks are divided into 512 byte **sectors**, with more unused space (**gap**) between the sectors on the outside of the platter.

When you break down the advertised **access time** of a hard drive, you will notice that most of that time is taken by movement of the heads (about 65%) and **rotational latency** (about 30%).

4.1.2. ide or scsi

Actually, the title should be **ata** or **scsi**, since ide is an ata compatible device. Most desktops use **ata devices**, most servers use **scsi**.

4.1.3. ata

An **ata controller** allows two devices per bus, one **master** and one **slave**. Unless your controller and devices support **cable select**, you have to set this manually with jumpers.

With the introduction of **sata** (serial ata), the original ata was renamed to **parallel ata**. Optical drives often use **atapi**, which is an ATA interface using the SCSI communication protocol.

4.1.4. scsi

A **scsi controller** allows more than two devices. When using **SCSI (small computer system interface)**, each device gets a unique **scsi id**. The **scsi controller** also needs a **scsi id**, do not use this id for a scsi-attached device.

Older 8-bit SCSI is now called **narrow**, whereas 16-bit is **wide**. When the bus speeds was doubled to 10Mhz, this was known as **fast SCSI**. Doubling to 20Mhz made it **ultra SCSI**. Take a look at http://en.wikipedia.org/wiki/SCSI for more SCSI standards.

4.1.5. block device

Random access hard disk devices have an abstraction layer called **block device** to enable formatting in fixed-size (usually 512 bytes) blocks. Blocks can be accessed independent of access to other blocks.

```
[root@centos65 ~]# lsblk
NAME                           MAJ:MIN RM   SIZE RO TYPE MOUNTPOINT
sda                              8:0    0    40G  0 disk
--sda1                           8:1    0   500M  0 part /boot
--sda2                           8:2    0 39.5G   0 part
  --VolGroup-lv_root (dm-0) 253:0    0 38.6G   0 lvm  /
  --VolGroup-lv_swap (dm-1) 253:1    0   928M  0 lvm  [SWAP]
sdb                              8:16   0    72G  0 disk
sdc                              8:32   0   144G  0 disk
```

A block device has the letter b to denote the file type in the output of **ls -l**.

```
[root@centos65 ~]# ls -l /dev/sd*
brw-rw----. 1 root disk 8,  0 Apr 19 10:12 /dev/sda
brw-rw----. 1 root disk 8,  1 Apr 19 10:12 /dev/sda1
brw-rw----. 1 root disk 8,  2 Apr 19 10:12 /dev/sda2
brw-rw----. 1 root disk 8, 16 Apr 19 10:12 /dev/sdb
brw-rw----. 1 root disk 8, 32 Apr 19 10:12 /dev/sdc
```

Note that a **character device** is a constant stream of characters, being denoted by a c in **ls -l**. Note also that the **ISO 9660** standard for cdrom uses a **2048 byte** block size.

Old hard disks (and floppy disks) use **cylinder-head-sector** addressing to access a sector on the disk. Most current disks use **LBA (Logical Block Addressing)**.

4.1.6. solid state drive

A **solid state drive** or **ssd** is a block device without moving parts. It is comparable to **flash memory**. An **ssd** is more expensive than a hard disk, but it typically has a much faster access time.

In this book we will use the following pictograms for **spindle disks** (in brown) and **solid state disks** (in blue).

4.2. device naming

4.2.1. ata (ide) device naming

All **ata** drives on your system will start with **/dev/hd** followed by a unit letter. The master hdd on the first **ata controller** is /dev/hda, the slave is /dev/hdb. For the second controller, the names of the devices are /dev/hdc and /dev/hdd.

Table 4.1. ide device naming

controller	connection	device name
ide0	master	/dev/hda
	slave	/dev/hdb
ide1	master	/dev/hdc
	slave	/dev/hdd

It is possible to have only **/dev/hda** and **/dev/hdd**. The first one is a single ata hard disk, the second one is the cdrom (by default configured as slave).

4.2.2. scsi device naming

scsi drives follow a similar scheme, but all start with **/dev/sd**. When you run out of letters (after /dev/sdz), you can continue with /dev/sdaa and /dev/sdab and so on. (We will see later on that **lvm** volumes are commonly seen as /dev/md0, /dev/md1 etc.)

Below a **sample** of how scsi devices on a Linux can be named. Adding a scsi disk or raid controller with a lower scsi address will change the naming scheme (shifting the higher scsi addresses one letter further in the alphabet).

Table 4.2. scsi device naming

device	scsi id	device name
disk 0	0	/dev/sda
disk 1	1	/dev/sdb
raid controller 0	5	/dev/sdc
raid controller 1	6	/dev/sdd

A modern Linux system will use **/dev/sd*** for scsi and sata devices, and also for sd-cards, usb-sticks, (legacy) ATA/IDE devices and solid state drives.

4.3. discovering disk devices

4.3.1. fdisk

You can start by using **/sbin/fdisk** to find out what kind of disks are seen by the kernel. Below the result on old Debian desktop, with two **ata-ide disks** present.

```
root@barry:~# fdisk -l | grep Disk
Disk /dev/hda: 60.0 GB, 60022480896 bytes
Disk /dev/hdb: 81.9 GB, 81964302336 bytes
```

And here an example of **sata and scsi disks** on a server with CentOS. Remember that **sata** disks are also presented to you with the **scsi** /dev/sd* notation.

```
[root@centos65 ~]# fdisk -l | grep 'Disk /dev/sd'
Disk /dev/sda: 42.9 GB, 42949672960 bytes
Disk /dev/sdb: 77.3 GB, 77309411328 bytes
Disk /dev/sdc: 154.6 GB, 154618822656 bytes
Disk /dev/sdd: 154.6 GB, 154618822656 bytes
```

Here is an overview of disks on a RHEL4u3 server with two real 72GB **scsi disks**. This server is attached to a **NAS** with four **NAS disks** of half a terabyte. On the NAS disks, four LVM (/dev/mdx) software RAID devices are configured.

```
[root@tsvtl1 ~]# fdisk -l | grep Disk
Disk /dev/sda: 73.4 GB, 73407488000 bytes
Disk /dev/sdb: 73.4 GB, 73407488000 bytes
Disk /dev/sdc: 499.0 GB, 499036192768 bytes
Disk /dev/sdd: 499.0 GB, 499036192768 bytes
Disk /dev/sde: 499.0 GB, 499036192768 bytes
Disk /dev/sdf: 499.0 GB, 499036192768 bytes
Disk /dev/md0: 271 MB, 271319040 bytes
Disk /dev/md2: 21.4 GB, 21476081664 bytes
Disk /dev/md3: 21.4 GB, 21467889664 bytes
Disk /dev/md1: 21.4 GB, 21476081664 bytes
```

You can also use **fdisk** to obtain information about one specific hard disk device.

```
[root@centos65 ~]# fdisk -l /dev/sdc

Disk /dev/sdc: 154.6 GB, 154618822656 bytes
255 heads, 63 sectors/track, 18798 cylinders
Units = cylinders of 16065 * 512 = 8225280 bytes
Sector size (logical/physical): 512 bytes / 512 bytes
I/O size (minimum/optimal): 512 bytes / 512 bytes
Disk identifier: 0x00000000
```

Later we will use fdisk to do dangerous stuff like creating and deleting partitions.

4.3.2. dmesg

Kernel boot messages can be seen after boot with **dmesg**. Since hard disk devices are detected by the kernel during boot, you can also use dmesg to find information about disk devices.

```
[root@centos65 ~]# dmesg | grep 'sd[a-z]' | head
sd 0:0:0:0: [sda] 83886080 512-byte logical blocks: (42.9 GB/40.0 GiB)
sd 0:0:0:0: [sda] Write Protect is off
sd 0:0:0:0: [sda] Mode Sense: 00 3a 00 00
sd 0:0:0:0: [sda] Write cache: enabled, read cache: enabled, doesn't support \
DPO or FUA
sda: sda1 sda2
sd 0:0:0:0: [sda] Attached SCSI disk
sd 3:0:0:0: [sdb] 150994944 512-byte logical blocks: (77.3 GB/72.0 GiB)
sd 3:0:0:0: [sdb] Write Protect is off
sd 3:0:0:0: [sdb] Mode Sense: 00 3a 00 00
sd 3:0:0:0: [sdb] Write cache: enabled, read cache: enabled, doesn't support \
DPO or FUA
```

Here is another example of **dmesg** on a computer with a 200GB ata disk.

```
paul@barry:~$ dmesg | grep -i "ata disk"
[    2.624149] hda: ST360021A, ATA DISK drive
[    2.904150] hdb: Maxtor 6Y080L0, ATA DISK drive
[    3.472148] hdd: WDC WD2000BB-98DWA0, ATA DISK drive
```

Third and last example of **dmesg** running on RHEL5.3.

```
root@rhel53 ~# dmesg | grep -i "scsi disk"
sd 0:0:2:0: Attached scsi disk sda
sd 0:0:3:0: Attached scsi disk sdb
sd 0:0:6:0: Attached scsi disk sdc
```

4.3.3. /sbin/lshw

The **lshw** tool will **list hardware**. With the right options **lshw** can show a lot of information about disks (and partitions).

Below a truncated screenshot on Debian 6:

```
root@debian6~# lshw -class volume | grep -A1 -B2 scsi
       description: Linux raid autodetect partition
       physical id: 1
       bus info: scsi@1:0.0.0,1
       logical name: /dev/sdb1
--
       description: Linux raid autodetect partition
       physical id: 1
       bus info: scsi@2:0.0.0,1
       logical name: /dev/sdc1
--
       description: Linux raid autodetect partition
       physical id: 1
       bus info: scsi@3:0.0.0,1
       logical name: /dev/sdd1
--
       description: Linux raid autodetect partition
       physical id: 1
       bus info: scsi@4:0.0.0,1
       logical name: /dev/sde1
--
       vendor: Linux
       physical id: 1
       bus info: scsi@0:0.0.0,1
       logical name: /dev/sda1
--
       vendor: Linux
       physical id: 2
       bus info: scsi@0:0.0.0,2
       logical name: /dev/sda2
--
       description: Extended partition
       physical id: 3
       bus info: scsi@0:0.0.0,3
       logical name: /dev/sda3
```

Redhat and CentOS do not have this tool (unless you add a repository).

4.3.4. /sbin/lsscsi

The **lsscsi** command provides a nice readable output of all scsi (and scsi emulated devices). This first screenshot shows **lsscsi** on a SPARC system.

```
root@shaka:~# lsscsi
[0:0:0:0]     disk    Adaptec  RAID5             V1.0  /dev/sda
[1:0:0:0]     disk    SEAGATE  ST336605FSUN36G   0438  /dev/sdb
root@shaka:~#
```

Below a screenshot of **lsscsi** on a QNAP NAS (which has four 750GB disks and boots from a usb stick).

```
lroot@debian6~# lsscsi
[0:0:0:0]     disk    SanDisk  Cruzer Edge       1.19  /dev/sda
[1:0:0:0]     disk    ATA      ST3750330AS       SD04  /dev/sdb
[2:0:0:0]     disk    ATA      ST3750330AS       SD04  /dev/sdc
[3:0:0:0]     disk    ATA      ST3750330AS       SD04  /dev/sdd
[4:0:0:0]     disk    ATA      ST3750330AS       SD04  /dev/sde
```

This screenshot shows the classic output of **lsscsi**.

```
root@debian6~# lsscsi -c
Attached devices:
Host: scsi0 Channel: 00 Target: 00 Lun: 00
  Vendor: SanDisk  Model: Cruzer Edge       Rev: 1.19
  Type:    Direct-Access                    ANSI SCSI revision: 02
Host: scsi1 Channel: 00 Target: 00 Lun: 00
  Vendor: ATA      Model: ST3750330AS       Rev: SD04
  Type:    Direct-Access                    ANSI SCSI revision: 05
Host: scsi2 Channel: 00 Target: 00 Lun: 00
  Vendor: ATA      Model: ST3750330AS       Rev: SD04
  Type:    Direct-Access                    ANSI SCSI revision: 05
Host: scsi3 Channel: 00 Target: 00 Lun: 00
  Vendor: ATA      Model: ST3750330AS       Rev: SD04
  Type:    Direct-Access                    ANSI SCSI revision: 05
Host: scsi4 Channel: 00 Target: 00 Lun: 00
  Vendor: ATA      Model: ST3750330AS       Rev: SD04
  Type:    Direct-Access                    ANSI SCSI revision: 05
```

4.3.5. /proc/scsi/scsi

Another way to locate **scsi** (or sd) devices is via **/proc/scsi/scsi**.

This screenshot is from a **sparc** computer with adaptec RAID5.

```
root@shaka:~# cat /proc/scsi/scsi
Attached devices:
Host: scsi0 Channel: 00 Id: 00 Lun: 00
  Vendor: Adaptec  Model: RAID5            Rev: V1.0
  Type:   Direct-Access                    ANSI SCSI revision: 02
Host: scsi1 Channel: 00 Id: 00 Lun: 00
  Vendor: SEAGATE  Model: ST336605FSUN36G  Rev: 0438
  Type:   Direct-Access                    ANSI SCSI revision: 03
root@shaka:~#
```

Here we run **cat /proc/scsi/scsi** on the QNAP from above (with Debian Linux).

```
root@debian6~# cat /proc/scsi/scsi
Attached devices:
Host: scsi0 Channel: 00 Id: 00 Lun: 00
  Vendor: SanDisk  Model: Cruzer Edge      Rev: 1.19
  Type:   Direct-Access                    ANSI  SCSI revision: 02
Host: scsi1 Channel: 00 Id: 00 Lun: 00
  Vendor: ATA      Model: ST3750330AS      Rev: SD04
  Type:   Direct-Access                    ANSI  SCSI revision: 05
Host: scsi2 Channel: 00 Id: 00 Lun: 00
  Vendor: ATA      Model: ST3750330AS      Rev: SD04
  Type:   Direct-Access                    ANSI  SCSI revision: 05
Host: scsi3 Channel: 00 Id: 00 Lun: 00
  Vendor: ATA      Model: ST3750330AS      Rev: SD04
  Type:   Direct-Access                    ANSI  SCSI revision: 05
Host: scsi4 Channel: 00 Id: 00 Lun: 00
  Vendor: ATA      Model: ST3750330AS      Rev: SD04
  Type:   Direct-Access                    ANSI  SCSI revision: 05
```

Note that some recent versions of Debian have this disabled in the kernel. You can enable it (after a kernel compile) using this entry:

```
# CONFIG_SCSI_PROC_FS is not set
```

Redhat and CentOS have this by default (if there are scsi devices present).

```
[root@centos65 ~]# cat /proc/scsi/scsi
Attached devices:
Host: scsi0 Channel: 00 Id: 00 Lun: 00
  Vendor: ATA      Model: VBOX HARDDISK    Rev: 1.0
  Type:   Direct-Access                    ANSI  SCSI revision: 05
Host: scsi3 Channel: 00 Id: 00 Lun: 00
  Vendor: ATA      Model: VBOX HARDDISK    Rev: 1.0
  Type:   Direct-Access                    ANSI  SCSI revision: 05
Host: scsi4 Channel: 00 Id: 00 Lun: 00
  Vendor: ATA      Model: VBOX HARDDISK    Rev: 1.0
  Type:   Direct-Access                    ANSI  SCSI revision: 05
```

4.4. erasing a hard disk

Before selling your old hard disk on the internet, it may be a good idea to erase it. By simply repartitioning, or by using the Microsoft Windows format utility, or even after an **mkfs** command, some people will still be able to read most of the data on the disk.

```
root@debian6~# aptitude search foremost autopsy sleuthkit | tr -s ' '
p autopsy - graphical interface to SleuthKit
p foremost - Forensics application to recover data
p sleuthkit - collection of tools for forensics analysis
```

Although technically the **/sbin/badblocks** tool is meant to look for bad blocks, you can use it to completely erase all data from a disk. Since this is really writing to every sector of the disk, it can take a long time!

```
root@RHELv4u2:~# badblocks -ws /dev/sdb
Testing with pattern 0xaa: done
Reading and comparing: done
Testing with pattern 0x55: done
Reading and comparing: done
Testing with pattern 0xff: done
Reading and comparing: done
Testing with pattern 0x00: done
Reading and comparing: done
```

The previous screenshot overwrites every sector of the disk **four times**. Erasing **once** with a tool like **dd** is enough to destroy all data.

Warning, this screenshot shows how to permanently destroy all data on a block device.

```
[root@rhel65 ~]# dd if=/dev/zero of=/dev/sdb
```

4.5. advanced hard disk settings

Tweaking of hard disk settings (dma, gap, ...) are not covered in this course. Several tools exists, **hdparm** and **sdparm** are two of them.

hdparm can be used to display or set information and parameters about an ATA (or SATA) hard disk device. The -i and -I options will give you even more information about the physical properties of the device.

```
root@laika:~# hdparm /dev/sdb

/dev/sdb:
 IO_support    =  0 (default 16-bit)
 readonly      =  0 (off)
 readahead     = 256 (on)
 geometry      = 12161/255/63, sectors = 195371568, start = 0
```

Below **hdparm** info about a 200GB IDE disk.

```
root@barry:~# hdparm /dev/hdd

/dev/hdd:
 multcount     =  0 (off)
 IO_support    =  0 (default)
 unmaskirq     =  0 (off)
 using_dma     =  1 (on)
 keepsettings  =  0 (off)
 readonly      =  0 (off)
 readahead     = 256 (on)
 geometry      = 24321/255/63, sectors = 390721968, start = 0
```

Here a screenshot of **sdparm** on Ubuntu 10.10.

```
root@ubu1010:~# aptitude install sdparm
...
root@ubu1010:~# sdparm /dev/sda | head -1
    /dev/sda: ATA        FUJITSU MJA2160B  0081
root@ubu1010:~# man sdparm
```

Use **hdparm** and **sdparm** with care.

4.6. practice: hard disk devices

About this lab: To practice working with hard disks, you will need some hard disks. When there are no physical hard disk available, you can use virtual disks in **vmware** or **VirtualBox**. The teacher will help you in attaching a couple of ATA and/or SCSI disks to a virtual machine. The results of this lab can be used in the next three labs (partitions, file systems, mounting).

It is adviced to attach three 1GB disks and three 2GB disks to the virtual machine. This will allow for some freedom in the practices of this chapter as well as the next chapters (raid, lvm, iSCSI).

1. Use **dmesg** to make a list of hard disk devices detected at boot-up.

2. Use **fdisk** to find the total size of all hard disk devices on your system.

3. Stop a virtual machine, add three virtual 1 gigabyte **scsi** hard disk devices and one virtual 400 megabyte **ide** hard disk device. If possible, also add another virtual 400 megabyte **ide** disk.

4. Use **dmesg** to verify that all the new disks are properly detected at boot-up.

5. Verify that you can see the disk devices in **/dev**.

6. Use **fdisk** (with **grep** and **/dev/null**) to display the total size of the new disks.

7. Use **badblocks** to completely erase one of the smaller hard disks.

8. Look at **/proc/scsi/scsi**.

9. If possible, install **lsscsi, lshw** and use them to list the disks.

4.7. solution: hard disk devices

1. Use **dmesg** to make a list of hard disk devices detected at boot-up.

```
Some possible answers...

dmesg | grep -i disk

Looking for ATA disks: dmesg | grep hd[abcd]

Looking for ATA disks: dmesg | grep -i "ata disk"

Looking for SCSI disks: dmesg | grep sd[a-f]

Looking for SCSI disks: dmesg | grep -i "scsi disk"
```

2. Use **fdisk** to find the total size of all hard disk devices on your system.

```
fdisk -l
```

3. Stop a virtual machine, add three virtual 1 gigabyte **scsi** hard disk devices and one virtual 400 megabyte **ide** hard disk device. If possible, also add another virtual 400 megabyte **ide** disk.

```
This exercise happens in the settings of vmware or VirtualBox.
```

4. Use **dmesg** to verify that all the new disks are properly detected at boot-up.

```
See 1.
```

5. Verify that you can see the disk devices in **/dev**.

```
SCSI+SATA: ls -l /dev/sd*

ATA: ls -l /dev/hd*
```

6. Use **fdisk** (with **grep** and **/dev/null**) to display the total size of the new disks.

```
root@rhel53 ~# fdisk -l 2>/dev/null | grep [MGT]B
Disk /dev/hda: 21.4 GB, 21474836480 bytes
Disk /dev/hdb: 1073 MB, 1073741824 bytes
Disk /dev/sda: 2147 MB, 2147483648 bytes
Disk /dev/sdb: 2147 MB, 2147483648 bytes
Disk /dev/sdc: 2147 MB, 2147483648 bytes
```

7. Use **badblocks** to completely erase one of the smaller hard disks.

```
#Verify the device (/dev/sdc??) you want to erase before typing this.
#
root@rhel53 ~# badblocks -ws /dev/sdc
Testing with pattern 0xaa: done
Reading and comparing: done
Testing with pattern 0x55: done
Reading and comparing: done
Testing with pattern 0xff: done
Reading and comparing: done
Testing with pattern 0x00: done
Reading and comparing: done
```

8. Look at **/proc/scsi/scsi**.

```
root@rhel53 ~# cat /proc/scsi/scsi
```

```
Attached devices:
Host: scsi0 Channel: 00 Id: 02 Lun: 00
  Vendor: VBOX     Model: HARDDISK         Rev: 1.0
  Type:   Direct-Access                    ANSI SCSI revision: 05
Host: scsi0 Channel: 00 Id: 03 Lun: 00
  Vendor: VBOX     Model: HARDDISK         Rev: 1.0
  Type:   Direct-Access                    ANSI SCSI revision: 05
Host: scsi0 Channel: 00 Id: 06 Lun: 00
  Vendor: VBOX     Model: HARDDISK         Rev: 1.0
  Type:   Direct-Access                    ANSI SCSI revision: 05
```

9. If possible, install **lsscsi**, **lshw** and use them to list the disks.

```
Debian,Ubuntu: aptitude install lsscsi lshw
```

```
Fedora: yum install lsscsi lshw
```

```
root@rhel53 ~# lsscsi
[0:0:2:0]    disk    VBOX     HARDDISK        1.0   /dev/sda
[0:0:3:0]    disk    VBOX     HARDDISK        1.0   /dev/sdb
[0:0:6:0]    disk    VBOX     HARDDISK        1.0   /dev/sdc
```

Chapter 5. disk partitions

This chapter continues on the **hard disk devices** from the previous one. Here we will put **partitions** on those devices.

This chapter prepares you for the next chapter, where we put **file systems** on our partitions.

5.1. about partitions

5.1.1. primary, extended and logical

Linux requires you to create one or more **partitions**. The next paragraphs will explain how to create and use partitions.

A partition's **geometry** and size is usually defined by a starting and ending cylinder (sometimes by sector). Partitions can be of type **primary** (maximum four), **extended** (maximum one) or **logical** (contained within the extended partition). Each partition has a **type field** that contains a code. This determines the computers operating system or the partitions file system.

Table 5.1. primary, extended and logical partitions

Partition Type	naming
Primary (max 4)	1-4
Extended (max 1)	1-4
Logical	5-

5.1.2. partition naming

We saw before that hard disk devices are named /dev/hdx or /dev/sdx with x depending on the hardware configuration. Next is the partition number, starting the count at 1. Hence the four (possible) primary partitions are numbered 1 to 4. Logical partition counting always starts at 5. Thus /dev/hda2 is the second partition on the first ATA hard disk device, and /dev/hdb5 is the first logical partition on the second ATA hard disk device. Same for SCSI, /dev/sdb3 is the third partition on the second SCSI disk.

Table 5.2. Partition naming

partition	device
/dev/hda1	first primary partition on /dev/hda
/dev/hda2	second primary or extended partition on /dev/hda
/dev/sda5	first logical drive on /dev/sda
/dev/sdb6	second logical on /dev/sdb

The picture below shows two (spindle) disks with partitions. Note that an extended partition is a container holding logical drives.

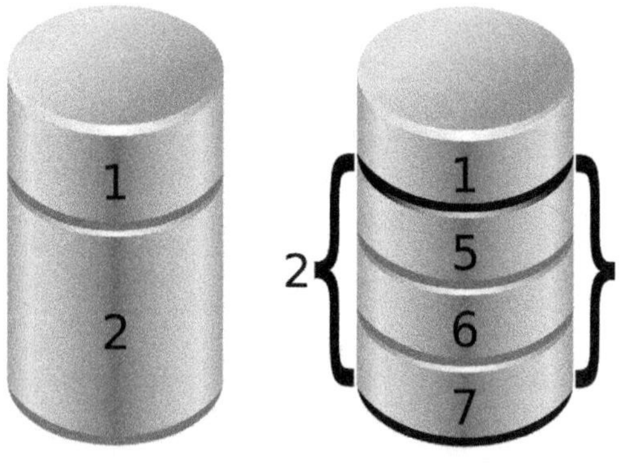

5.2. discovering partitions

5.2.1. fdisk -l

In the **fdisk -l** example below you can see that two partitions exist on **/dev/sdb**. The first partition spans 31 cylinders and contains a Linux swap partition. The second partition is much bigger.

```
root@laika:~# fdisk -l /dev/sdb

Disk /dev/sdb: 100.0 GB, 100030242816 bytes
255 heads, 63 sectors/track, 12161 cylinders
Units = cylinders of 16065 * 512 = 8225280 bytes

   Device Boot    Start       End      Blocks   Id  System
/dev/sdb1             1        31      248976   82  Linux swap / Solaris
/dev/sdb2            32     12161    97434225   83  Linux
root@laika:~#
```

5.2.2. /proc/partitions

The **/proc/partitions** file contains a table with major and minor number of partitioned devices, their number of blocks and the device name in **/dev**. Verify with **/proc/devices** to link the major number to the proper device.

```
paul@RHELv4u4:~$ cat /proc/partitions
major minor  #blocks  name

   3     0     524288 hda
   3    64     734003 hdb
   8     0    8388608 sda
   8     1     104391 sda1
   8     2    8281507 sda2
   8    16    1048576 sdb
   8    32    1048576 sdc
   8    48    1048576 sdd
 253     0    7176192 dm-0
 253     1    1048576 dm-1
```

The **major** number corresponds to the device type (or driver) and can be found in **/proc/devices**. In this case 3 corresponds to **ide** and 8 to **sd**. The **major** number determines the **device driver** to be used with this device.

The **minor** number is a unique identification of an instance of this device type. The **devices.txt** file in the kernel tree contains a full list of major and minor numbers.

5.2.3. parted and others

You may be interested in alternatives to **fdisk** like **parted**, **cfdisk**, **sfdisk** and **gparted**. This course mainly uses **fdisk** to partition hard disks.

parted is recommended by some Linux distributions for handling storage with **gpt** instead of **mbr**.

Below a screenshot of **parted** on CentOS.

```
[root@centos65 ~]# rpm -q parted
parted-2.1-21.el6.x86_64
[root@centos65 ~]# parted /dev/sda
GNU Parted 2.1
Using /dev/sda
Welcome to GNU Parted! Type 'help' to view a list of commands.
(parted) print
Model: ATA VBOX HARDDISK (scsi)
Disk /dev/sda: 42.9GB
Sector size (logical/physical): 512B/512B
Partition Table: msdos

Number  Start   End     Size    Type     File system  Flags
 1      1049kB  525MB   524MB   primary  ext4         boot
 2      525MB   42.9GB  42.4GB  primary               lvm

(parted)
```

5.3. partitioning new disks

In the example below, we bought a new disk for our system. After the new hardware is properly attached, you can use **fdisk** and **parted** to create the necessary partition(s). This example uses **fdisk**, but there is nothing wrong with using **parted**.

5.3.1. recognising the disk

First, we check with **fdisk -l** whether Linux can see the new disk. Yes it does, the new disk is seen as /dev/sdb, but it does not have any partitions yet.

```
root@RHELv4u2:~# fdisk -l

Disk /dev/sda: 12.8 GB, 12884901888 bytes
255 heads, 63 sectors/track, 1566 cylinders
Units = cylinders of 16065 * 512 = 8225280 bytes

Device Boot      Start       End       Blocks    Id  System
/dev/sda1   *        1        13       104391    83  Linux
/dev/sda2           14      1566     12474472+   8e  Linux LVM

Disk /dev/sdb: 1073 MB, 1073741824 bytes
255 heads, 63 sectors/track, 130 cylinders
Units = cylinders of 16065 * 512 = 8225280 bytes

Disk /dev/sdb doesn't contain a valid partition table
```

5.3.2. opening the disk with fdisk

Then we create a partition with fdisk on /dev/sdb. First we start the fdisk tool with /dev/sdb as argument. Be very very careful not to partition the wrong disk!!

```
root@RHELv4u2:~# fdisk /dev/sdb
Device contains neither a valid DOS partition table, nor Sun, SGI...
Building a new DOS disklabel. Changes will remain in memory only,
until you decide to write them. After that, of course, the previous
content won't be recoverable.

Warning: invalid flag 0x0000 of partition table 4 will be corrected...
```

5.3.3. empty partition table

Inside the fdisk tool, we can issue the **p** command to see the current disks partition table.

```
Command (m for help): p

Disk /dev/sdb: 1073 MB, 1073741824 bytes
255 heads, 63 sectors/track, 130 cylinders
Units = cylinders of 16065 * 512 = 8225280 bytes

Device Boot      Start         End      Blocks   Id  System
```

5.3.4. create a new partition

No partitions exist yet, so we issue **n** to create a new partition. We choose p for primary, 1 for the partition number, 1 for the start cylinder and 14 for the end cylinder.

```
Command (m for help): n
Command action
e   extended
p   primary partition (1-4)
p
Partition number (1-4): 1
First cylinder (1-130, default 1):
Using default value 1
Last cylinder or +size or +sizeM or +sizeK (1-130, default 130): 14
```

We can now issue p again to verify our changes, but they are not yet written to disk. This means we can still cancel this operation! But it looks good, so we use **w** to write the changes to disk, and then quit the fdisk tool.

```
Command (m for help): p

Disk /dev/sdb: 1073 MB, 1073741824 bytes
255 heads, 63 sectors/track, 130 cylinders
Units = cylinders of 16065 * 512 = 8225280 bytes

Device Boot      Start         End      Blocks   Id  System
/dev/sdb1            1          14      112423+  83  Linux

Command (m for help): w
The partition table has been altered!

Calling ioctl() to re-read partition table.
Syncing disks.
root@RHELv4u2:~#
```

5.3.5. display the new partition

Let's verify again with **fdisk -l** to make sure reality fits our dreams. Indeed, the screenshot below now shows a partition on /dev/sdb.

```
root@RHELv4u2:~# fdisk -l

Disk /dev/sda: 12.8 GB, 12884901888 bytes
255 heads, 63 sectors/track, 1566 cylinders
Units = cylinders of 16065 * 512 = 8225280 bytes

Device Boot      Start         End      Blocks   Id  System
/dev/sda1   *        1          13      104391   83  Linux
/dev/sda2           14        1566    12474472+  8e  Linux LVM

Disk /dev/sdb: 1073 MB, 1073741824 bytes
255 heads, 63 sectors/track, 130 cylinders
Units = cylinders of 16065 * 512 = 8225280 bytes

Device Boot      Start         End      Blocks   Id  System
/dev/sdb1            1          14      112423+  83  Linux
root@RHELv4u2:~#
```

5.4. about the partition table

5.4.1. master boot record

The **partition table** information (primary and extended partitions) is written in the **master boot record** or **mbr**. You can use **dd** to copy the mbr to a file.

This example copies the master boot record from the first SCSI hard disk.

```
dd if=/dev/sda of=/SCSIdisk.mbr bs=512 count=1
```

The same tool can also be used to wipe out all information about partitions on a disk. This example writes zeroes over the master boot record.

```
dd if=/dev/zero of=/dev/sda bs=512 count=1
```

Or to wipe out the whole partition or disk.

```
dd if=/dev/zero of=/dev/sda
```

5.4.2. partprobe

Don't forget that after restoring a **master boot record** with **dd**, that you need to force the kernel to reread the partition table with **partprobe**. After running **partprobe**, the partitions can be used again.

```
[root@RHEL5 ~]# partprobe
[root@RHEL5 ~]#
```

5.4.3. logical drives

The **partition table** does not contain information about **logical drives**. So the **dd** backup of the **mbr** only works for primary and extended partitions. To backup the partition table including the logical drives, you can use **sfdisk**.

This example shows how to backup all partition and logical drive information to a file.

```
sfdisk -d /dev/sda > parttable.sda.sfdisk
```

The following example copies the **mbr** and all **logical drive** info from /dev/sda to /dev/sdb.

```
sfdisk -d /dev/sda | sfdisk /dev/sdb
```

5.5. GUID partition table

gpt was developed because of the limitations of the 1980s **mbr** partitioning scheme (for example only four partitions can be defined, and they have a maximum size two terabytes).

Since 2010 **gpt** is a part of the **uefi** specification, but it is also used on **bios** systems.

Newer versions of **fdisk** work fine with **gpt**, but most production servers today (mid 2015) still have an older **fdisk.**. You can use **parted** instead.

5.6. labeling with parted

parted is an interactive tool, just like **fdisk**. Type **help** in **parted** for a list of commands and options.

This screenshot shows how to start **parted** to manage partitions on **/dev/sdb**.

```
[root@rhel71 ~]# parted /dev/sdb
GNU Parted 3.1
Using /dev/sdb
Welcome to GNU Parted! Type 'help' to view a list of commands.
(parted)
```

Each command also has built-in help. For example **help mklabel** will list all supported labels. Note that we only discussed **mbr**(msdos) and **gpt** in this book.

```
(parted) help mklabel
 mklabel,mktable LABEL-TYPE              create a new disklabel (partition table)

    LABEL-TYPE is one of: aix, amiga, bsd, dvh, gpt, mac, msdos, pc98, sun, loop
(parted)
```

We create an **mbr** label.

```
(parted) mklabel msdos>
Warning: The existing disk label on /dev/sdb will be destroyed and all data on
this disk will be lost. Do you want to continue?
Yes/No? yes
(parted) mklabel gpt
Warning: The existing disk label on /dev/sdb will be destroyed and all data on
this disk will be lost. Do you want to continue?
Yes/No? Y
(parted)
```

5.6.1. partitioning with parted

Once labeled it is easy to create partitions with **parted**. This screenshot starts with an unpartitioned (but **gpt** labeled) disk.

```
(parted) print
Model: ATA VBOX HARDDISK (scsi)
Disk /dev/sdb: 8590MB
Sector size (logical/physical): 512B/512B
Partition Table: gpt
Disk Flags:

Number  Start  End  Size  File system  Name  Flags

(parted)
```

This example shows how to create two primary partitions of equal size.

```
(parted) mkpart primary 0 50%
Warning: The resulting partition is not properly aligned for best performance.
Ignore/Cancel? I
(parted) mkpart primary 50% 100%
(parted)
```

Verify with **print** and exit with **quit**. Since **parted** works directly on the disk, there is no need to **w(rite)** like in **fdisk**.

```
(parted) print
Model: ATA VBOX HARDDISK (scsi)
Disk /dev/sdb: 8590MB
Sector size (logical/physical): 512B/512B
Partition Table: gpt
Disk Flags:

Number  Start   End     Size    File system  Name     Flags
 1      17.4kB  4295MB  4295MB               primary
 2      4295MB  8589MB  4294MB               primary

(parted) quit
Information: You may need to update /etc/fstab.

[root@rhel71 ~]#
```

5.7. practice: partitions

1. Use **fdisk -l** to display existing partitions and sizes.

2. Use **df -h** to display existing partitions and sizes.

3. Compare the output of **fdisk** and **df**.

4. Create a 200MB primary partition on a small disk.

5. Create a 400MB primary partition and two 300MB logical drives on a big disk.

6. Use **df -h** and **fdisk -l** to verify your work.

7. Compare the output again of **fdisk** and **df**. Do both commands display the new partitions ?

8. Create a backup with **dd** of the **mbr** that contains your 200MB primary partition.

9. Take a backup of the **partition table** containing your 400MB primary and 300MB logical drives. Make sure the logical drives are in the backup.

10. (optional) Remove all your partitions with fdisk. Then restore your backups.

5.8. solution: partitions

1. Use **fdisk -l** to display existing partitions and sizes.

```
as root: # fdisk -l
```

2. Use **df -h** to display existing partitions and sizes.

```
df -h
```

3. Compare the output of **fdisk** and **df**.

```
Some partitions will be listed in both outputs (maybe /dev/sda1 or /dev/hda1).
```

4. Create a 200MB primary partition on a small disk.

```
Choose one of the disks you added (this example uses /dev/sdc).
root@rhel53 ~# fdisk /dev/sdc
...
Command (m for help): n
Command action
   e   extended
   p   primary partition (1-4)
p
Partition number (1-4): 1
First cylinder (1-261, default 1): 1
Last cylinder or +size or +sizeM or +sizeK (1-261, default 261): +200m
Command (m for help): w
The partition table has been altered!
Calling ioctl() to re-read partition table.
Syncing disks.
```

5. Create a 400MB primary partition and two 300MB logical drives on a big disk.

```
Choose one of the disks you added (this example uses /dev/sdb)

fdisk /dev/sdb

inside fdisk : n p 1 +400m enter --- n e 2 enter enter --- n l +300m (twice)
```

6. Use **df -h** and **fdisk -l** to verify your work.

```
fdisk -l ; df -h
```

7. Compare the output again of **fdisk** and **df**. Do both commands display the new partitions ?

The newly created partitions are visible with **fdisk**.

But they are not displayed by **df**.

8. Create a backup with **dd** of the **mbr** that contains your 200MB primary partition.

```
dd if=/dev/sdc of=bootsector.sdc.dd count=1 bs=512
```

9. Take a backup of the **partition table** containing your 400MB primary and 300MB logical drives. Make sure the logical drives are in the backup.

```
sfdisk -d /dev/sdb > parttable.sdb.sfdisk
```

Chapter 6. file systems

When you are finished partitioning the hard disk, you can put a **file system** on each partition.

This chapter builds on the **partitions** from the previous chapter, and prepares you for the next one where we will **mount** the filesystems.

6.1. about file systems

A file system is a way of organizing files on your partition. Besides file-based storage, file systems usually include **directories** and **access control**, and contain meta information about files like access times, modification times and file ownership.

The properties (length, character set, ...) of filenames are determined by the file system you choose. Directories are usually implemented as files, you will have to learn how this is implemented! Access control in file systems is tracked by user ownership (and group owner- and membership) in combination with one or more access control lists.

6.1.1. man fs

The manual page about filesystems is accessed by typing **man fs**.

```
[root@rhel65 ~]# man fs
```

6.1.2. /proc/filesystems

The Linux kernel will inform you about currently loaded file system drivers in **/proc/filesystems**.

```
root@rhel53 ~# cat /proc/filesystems  | grep -v nodev
 ext2
 iso9660
 ext3
```

6.1.3. /etc/filesystems

The **/etc/filesystems** file contains a list of autodetected filesystems (in case the **mount** command is used without the **-t** option.

Help for this file is provided by **man mount**.

```
[root@rhel65 ~]# man mount
```

6.2. common file systems

6.2.1. ext2 and ext3

Once the most common Linux file systems is the **ext2** (the second extended) file system. A disadvantage is that file system checks on ext2 can take a long time.

ext2 was being replaced by **ext3** on most Linux machines. They are essentially the same, except for the **journaling** which is only present in ext3.

Journaling means that changes are first written to a journal on the disk. The journal is flushed regularly, writing the changes in the file system. Journaling keeps the file system in a consistent state, so you don't need a file system check after an unclean shutdown or power failure.

6.2.2. creating ext2 and ext3

You can create these file systems with the **/sbin/mkfs** or **/sbin/mke2fs** commands. Use **mke2fs -j** to create an **ext3** file system.

You can convert an ext2 to ext3 with **tune2fs -j**. You can mount an ext3 file system as ext2, but then you lose the journaling. Do not forget to run **mkinitrd** if you are booting from this device.

6.2.3. ext4

The newest incarnation of the ext file system is named **ext4** and is available in the Linux kernel since 2008. **ext4** supports larger files (up to 16 terabyte) and larger file systems than **ext3** (and many more features).

Development started by making **ext3** fully capable for 64-bit. When it turned out the changes were significant, the developers decided to name it **ext4**.

6.2.4. xfs

Redhat Enterprise Linux 7 will have **XFS** as the default file system. This is a highly scalable high-performance file system.

xfs was created for **Irix** and for a couple of years it was also used in **FreeBSD**. It is supported by the Linux kernel, but rarely used in dsitributions outside of the Redhat/CentOS realm.

6.2.5. vfat

The **vfat** file system exists in a couple of forms : **fat12** for floppy disks, **fat16** on **ms-dos**, and **fat32** for larger disks. The Linux **vfat** implementation supports all of these, but vfat lacks a lot of features like security and links. **fat** disks can be read by every operating system, and are used a lot for digital cameras, **usb** sticks and to exchange data between different OS'ses on a home user's computer.

6.2.6. iso 9660

iso 9660 is the standard format for cdroms. Chances are you will encounter this file system also on your hard disk in the form of images of cdroms (often with the .iso extension). The **iso 9660** standard limits filenames to the 8.3 format. The Unix world didn't like this, and thus added the **rock ridge** extensions, which allows for filenames up to 255 characters and Unix-style file-modes, ownership and symbolic links. Another extensions to **iso 9660** is **joliet**, which adds 64 unicode characters to the filename. The **el torito** standard extends **iso 9660** to be able to boot from CD-ROM's.

6.2.7. udf

Most optical media today (including cd's and dvd's) use **udf**, the Universal Disk Format.

6.2.8. swap

All things considered, swap is not a file system. But to use a partition as a **swap partition** it must be formatted and mounted as swap space.

6.2.9. gfs

Linux clusters often use a dedicated cluster filesystem like GFS, GFS2, ClusterFS, ...

6.2.10. and more...

You may encounter **reiserfs** on older Linux systems. Maybe you will see Sun's **zfs** or the open source **btrfs**. This last one requires a chapter on itself.

6.2.11. /proc/filesystems

The **/proc/filesystems** file displays a list of supported file systems. When you mount a file system without explicitly defining one, then mount will first try to probe **/etc/filesystems** and then probe **/proc/filesystems** for all the filesystems without the **nodev** label. If **/etc/filesystems** ends with a line containing only an asterisk (*) then both files are probed.

```
paul@RHELv4u4:~$ cat /proc/filesystems
nodev   sysfs
nodev   rootfs
nodev   bdev
nodev   proc
nodev   sockfs
nodev   binfmt_misc
nodev   usbfs
nodev   usbdevfs
nodev   futexfs
nodev   tmpfs
nodev   pipefs
nodev   eventpollfs
nodev   devpts
        ext2
nodev   ramfs
nodev   hugetlbfs
        iso9660
nodev   relayfs
nodev   mqueue
nodev   selinuxfs
        ext3
nodev   rpc_pipefs
nodev   vmware-hgfs
nodev   autofs
paul@RHELv4u4:~$
```

6.3. putting a file system on a partition

We now have a fresh partition. The system binaries to make file systems can be found with ls.

```
[root@RHEL4b ~]# ls -lS /sbin/mk*
-rwxr-xr-x  3 root root 34832 Apr 24  2006 /sbin/mke2fs
-rwxr-xr-x  3 root root 34832 Apr 24  2006 /sbin/mkfs.ext2
-rwxr-xr-x  3 root root 34832 Apr 24  2006 /sbin/mkfs.ext3
-rwxr-xr-x  3 root root 28484 Oct 13  2004 /sbin/mkdosfs
-rwxr-xr-x  3 root root 28484 Oct 13  2004 /sbin/mkfs.msdos
-rwxr-xr-x  3 root root 28484 Oct 13  2004 /sbin/mkfs.vfat
-rwxr-xr-x  1 root root 20313 Apr 10  2006 /sbin/mkinitrd
-rwxr-x---  1 root root 15444 Oct  5  2004 /sbin/mkzonedb
-rwxr-xr-x  1 root root 15300 May 24  2006 /sbin/mkfs.cramfs
-rwxr-xr-x  1 root root 13036 May 24  2006 /sbin/mkswap
-rwxr-xr-x  1 root root  6912 May 24  2006 /sbin/mkfs
-rwxr-xr-x  1 root root  5905 Aug  3  2004 /sbin/mkbootdisk
[root@RHEL4b ~]#
```

It is time for you to read the manual pages of **mkfs** and **mke2fs**. In the example below, you see the creation of an **ext2 file system** on /dev/sdb1. In real life, you might want to use options like -m0 and -j.

```
root@RHELv4u2:~# mke2fs /dev/sdb1
mke2fs 1.35 (28-Feb-2004)
Filesystem label=
OS type: Linux
Block size=1024 (log=0)
Fragment size=1024 (log=0)
28112 inodes, 112420 blocks
5621 blocks (5.00%) reserved for the super user
First data block=1
Maximum filesystem blocks=67371008
14 block groups
8192 blocks per group, 8192 fragments per group
2008 inodes per group
Superblock backups stored on blocks:
8193, 24577, 40961, 57345, 73729

Writing inode tables: done
Writing superblocks and filesystem accounting information: done

This filesystem will be automatically checked every 37 mounts or
180 days, whichever comes first.  Use tune2fs -c or -i to override.
```

6.4. tuning a file system

You can use **tune2fs** to list and set file system settings. The first screenshot lists the reserved space for root (which is set at five percent).

```
[root@rhel4 ~]# tune2fs -l /dev/sda1 | grep -i "block count"
Block count:              104388
Reserved block count:     5219
[root@rhel4 ~]#
```

This example changes this value to ten percent. You can use tune2fs while the file system is active, even if it is the root file system (as in this example).

```
[root@rhel4 ~]# tune2fs -m10 /dev/sda1
tune2fs 1.35 (28-Feb-2004)
Setting reserved blocks percentage to 10 (10430 blocks)
[root@rhel4 ~]# tune2fs -l /dev/sda1 | grep -i "block count"
Block count:              104388
Reserved block count:     10430
[root@rhel4 ~]#
```

6.5. checking a file system

The **fsck** command is a front end tool used to check a file system for errors.

```
[root@RHEL4b ~]# ls /sbin/*fsck*
/sbin/dosfsck  /sbin/fsck        /sbin/fsck.ext2  /sbin/fsck.msdos
/sbin/e2fsck   /sbin/fsck.cramfs /sbin/fsck.ext3  /sbin/fsck.vfat
[root@RHEL4b ~]#
```

The last column in **/etc/fstab** is used to determine whether a file system should be checked at boot-up.

```
[paul@RHEL4b ~]$ grep ext /etc/fstab
/dev/VolGroup00/LogVol00    /              ext3    defaults        1 1
LABEL=/boot                 /boot          ext3    defaults        1 2
[paul@RHEL4b ~]$
```

Manually checking a mounted file system results in a warning from fsck.

```
[root@RHEL4b ~]# fsck /boot
fsck 1.35 (28-Feb-2004)
e2fsck 1.35 (28-Feb-2004)
/dev/sda1 is mounted.

WARNING!!!  Running e2fsck on a mounted filesystem may cause
SEVERE filesystem damage.

Do you really want to continue (y/n)? no

check aborted.
```

But after unmounting fsck and **e2fsck** can be used to check an ext2 file system.

```
[root@RHEL4b ~]# fsck  /boot
fsck 1.35 (28-Feb-2004)
e2fsck 1.35 (28-Feb-2004)
/boot: clean, 44/26104 files, 17598/104388 blocks
[root@RHEL4b ~]# fsck -p /boot
fsck 1.35 (28-Feb-2004)
/boot: clean, 44/26104 files, 17598/104388 blocks
[root@RHEL4b ~]# e2fsck -p /dev/sda1
/boot: clean, 44/26104 files, 17598/104388 blocks
```

6.6. practice: file systems

1. List the filesystems that are known by your system.

2. Create an **ext2** filesystem on the 200MB partition.

3. Create an **ext3** filesystem on one of the 300MB logical drives.

4. Create an **ext4** on the 400MB partition.

5. Set the reserved space for root on the ext3 filesystem to 0 percent.

6. Verify your work with **fdisk** and **df**.

7. Perform a file system check on all the new file systems.

6.7. solution: file systems

1. List the filesystems that are known by your system.

```
man fs
```

```
cat /proc/filesystems
```

```
cat /etc/filesystems (not on all Linux distributions)
```

2. Create an **ext2** filesystem on the 200MB partition.

```
mke2fs /dev/sdc1 (replace sdc1 with the correct partition)
```

3. Create an **ext3** filesystem on one of the 300MB logical drives.

```
mke2fs -j /dev/sdb5 (replace sdb5 with the correct partition)
```

4. Create an **ext4** on the 400MB partition.

```
mkfs.ext4 /dev/sdb1 (replace sdb1 with the correct partition)
```

5. Set the reserved space for root on the ext3 filesystem to 0 percent.

```
tune2fs -m 0 /dev/sdb5
```

6. Verify your work with **fdisk** and **df**.

```
mkfs (mke2fs) makes no difference in the output of these commands
```

```
The big change is in the next topic: mounting
```

7. Perform a file system check on all the new file systems.

```
fsck /dev/sdb1
fsck /dev/sdc1
fsck /dev/sdb5
```

Chapter 7. mounting

Once you've put a file system on a partition, you can **mount** it. Mounting a file system makes it available for use, usually as a directory. We say **mounting a file system** instead of mounting a partition because we will see later that we can also mount file systems that do not exists on partitions.

On all **Unix** systems, every file and every directory is part of one big file tree. To access a file, you need to know the full path starting from the root directory. When adding a **file system** to your computer, you need to make it available somewhere in the file tree. The directory where you make a file system available is called a **mount point**.

7.1. mounting local file systems

7.1.1. mkdir

This example shows how to create a new **mount point** with **mkdir**.

```
root@RHELv4u2:~# mkdir /home/project42
```

7.1.2. mount

When the **mount point** is created, and a **file system** is present on the partition, then **mount** can **mount** the **file system** on the **mount point directory**.

```
root@RHELv4u2:~# mount -t ext2 /dev/sdb1 /home/project42/
```

Once mounted, the new file system is accessible to users.

7.1.3. /etc/filesystems

Actually the explicit **-t ext2** option to set the file system is not always necessary. The **mount** command is able to automatically detect a lot of file systems.

When mounting a file system without specifying explicitly the file system, then **mount** will first probe **/etc/filesystems**. Mount will skip lines with the **nodev** directive.

```
paul@RHELv4u4:~$ cat /etc/filesystems
ext3
ext2
nodev proc
nodev devpts
iso9660
vfat
hfs
```

7.1.4. /proc/filesystems

When **/etc/filesystems** does not exist, or ends with a single * on the last line, then **mount** will read **/proc/filesystems**.

```
[root@RHEL52 ~]# cat /proc/filesystems | grep -v ^nodev
 ext2
 iso9660
 ext3
```

7.1.5. umount

You can **unmount** a mounted file system using the **umount** command.

```
root@pasha:~# umount /home/reet
```

7.2. displaying mounted file systems

To display all mounted file systems, issue the **mount** command. Or look at the files **/proc/mounts** and **/etc/mtab**.

7.2.1. mount

The simplest and most common way to view all mounts is by issuing the **mount** command without any arguments.

```
root@RHELv4u2:~# mount | grep /dev/sdb
/dev/sdb1 on /home/project42 type ext2 (rw)
```

7.2.2. /proc/mounts

The kernel provides the info in **/proc/mounts** in file form, but **/proc/mounts** does not exist as a file on any hard disk. Looking at **/proc/mounts** is looking at information that comes directly from the kernel.

```
root@RHELv4u2:~# cat /proc/mounts | grep /dev/sdb
/dev/sdb1 /home/project42 ext2 rw 0 0
```

7.2.3. /etc/mtab

The **/etc/mtab** file is not updated by the kernel, but is maintained by the **mount** command. Do not edit **/etc/mtab** manually.

```
root@RHELv4u2:~# cat /etc/mtab | grep /dev/sdb
/dev/sdb1 /home/project42 ext2 rw 0 0
```

7.2.4. df

A more user friendly way to look at mounted file systems is **df**. The **df (diskfree)** command has the added benefit of showing you the free space on each mounted disk. Like a lot of Linux commands, **df** supports the **-h** switch to make the output more **human readable**.

```
root@RHELv4u2:~# df
Filesystem            1K-blocks      Used Available Use% Mounted on
/dev/mapper/VolGroup00-LogVol00
11707972   6366996   4746240  58% /
/dev/sda1               101086      9300     86567  10% /boot
none                    127988         0    127988   0% /dev/shm
/dev/sdb1               108865      1550    101694   2% /home/project42
root@RHELv4u2:~# df -h
Filesystem            Size  Used Avail Use% Mounted on
/dev/mapper/VolGroup00-LogVol00
12G  6.1G  4.6G  58% /
/dev/sda1              99M  9.1M   85M  10% /boot
none                  125M     0  125M   0% /dev/shm
/dev/sdb1             107M  1.6M  100M   2% /home/project42
```

7.2.5. df -h

In the **df -h** example below you can see the size, free space, used gigabytes and percentage and mount point of a partition.

```
root@laika:~# df -h | egrep -e "(sdb2|File)"
Filesystem            Size Used Avail Use% Mounted on
/dev/sdb2              92G   83G  8.6G  91% /media/sdb2
```

7.2.6. du

The **du** command can summarize **disk usage** for files and directories. By using **du** on a mount point you effectively get the disk space used on a file system.

While **du** can go display each subdirectory recursively, the **-s** option will give you a total summary for the parent directory. This option is often used together with **-h**. This means **du -sh** on a mount point gives the total amount used by the file system in that partition.

```
root@debian6~# du -sh /boot /srv/wolf
6.2M /boot
1.1T /srv/wolf
```

7.3. from start to finish

Below is a screenshot that show a summary roadmap starting with detection of the hardware (/dev/sdb) up until mounting on **/mnt**.

```
[root@centos65 ~]# dmesg | grep '\[sdb\]'
sd 3:0:0:0: [sdb] 150994944 512-byte logical blocks: (77.3 GB/72.0 GiB)
sd 3:0:0:0: [sdb] Write Protect is off
sd 3:0:0:0: [sdb] Mode Sense: 00 3a 00 00
sd 3:0:0:0: [sdb] Write cache: enabled, read cache: enabled, doesn't support \
DPO or FUA
sd 3:0:0:0: [sdb] Attached SCSI disk

[root@centos65 ~]# parted /dev/sdb

(parted) mklabel msdos
(parted) mkpart primary ext4 1 77000
(parted) print
Model: ATA VBOX HARDDISK (scsi)
Disk /dev/sdb: 77.3GB
Sector size (logical/physical): 512B/512B
Partition Table: msdos

Number  Start   End     Size    Type     File system  Flags
 1      1049kB  77.0GB  77.0GB  primary

(parted) quit
[root@centos65 ~]# mkfs.ext4 /dev/sdb1
mke2fs 1.41.12 (17-May-2010)
Filesystem label=
OS type: Linux
Block size=4096 (log=2)
Fragment size=4096 (log=2)
Stride=0 blocks, Stripe width=0 blocks
4702208 inodes, 18798592 blocks
939929 blocks (5.00%) reserved for the super user
First data block=0
Maximum filesystem blocks=4294967296
574 block groups
32768 blocks per group, 32768 fragments per group
8192 inodes per group
( output truncated )
...
[root@centos65 ~]# mount /dev/sdb1 /mnt
[root@centos65 ~]# mount | grep mnt
/dev/sdb1 on /mnt type ext4 (rw)
[root@centos65 ~]# df -h | grep mnt
/dev/sdb1              71G  180M   67G   1% /mnt
[root@centos65 ~]# du -sh /mnt
20K     /mnt
[root@centos65 ~]# umount /mnt
```

7.4. permanent mounts

Until now, we performed all mounts manually. This works nice, until the next reboot. Luckily there is a way to tell your computer to automatically mount certain file systems during boot.

7.4.1. /etc/fstab

The file system table located in **/etc/fstab** contains a list of file systems, with an option to automtically mount each of them at boot time.

Below is a sample **/etc/fstab** file.

```
root@RHELv4u2:~# cat /etc/fstab
/dev/VolGroup00/LogVol00 /                     ext3    defaults          1 1
LABEL=/boot              /boot                 ext3    defaults          1 2
none                     /dev/pts              devpts  gid=5,mode=620    0 0
none                     /dev/shm              tmpfs   defaults          0 0
none                     /proc                 proc    defaults          0 0
none                     /sys                  sysfs   defaults          0 0
/dev/VolGroup00/LogVol01 swap                  swap    defaults          0 0
```

By adding the following line, we can automate the mounting of a file system.

```
/dev/sdb1                /home/project42      ext2    defaults    0 0
```

7.4.2. mount /mountpoint

Adding an entry to **/etc/fstab** has the added advantage that you can simplify the **mount** command. The command in the screenshot below forces **mount** to look for the partition info in **/etc/fstab**.

```
root@rhel65:~# mount /home/project42
```

7.5. securing mounts

File systems can be secured with several **mount options**. Here are some examples.

7.5.1. ro

The **ro** option will mount a file system as read only, preventing anyone from writing.

```
root@rhel53 ~# mount -t ext2 -o ro /dev/hdb1 /home/project42
root@rhel53 ~# touch /home/project42/testwrite
touch: cannot touch `/home/project42/testwrite': Read-only file system
```

7.5.2. noexec

The **noexec** option will prevent the execution of binaries and scripts on the mounted file system.

```
root@rhel53 ~# mount -t ext2 -o noexec /dev/hdb1 /home/project42
root@rhel53 ~# cp /bin/cat /home/project42
root@rhel53 ~# /home/project42/cat /etc/hosts
-bash: /home/project42/cat: Permission denied
root@rhel53 ~# echo echo hello > /home/project42/helloscript
root@rhel53 ~# chmod +x /home/project42/helloscript
root@rhel53 ~# /home/project42/helloscript
-bash: /home/project42/helloscript: Permission denied
```

7.5.3. nosuid

The **nosuid** option will ignore **setuid** bit set binaries on the mounted file system.

Note that you can still set the **setuid** bit on files.

```
root@rhel53 ~# mount -o nosuid /dev/hdb1 /home/project42
root@rhel53 ~# cp /bin/sleep /home/project42/
root@rhel53 ~# chmod 4555 /home/project42/sleep
root@rhel53 ~# ls -l /home/project42/sleep
-r-sr-xr-x 1 root root 19564 Jun 24 17:57 /home/project42/sleep
```

But users cannot exploit the **setuid** feature.

```
root@rhel53 ~# su - paul
[paul@rhel53 ~]$ /home/project42/sleep 500 &
[1] 2876
[paul@rhel53 ~]$ ps -f 2876
UID        PID  PPID  C STIME TTY      STAT   TIME CMD
paul      2876  2853  0 17:58 pts/0    S      0:00 /home/project42/sleep 500
[paul@rhel53 ~]$
```

7.5.4. noacl

To prevent cluttering permissions with **acl's**, use the **noacl** option.

```
root@rhel53 ~# mount -o noacl /dev/hdb1 /home/project42
```

More **mount options** can be found in the manual page of **mount**.

7.6. mounting remote file systems

7.6.1. smb/cifs

The Samba team (samba.org) has a Unix/Linux service that is compatible with the SMB/CIFS protocol. This protocol is mainly used by networked Microsoft Windows computers.

Connecting to a Samba server (or to a Microsoft computer) is also done with the mount command.

This example shows how to connect to the **10.0.0.42** server, to a share named **data2**.

```
[root@centos65 ~]# mount -t cifs -o user=paul //10.0.0.42/data2 /home/data2
Password:
[root@centos65 ~]# mount | grep cifs
//10.0.0.42/data2 on /home/data2 type cifs (rw)
```

The above requires **yum install cifs-client**.

7.6.2. nfs

Unix servers often use **nfs** (aka the network file system) to share directories over the network. Setting up an nfs server is discussed later. Connecting as a client to an nfs server is done with **mount**, and is very similar to connecting to local storage.

This command shows how to connect to the nfs server named **server42**, which is sharing the directory **/srv/data**. The **mount point** at the end of the command (**/home/data**) must already exist.

```
[root@centos65 ~]# mount -t nfs server42:/srv/data /home/data
[root@centos65 ~]#
```

If this **server42** has ip-address **10.0.0.42** then you can also write:

```
[root@centos65 ~]# mount -t nfs 10.0.0.42:/srv/data /home/data
[root@centos65 ~]# mount | grep data
10.0.0.42:/srv/data on /home/data type nfs (rw,vers=4,addr=10.0.0.42,clienta\
ddr=10.0.0.33)
```

7.6.3. nfs specific mount options

```
bg If mount fails, retry in background.
fg (default)If mount fails, retry in foreground.
soft Stop trying to mount after X attempts.
hard (default)Continue trying to mount.
```

The **soft+bg** options combined guarantee the fastest client boot if there are NFS problems.

```
retrans=X Try X times to connect (over udp).
tcp Force tcp (default and supported)
udp Force udp (unsupported)
```

7.7. practice: mounting file systems

1. Mount the small 200MB partition on /home/project22.

2. Mount the big 400MB primary partition on /mnt, the copy some files to it (everything in /etc). Then umount, and mount the file system as read only on /srv/nfs/salesnumbers. Where are the files you copied ?

3. Verify your work with **fdisk**, **df** and **mount**. Also look in **/etc/mtab** and **/proc/mounts**.

4. Make both mounts permanent, test that it works.

5. What happens when you mount a file system on a directory that contains some files ?

6. What happens when you mount two file systems on the same mount point ?

7. (optional) Describe the difference between these commands: find, locate, updatedb, makewhatis, whereis, apropos, which and type.

8. (optional) Perform a file system check on the partition mounted at /srv/nfs/salesnumbers.

7.8. solution: mounting file systems

1. Mount the small 200MB partition on /home/project22.

```
mkdir /home/project22
mount /dev/sdc1 /home/project22
```

2. Mount the big 400MB primary partition on /mnt, the copy some files to it (everything in /etc). Then umount, and mount the file system as read only on /srv/nfs/salesnumbers. Where are the files you copied ?

```
mount /dev/sdb1 /mnt
cp -r /etc /mnt
ls -l /mnt

umount /mnt
ls -l /mnt

mkdir -p /srv/nfs/salesnumbers
mount /dev/sdb1 /srv/nfs/salesnumbers
```

```
You see the files in /srv/nfs/salenumbers now...

But physically they are on ext3 on partition /dev/sdb1
```

3. Verify your work with **fdisk**, **df** and **mount**. Also look in **/etc/mtab** and **/proc/mounts**.

```
fdisk -l
df -h
mount
```

```
All three the above commands should show your mounted partitions.
```

```
grep project22 /etc/mtab
grep project22 /proc/mounts
```

4. Make both mounts permanent, test that it works.

```
add the following lines to /etc/fstab

/dev/sdc1 /home/project22 auto defaults 0 0
/dev/sdb1 /srv/nfs/salesnumbers auto defaults 0 0
```

5. What happens when you mount a file system on a directory that contains some files ?

```
The files are hidden until umount.
```

6. What happens when you mount two file systems on the same mount point ?

```
Only the last mounted fs is visible.
```

7. (optional) Describe the difference between these commands: find, locate, updatedb, makewhatis, whereis, apropos, which and type.

```
man find
man locate
...
```

8. (optional) Perform a file system check on the partition mounted at /srv/nfs/salesnumbers.

```
# umount /srv/nfs/salesnumbers (optional but recommended)
# fsck /dev/sdb1
```

Chapter 8. troubleshooting tools

This chapter introduces some tools that go beyond **df -h** and **du -sh**. Tools that will enable you to troubleshoot a variety of issues with **file systems** and storage.

8.1. lsof

List open files with **lsof**.

When invoked without options, **lsof** will list all open files. You can see the command (init in this case), its PID (1) and the user (root) has openend the root directory and **/sbin/init**. The FD (file descriptor) columns shows that / is both the root directory (rtd) and current working directory (cwd) for the /sbin/init command. The FD column displays **rtd** for root directory, **cwd** for current directory and **txt** for text (both including data and code).

```
root@debian7:~# lsof | head -4
COMMAND PID  TID   USER   FD     TYPE      DEVICE SIZE/OFF       NODE NAME
init      1        root  cwd      DIR       254,0     4096          2 /
init      1        root  rtd      DIR       254,0     4096          2 /
init      1        root  txt      REG       254,0    36992     130856 /sbin/init
```

Other options in the FD column besides w for writing, are r for reading and u for both reading and writing. You can look at open files for a process id by typing **lsof -p PID**. For **init** this would look like this:

```
lsof -p 1
```

The screenshot below shows basic use of **lsof** to prove that **vi** keeps a **.swp** file open (even when stopped in background) on our freshly mounted file system.

```
[root@RHEL65 ~]# df -h | grep sdb
/dev/sdb1                         541M   17M  497M   4% /srv/project33
[root@RHEL65 ~]# vi /srv/project33/busyfile.txt
[1]+  Stopped                 vi /srv/project33/busyfile.txt
[root@RHEL65 ~]# lsof /srv/*
COMMAND  PID USER  FD  TYPE DEVICE SIZE/OFF NODE NAME
vi      3243 root  3u  REG   8,17    4096   12 /srv/project33/.busyfile.txt.swp
```

Here we see that **rsyslog** has a couple of log files open for writing (the FD column).

```
root@debian7:~# lsof /var/log/*
COMMAND    PID USER   FD   TYPE DEVICE SIZE/OFF    NODE NAME
rsyslogd 2013 root    1w   REG  254,0   454297 1308187 /var/log/syslog
rsyslogd 2013 root    2w   REG  254,0   419328 1308189 /var/log/kern.log
rsyslogd 2013 root    5w   REG  254,0   116725 1308200 /var/log/debug
rsyslogd 2013 root    6w   REG  254,0   309847 1308201 /var/log/messages
rsyslogd 2013 root    7w   REG  254,0    17591 1308188 /var/log/daemon.log
rsyslogd 2013 root    8w   REG  254,0   101768 1308186 /var/log/auth.log
```

You can specify a specific user with **lsof -u**. This example shows the current working directory for a couple of command line programs.

```
[paul@RHEL65 ~]$ lsof -u paul | grep home
bash     3302 paul  cwd    DIR  253,0      4096   788024 /home/paul
lsof     3329 paul  cwd    DIR  253,0      4096   788024 /home/paul
grep     3330 paul  cwd    DIR  253,0      4096   788024 /home/paul
lsof     3331 paul  cwd    DIR  253,0      4096   788024 /home/paul
```

The -u switch of **lsof** also supports the ^ character meaning 'not'. To see all open files, but not those open by root:

```
lsof -u^root
```

8.2. fuser

The **fuser** command will display the 'user' of a file system.

In this example we still have a vi process in background and we use **fuser** to find the process id of the process using this file system.

```
[root@RHEL65 ~]# jobs
[1]+  Stopped                 vi /srv/project33/busyfile.txt
[root@RHEL65 ~]# fuser -m /srv/project33/
/srv/project33/:         3243
```

Adding the **-u** switch will also display the user name.

```
[root@RHEL65 ~]# fuser -m -u /srv/project33/
/srv/project33/:         3243(root)
```

You can quickly kill all processes that are using a specific file (or directory) with the -k switch.

```
[root@RHEL65 ~]# fuser -m -k -u /srv/project33/
/srv/project33/:         3243(root)
[1]+  Killed                  vi /srv/project33/busyfile.txt
[root@RHEL65 ~]# fuser -m -u /srv/project33/
[root@RHEL65 ~]#
```

This example shows all processes that are using the current directory (bash and vi in this case).

```
root@debian7:~/test42# vi file42

[1]+  Stopped                 vi file42
root@debian7:~/test42# fuser -v .
                     USER        PID ACCESS COMMAND
/root/test42:        root       2909 ..c.. bash
                     root       3113 ..c.. vi
```

This example shows that the **vi** command actually accesses **/usr/bin/vim.basic** as an **executable** file.

```
root@debian7:~/test42# fuser -v $(which vi)
                     USER        PID ACCESS COMMAND
/usr/bin/vim.basic:  root       3113 ...e. vi
```

The last example shows how to find the process that is accessing a specific file.

```
[root@RHEL65 ~]# vi /srv/project33/busyfile.txt

[1]+  Stopped                 vi /srv/project33/busyfile.txt
[root@RHEL65 ~]# fuser -v -m /srv/project33/busyfile.txt
                     USER        PID ACCESS COMMAND
/srv/project33/busyfile.txt:
                     root      13938 F.... vi
[root@RHEL65 ~]# ps -fp 13938
UID        PID  PPID  C STIME TTY          TIME CMD
root     13938  3110  0 15:47 pts/0    00:00:00 vi /srv/project33/busyfile.txt
```

8.3. chroot

The **chroot** command creates a shell with an alternate root directory. It effectively hides anything outside of this directory.

In the example below we assume that our system refuses to start (maybe because there is a problem with **/etc/fstab** or the mounting of the root file system).

We start a live system (booted from cd/dvd/usb) to troubleshoot our server. The live system will not use our main hard disk as root device

```
root@livecd:~# df -h | grep root
rootfs          186M   11M  175M   6% /
/dev/loop0      807M  807M     0 100% /lib/live/mount/rootfs/filesystem.squashfs
root@livecd:~# mount | grep root
/dev/loop0 on /lib/live/mount/rootfs/filesystem.squashfs type squashfs (ro)
```

We create some test file on the current rootfs.

```
root@livecd:~# touch /file42
root@livecd:~# mkdir /dir42
root@livecd:~# ls /
bin   dir42   home        lib64  opt   run      srv  usr
boot  etc     initrd.img  media  proc  sbin     sys  var
dev   file42  lib         mnt    root  selinux  tmp  vmlinuz
```

First we mount the root file system from the disk (which is on **lvm** so we use **/dev/mapper** instead of **/dev/sda5**).

```
root@livecd:~# mount /dev/mapper/packer--debian--7-root /mnt
```

We are now ready to **chroot** into the rootfs on disk.

```
root@livecd:~# cd /mnt
root@livecd:/mnt# chroot /mnt
root@livecd:/# ls /
bin   dev   initrd.img  lost+found  opt   run      srv  usr      vmlinuz
boot  etc   lib         media       proc  sbin     sys  vagrant
data  home  lib64       mnt         root  selinux  tmp  var
```

Our test files (file42 and dir42) are not visible because they are out of the **chrooted** environment.

Note that the **hostname** of the chrooted environment is identical to the existing hostname.

To exit the **chrooted** file system:

```
root@livecd:/# exit
exit
root@livecd:~# ls /
bin   dir42   home        lib64  opt   run      srv  usr
boot  etc     initrd.img  media  proc  sbin     sys  var
dev   file42  lib         mnt    root  selinux  tmp  vmlinuz
```

8.4. iostat

iostat reports IO statitics every given period of time. It also includes a small cpu usage summary. This example shows **iostat** running every ten seconds with **/dev/sdc** and **/dev/sde** showing a lot of write activity.

```
[root@RHEL65 ~]# iostat 10 3
Linux 2.6.32-431.el6.x86_64 (RHEL65)   06/16/2014    _x86_64_     (1 CPU)

avg-cpu:  %user   %nice %system %iowait  %steal   %idle
           5.81    0.00    3.15    0.18    0.00   90.85

Device:            tps   Blk_read/s   Blk_wrtn/s   Blk_read   Blk_wrtn
sda              42.08      1204.10      1634.88    1743708    2367530
sdb               1.20         7.69        45.78      11134      66292
sdc               0.92         5.30        45.82       7672      66348
sdd               0.91         5.29        45.78       7656      66292
sde               1.04         6.28        91.49       9100     132496
sdf               0.70         3.40        91.46       4918     132440
sdg               0.69         3.40        91.46       4918     132440
dm-0            191.68      1045.78      1362.30    1514434    1972808
dm-1             49.26       150.54       243.55     218000     352696

avg-cpu:  %user   %nice %system %iowait  %steal   %idle
          56.11    0.00   16.83    0.10    0.00   26.95

Device:            tps   Blk_read/s   Blk_wrtn/s   Blk_read   Blk_wrtn
sda             257.01     10185.97        76.95     101656        768
sdb               0.00         0.00         0.00          0          0
sdc               3.81         1.60      2953.11         16      29472
sdd               0.00         0.00         0.00          0          0
sde               4.91         1.60      4813.63         16      48040
sdf               0.00         0.00         0.00          0          0
sdg               0.00         0.00         0.00          0          0
dm-0            283.77     10185.97        76.95     101656        768
dm-1              0.00         0.00         0.00          0          0

avg-cpu:  %user   %nice %system %iowait  %steal   %idle
          67.65    0.00   31.11    0.11    0.00    1.13

Device:            tps   Blk_read/s   Blk_wrtn/s   Blk_read   Blk_wrtn
sda             466.86     26961.09       178.28     238336       1576
sdb               0.00         0.00         0.00          0          0
sdc              31.45         0.90     24997.29          8     220976
sdd               0.00         0.00         0.00          0          0
sde               0.34         0.00         5.43          0         48
sdf               0.00         0.00         0.00          0          0
sdg               0.00         0.00         0.00          0          0
dm-0            503.62     26938.46       178.28     238136       1576
dm-1              2.83        22.62         0.00        200          0

[root@RHEL65 ~]#
```

Other options are to specify the disks you want to monitor (every 5 seconds here):

```
iostat sdd sde sdf 5
```

Or to show statistics per partition:

```
iostat -p sde -p sdf 5
```

8.5. iotop

iotop works like the **top** command but orders processes by input/output instead of by CPU.

By default **iotop** will show all processes. This example uses **iotop -o** to only display processes with actual I/O.

```
[root@RHEL65 ~]# iotop -o

Total DISK READ: 8.63 M/s | Total DISK WRITE: 0.00 B/s
  TID  PRIO  USER  DISK READ  DISK WRITE  SWAPIN     IO>    COMMAND
15000 be/4 root     2.43 M/s    0.00 B/s  0.00 % 14.60 % tar cjf /srv/di...
25000 be/4 root     6.20 M/s    0.00 B/s  0.00 %  6.15 % tar czf /srv/di...
24988 be/4 root     0.00 B/s    7.21 M/s  0.00 %  0.00 % gzip
25003 be/4 root     0.00 B/s 1591.19 K/s  0.00 %  0.00 % gzip
25004 be/4 root     0.00 B/s  193.51 K/s  0.00 %  0.00 % bzip2
```

Use the **-b** switch to create a log of **iotop** output (instead of the default interactive view).

```
[root@RHEL65 ~]# iotop -bod 10
Total DISK READ: 12.82 M/s | Total DISK WRITE: 5.69 M/s
  TID  PRIO  USER  DISK READ  DISK WRITE  SWAPIN      IO    COMMAND
25153 be/4 root     2.05 M/s    0.00 B/s  0.00 %  7.81 % tar cjf /srv/di...
25152 be/4 root    10.77 M/s    0.00 B/s  0.00 %  2.94 % tar czf /srv/di...
25144 be/4 root   408.54 B/s    0.00 B/s  0.00 %  0.05 % python /usr/sbi...
12516 be/3 root     0.00 B/s 1491.33 K/s  0.00 %  0.04 % [jbd2/sdc1-8]
12522 be/3 root     0.00 B/s   45.48 K/s  0.00 %  0.01 % [jbd2/sde1-8]
25158 be/4 root     0.00 B/s    0.00 B/s  0.00 %  0.00 % [flush-8:64]
25155 be/4 root     0.00 B/s  493.12 K/s  0.00 %  0.00 % bzip2
25156 be/4 root     0.00 B/s    2.81 M/s  0.00 %  0.00 % gzip
25159 be/4 root     0.00 B/s  528.63 K/s  0.00 %  0.00 % [flush-8:32]
```

This is an example of **iotop** to track disk I/O every ten seconds for one user named **vagrant** (and only one process of this user, but this can be omitted). The **-a** switch accumulates I/O over time.

```
[root@RHEL65 ~]# iotop -q -a -u vagrant -b -p 5216 -d 10 -n 10
Total DISK READ: 0.00 B/s | Total DISK WRITE: 0.00 B/s
  TID  PRIO  USER     DISK READ  DISK WRITE  SWAPIN      IO    COMMAND
 5216 be/4 vagrant      0.00 B      0.00 B  0.00 %  0.00 % gzip
Total DISK READ: 818.22 B/s | Total DISK WRITE: 20.78 M/s
 5216 be/4 vagrant      0.00 B    213.89 M  0.00 %  0.00 % gzip
Total DISK READ: 2045.95 B/s | Total DISK WRITE: 23.16 M/s
 5216 be/4 vagrant      0.00 B    430.70 M  0.00 %  0.00 % gzip
Total DISK READ: 1227.50 B/s | Total DISK WRITE: 22.37 M/s
 5216 be/4 vagrant      0.00 B    642.02 M  0.00 %  0.00 % gzip
Total DISK READ: 818.35 B/s | Total DISK WRITE: 16.44 M/s
 5216 be/4 vagrant      0.00 B    834.09 M  0.00 %  0.00 % gzip
Total DISK READ: 6.95 M/s | Total DISK WRITE: 8.74 M/s
 5216 be/4 vagrant      0.00 B    920.69 M  0.00 %  0.00 % gzip
Total DISK READ: 21.71 M/s | Total DISK WRITE: 11.99 M/s
```

8.6. vmstat

While **vmstat** is mainly a memory monitoring tool, it is worth mentioning here for its reporting on summary I/O data for block devices and swap space.

This example shows some disk activity (underneath the **-----io----** column), without swapping.

```
[root@RHEL65 ~]# vmstat 5 10
procs -----------memory---------- ---swap-- -----io---- --system-- -----cpu-----
 r  b   swpd   free   buff  cache   si   so    bi    bo   in   cs us sy id wa st
 0  0   5420   9092  14020 340876    7   12   235   252   77  100  2  1 98  0  0
 2  0   5420   6104  13840 338176    0    0  7401  7812  747 1887 38 12 50  0  0
 2  0   5420  10136  13696 336012    0    0 11334    14 1725 4036 76 24  0  0  0
 0  0   5420  14160  13404 341552    0    0 10161  9914 1174 1924 67 15 18  0  0
 0  0   5420  14300  13420 341564    0    0     0    16   28   18  0  0 100  0  0
 0  0   5420  14300  13420 341564    0    0     0     0   22   16  0  0 100  0  0
...
[root@RHEL65 ~]#
```

You can benefit from **vmstat**'s ability to display memory in kilobytes, megabytes or even kibibytes and mebibytes using -S (followed by k K m or M).

```
[root@RHEL65 ~]# vmstat -SM 5 10
procs -----------memory---------- ---swap-- -----io---- --system-- -----cpu-----
 r  b   swpd   free   buff  cache   si   so    bi    bo   in   cs us sy id wa st
 0  0      5     14     11    334    0    0   259   255   79  107  2  1 97  0  0
 0  0      5     14     11    334    0    0     0     2   21   18  0  0 100  0  0
 0  0      5     15     11    334    0    0     6     0   35   31  0  0 100  0  0
 2  0      5      6     11    336    0    0 17100  7814 1378 2945 48 21 31  0  0
 2  0      5      6     11    336    0    0 13193    14 1662 3343 78 22  0  0  0
 2  0      5     13     11    330    0    0 11656  9781 1419 2642 82 18  0  0  0
 2  0      5      9     11    334    0    0 10705  2716 1504 2657 81 19  0  0  0
 1  0      5     14     11    336    0    0  6467  3788  765 1384 43  9 48  0  0
 0  0      5     14     11    336    0    0     0    13   28   24  0  0 100  0  0
 0  0      5     14     11    336    0    0     0     0   20   15  0  0 100  0  0
[root@RHEL65 ~]#
```

vmstat is also discussed in other chapters.

8.7. practice: troubleshooting tools

0. It is imperative that you practice these tools **before** trouble arises. It will help you get familiar with the tools and allow you to create a base line of normal behaviour for your systems.

1. Read the theory on **fuser** and explore its man page. Use this command to find files that you open yourself.

2. Read the theory on **lsof** and explore its man page. Use this command to find files that you open yourself.

3. Boot a live image on an existing computer (virtual or real) and **chroot** into to it.

4. Start one or more disk intensive jobs and monitor them with **iostat** and **iotop** (compare to **vmstat**).

8.8. solution: troubleshooting tools

0. It is imperative that you practice these tools **before** trouble arises. It will help you get familiar with the tools and allow you to create a base line of normal behaviour for your systems.

1. Read the theory on **fuser** and explore its man page. Use this command to find files that you open yourself.

2. Read the theory on **lsof** and explore its man page. Use this command to find files that you open yourself.

3. Boot a live image on an existing computer (virtual or real) and **chroot** into to it.

4. Start one or more disk intensive jobs and monitor them with **iostat** and **iotop** (compare to **vmstat**).

Chapter 9. introduction to uuid's

A **uuid** or **universally unique identifier** is used to uniquely identify objects. This 128bit standard allows anyone to create a unique **uuid**.

This chapter takes a brief look at **uuid's**.

9.1. about unique objects

Older versions of Linux have a **vol_id** utility to display the **uuid** of a file system.

```
root@debian5:~# vol_id --uuid /dev/sda1
193c3c9b-2c40-9290-8b71-4264ee4d4c82
```

Red Hat Enterprise Linux 5 puts **vol_id** in **/lib/udev/vol_id**, which is not in the $PATH. The syntax is also a bit different from Debian/Ubuntu/Mint.

```
root@rhel53 ~# /lib/udev/vol_id -u /dev/hda1
48a6a316-9ca9-4214-b5c6-e7b33a77e860
```

This utility is not available in standard installations of RHEL6 or Debian6.

9.2. tune2fs

Use **tune2fs** to find the **uuid** of a file system.

```
[root@RHEL5 ~]# tune2fs -l /dev/sda1 | grep UUID
Filesystem UUID:          11cfc8bc-07c0-4c3f-9f64-78422ef1dd5c
[root@RHEL5 ~]# /lib/udev/vol_id -u /dev/sda1
11cfc8bc-07c0-4c3f-9f64-78422ef1dd5c
```

9.3. uuid

There is more information in the manual of **uuid**, a tool that can generate uuid's.

```
[root@rhel65 ~]# yum install uuid
(output truncated)
[root@rhel65 ~]# man uuid
```

9.4. uuid in /etc/fstab

You can use the **uuid** to make sure that a volume is universally uniquely identified in **/etc/fstab**. The device name can change depending on the disk devices that are present at boot time, but a **uuid** never changes.

First we use **tune2fs** to find the **uuid**.

```
[root@RHEL5 ~]# tune2fs -l /dev/sdc1 | grep UUID
Filesystem UUID:          7626d73a-2bb6-4937-90ca-e451025d64e8
```

Then we check that it is properly added to **/etc/fstab**, the **uuid** replaces the variable devicename /dev/sdc1.

```
[root@RHEL5 ~]# grep UUID /etc/fstab
UUID=7626d73a-2bb6-4937-90ca-e451025d64e8 /home/pro42 ext3 defaults 0 0
```

Now we can mount the volume using the mount point defined in **/etc/fstab**.

```
[root@RHEL5 ~]# mount /home/pro42
[root@RHEL5 ~]# df -h | grep 42
/dev/sdc1             397M   11M  366M   3% /home/pro42
```

The real test now, is to remove **/dev/sdb** from the system, reboot the machine and see what happens. After the reboot, the disk previously known as **/dev/sdc** is now **/dev/sdb**.

```
[root@RHEL5 ~]# tune2fs -l /dev/sdb1 | grep UUID
Filesystem UUID:          7626d73a-2bb6-4937-90ca-e451025d64e8
```

And thanks to the **uuid** in **/etc/fstab**, the mountpoint is mounted on the same disk as before.

```
[root@RHEL5 ~]# df -h | grep sdb
/dev/sdb1             397M   11M  366M   3% /home/pro42
```

9.5. uuid as a boot device

Recent Linux distributions (Debian, Ubuntu, ...) use **grub** with a **uuid** to identify the root file system.

This example shows how a **root=/dev/sda1** is replaced with a **uuid**.

```
title           Ubuntu 9.10, kernel 2.6.31-19-generic
uuid            f001ba5d-9077-422a-9634-8d23d57e782a
kernel          /boot/vmlinuz-2.6.31-19-generic \
root=UUID=f001ba5d-9077-422a-9634-8d23d57e782a ro quiet splash
initrd          /boot/initrd.img-2.6.31-19-generic
```

The screenshot above contains only four lines. The line starting with **root=** is the continuation of the **kernel** line.

RHEL and CentOS boot from LVM after a default install.

9.6. practice: uuid and filesystems

1. Find the **uuid** of one of your **ext3** partitions with **tune2fs** (and **vol_id** if you are on RHEL5).

2. Use this **uuid** in **/etc/fstab** and test that it works with a simple **mount**.

3. (optional) Test it also by removing a disk (so the device name is changed). You can edit settings in vmware/Virtualbox to remove a hard disk.

4. Display the **root=** directive in **/boot/grub/menu.lst**. (We see later in the course how to maintain this file.)

5. (optional on ubuntu) Replace the **/dev/xxx** in **/boot/grub/menu.lst** with a **uuid** (use an extra stanza for this). Test that it works.

9.7. solution: uuid and filesystems

1. Find the **uuid** of one of your **ext3** partitions with **tune2fs** (and **vol_id** if you are on RHEL5).

```
root@rhel55:~# /lib/udev/vol_id -u /dev/hda1
60926898-2c78-49b4-a71d-c1d6310c87cc

root@ubu1004:~# tune2fs -l /dev/sda2 | grep UUID
Filesystem UUID:          3007b743-1dce-2d62-9a59-cf25f85191b7
```

2. Use this **uuid** in **/etc/fstab** and test that it works with a simple **mount**.

```
tail -1 /etc/fstab
UUID=60926898-2c78-49b4-a71d-c1d6310c87cc /home/pro42 ext3 defaults 0 0
```

3. (optional) Test it also by removing a disk (so the device name is changed). You can edit settings in vmware/Virtualbox to remove a hard disk.

4. Display the **root=** directive in **/boot/grub/menu.lst**. (We see later in the course how to maintain this file.)

```
paul@deb503:~$ grep ^[^#] /boot/grub/menu.lst | grep root=
kernel          /boot/vmlinuz-2.6.26-2-686 root=/dev/hda1 ro selinux=1 quiet
kernel          /boot/vmlinuz-2.6.26-2-686 root=/dev/hda1 ro selinux=1 single
```

5. (optional on ubuntu) Replace the **/dev/xxx** in **/boot/grub/menu.lst** with a **uuid** (use an extra stanza for this). Test that it works.

Chapter 10. introduction to raid

10.1. hardware or software

Redundant Array of Independent (originally Inexpensive) Disks or **RAID** can be set up using hardware or software. Hardware RAID is more expensive, but offers better performance. Software RAID is cheaper and easier to manage, but it uses your CPU and your memory.

Where ten years ago nobody was arguing about the best choice being hardware RAID, this has changed since technologies like mdadm, lvm and even zfs focus more on managability. The workload on the cpu for software RAID used to be high, but cpu's have gotten a lot faster.

10.2. raid levels

10.2.1. raid 0

raid 0 uses two or more disks, and is often called **striping** (or stripe set, or striped volume). Data is divided in **chunks**, those chunks are evenly spread across every disk in the array. The main advantage of **raid 0** is that you can create **larger drives**. **raid 0** is the only **raid** without redundancy.

10.2.2. jbod

jbod uses two or more disks, and is often called **concatenating** (spanning, spanned set, or spanned volume). Data is written to the first disk, until it is full. Then data is written to the second disk... The main advantage of **jbod** (Just a Bunch of Disks) is that you can create **larger drives**. JBOD offers no redundancy.

10.2.3. raid 1

raid 1 uses exactly two disks, and is often called **mirroring** (or mirror set, or mirrored volume). All data written to the array is written on each disk. The main advantage of raid 1 is **redundancy**. The main disadvantage is that you lose at least half of your available disk space (in other words, you at least double the cost).

10.2.4. raid 2, 3 and 4 ?

raid 2 uses bit level striping, **raid 3** byte level, and **raid 4** is the same as **raid 5**, but with a dedicated parity disk. This is actually slower than **raid 5**, because every write would have to write parity to this one (bottleneck) disk. It is unlikely that you will ever see these **raid** levels in production.

10.2.5. raid 5

raid 5 uses **three** or more disks, each divided into chunks. Every time chunks are written to the array, one of the disks will receive a **parity** chunk. Unlike **raid 4**, the parity chunk will alternate between all disks. The main advantage of this is that **raid 5** will allow for full data recovery in case of **one** hard disk failure.

10.2.6. raid 6

raid 6 is very similar to **raid 5**, but uses two parity chunks. **raid 6** protects against two hard disk failures. Oracle Solaris **zfs** calls this **raidz2** (and also had **raidz3** with triple parity).

10.2.7. raid 0+1

raid 0+1 is a mirror(1) of stripes(0). This means you first create two **raid 0 stripe** sets, and then you set them up as a mirror set. For example, when you have six 100GB disks, then the stripe sets are each 300GB. Combined in a mirror, this makes 300GB total. **raid 0+1** will survive one disk failure. It will only survive the second disk failure if this disk is in the same stripe set as the previous failed disk.

10.2.8. raid 1+0

raid 1+0 is a stripe(0) of mirrors(1). For example, when you have six 100GB disks, then you first create three mirrors of 100GB each. You then stripe them together into a 300GB drive. In this example, as long as not all disks in the same mirror fail, it can survive up to three hard disk failures.

10.2.9. raid 50

raid 5+0 is a stripe(0) of **raid 5** arrays. Suppose you have nine disks of 100GB, then you can create three **raid 5** arrays of 200GB each. You can then combine them into one large stripe set.

10.2.10. many others

There are many other nested **raid** combinations, like **raid** 30, 51, 60, 100, 150, ...

10.3. building a software raid5 array

10.3.1. do we have three disks?

First, you have to attach some disks to your computer. In this scenario, three brand new disks of eight gigabyte each are added. Check with **fdisk -l** that they are connected.

```
[root@rhel6c ~]# fdisk -l 2> /dev/null | grep MB
Disk /dev/sdb: 8589 MB, 8589934592 bytes
Disk /dev/sdc: 8589 MB, 8589934592 bytes
Disk /dev/sdd: 8589 MB, 8589934592 bytes
```

10.3.2. fd partition type

The next step is to create a partition of type **fd** on every disk. The **fd** type is to set the partition as **Linux RAID autodetect**. See this (truncated) screenshot:

```
[root@rhel6c ~]# fdisk /dev/sdd
...
Command (m for help): n
Command action
   e   extended
   p   primary partition (1-4)
p
Partition number (1-4): 1
First cylinder (1-1044, default 1):
Using default value 1
Last cylinder, +cylinders or +size{K,M,G} (1-1044, default 1044):
Using default value 1044

Command (m for help): t
Selected partition 1
Hex code (type L to list codes): fd
Changed system type of partition 1 to fd (Linux raid autodetect)

Command (m for help): w
The partition table has been altered!

Calling ioctl() to re-read partition table.
Syncing disks.
```

10.3.3. verify all three partitions

Now all three disks are ready for **raid 5**, so we have to tell the system what to do with these disks.

```
[root@rhel6c ~]# fdisk -l 2> /dev/null | grep raid
/dev/sdb1         1        1044     8385898+  fd  Linux raid autodetect
/dev/sdc1         1        1044     8385898+  fd  Linux raid autodetect
/dev/sdd1         1        1044     8385898+  fd  Linux raid autodetect
```

10.3.4. create the raid5

The next step used to be *create the **raid table** in **/etc/raidtab***. Nowadays, you can just issue the command **mdadm** with the correct parameters.

The command below is split on two lines to fit this print, but you should type it on one line, without the backslash (\).

```
[root@rhel6c ~]# mdadm --create /dev/md0 --chunk=64 --level=5 --raid-\
devices=3 /dev/sdb1 /dev/sdc1 /dev/sdd1
mdadm: Defaulting to version 1.2 metadata
mdadm: array /dev/md0 started.
```

Below a partial screenshot how fdisk -l sees the **raid 5**.

```
[root@rhel6c ~]# fdisk -l /dev/md0

Disk /dev/md0: 17.2 GB, 17172135936 bytes
2 heads, 4 sectors/track, 4192416 cylinders
Units = cylinders of 8 * 512 = 4096 bytes
Sector size (logical/physical): 512 bytes / 512 bytes
I/O size (minimum/optimal): 65536 bytes / 131072 bytes
Disk identifier: 0x00000000

Disk /dev/md0 doesn't contain a valid partition table
```

We could use this software **raid 5** array in the next topic: **lvm**.

10.3.5. /proc/mdstat

The status of the raid devices can be seen in **/proc/mdstat**. This example shows a **raid 5** in the process of rebuilding.

```
[root@rhel6c ~]# cat /proc/mdstat
Personalities : [raid6] [raid5] [raid4]
md0 : active raid5 sdd1[3] sdc1[1] sdb1[0]
      16769664 blocks super 1.2 level 5, 64k chunk, algorithm 2 [3/2] [UU_]
      [============>.......]  recovery = 62.8% (5266176/8384832) finish=0\
.3min speed=139200K/sec
```

This example shows an active software **raid 5**.

```
[root@rhel6c ~]# cat /proc/mdstat
Personalities : [raid6] [raid5] [raid4]
md0 : active raid5 sdd1[3] sdc1[1] sdb1[0]
    16769664 blocks super 1.2 level 5, 64k chunk, algorithm 2 [3/3] [UUU]
```

10.3.6. mdadm --detail

Use **mdadm --detail** to get information on a raid device.

```
[root@rhel6c ~]# mdadm --detail /dev/md0
/dev/md0:
        Version : 1.2
  Creation Time : Sun Jul 17 13:48:41 2011
     Raid Level : raid5
     Array Size : 16769664 (15.99 GiB 17.17 GB)
  Used Dev Size : 8384832 (8.00 GiB 8.59 GB)
   Raid Devices : 3
  Total Devices : 3
    Persistence : Superblock is persistent

    Update Time : Sun Jul 17 13:49:43 2011
          State : clean
 Active Devices : 3
Working Devices : 3
 Failed Devices : 0
  Spare Devices : 0

         Layout : left-symmetric
     Chunk Size : 64K

           Name : rhel6c:0  (local to host rhel6c)
           UUID : c10fd9c3:08f9a25f:be913027:999c8e1f
         Events : 18

    Number   Major   Minor   RaidDevice State
       0       8       17        0      active sync   /dev/sdb1
       1       8       33        1      active sync   /dev/sdc1
       3       8       49        2      active sync   /dev/sdd1
```

10.3.7. removing a software raid

The software raid is visible in **/proc/mdstat** when active. To remove the raid completely so you can use the disks for other purposes, you stop (de-activate) it with **mdadm**.

```
[root@rhel6c ~]# mdadm --stop /dev/md0
mdadm: stopped /dev/md0
```

The disks can now be repartitioned.

10.3.8. further reading

Take a look at the man page of **mdadm** for more information. Below an example command to add a new partition while removing a faulty one.

```
mdadm /dev/md0 --add /dev/sdd1 --fail /dev/sdb1 --remove /dev/sdb1
```

10.4. practice: raid

1. Add three virtual disks of 1GB each to a virtual machine.
2. Create a software **raid 5** on the three disks. (It is not necessary to put a filesystem on it)
3. Verify with **fdisk** and in **/proc** that the **raid 5** exists.
4. Stop and remove the **raid 5**.
5. Create a **raid 1** to mirror two disks.

10.5. solution: raid

1. Add three virtual disks of 1GB each to a virtual machine.

2. Create a software **raid 5** on the three disks. (It is not necessary to put a filesystem on it)

3. Verify with **fdisk** and in **/proc** that the **raid 5** exists.

4. Stop and remove the **raid 5**.

5. Create a **raid 1** to mirror two disks.

```
[root@rhel6c ~]# mdadm --create /dev/md0 --level=1 --raid-devices=2 \
/dev/sdb1 /dev/sdc1
mdadm: Defaulting to version 1.2 metadata
mdadm: array /dev/md0 started.
[root@rhel6c ~]# cat /proc/mdstat
Personalities : [raid6] [raid5] [raid4] [raid1]
md0 : active raid1 sdc1[1] sdb1[0]
      8384862 blocks super 1.2 [2/2] [UU]
      [====>................]  resync = 20.8% (1745152/8384862) \
finish=0.5min speed=218144K/sec
```

Chapter 11. logical volume management

Most **lvm** implementations support **physical storage grouping**, **logical volume resizing** and **data migration**.

Physical storage grouping is a fancy name for grouping multiple block devices (hard disks, but also iSCSI etc) into a logical mass storage device. To enlarge this physical group, block devices (including partitions) can be added at a later time.

The size of **lvm volumes** on this **physical group** is independent of the individual size of the components. The total size of the group is the limit.

One of the nice features of **lvm** is the logical volume resizing. You can increase the size of an **lvm volume**, sometimes even without any downtime. Additionally, you can migrate data away from a failing hard disk device, create mirrors and create snapshots.

11.1. introduction to lvm

11.1.1. problems with standard partitions

There are some problems when working with hard disks and standard partitions. Consider a system with a small and a large hard disk device, partitioned like this. The first disk (/dev/sda) is partitioned in two, the second disk (/dev/sdb) has two partitions and some empty space.

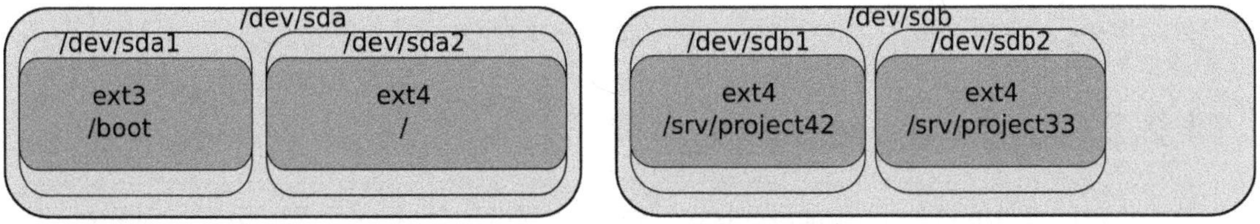

In the example above, consider the options when you want to enlarge the space available for **/srv/project42**. What can you do ? The solution will always force you to unmount the file system, take a backup of the data, remove and recreate partitions, and then restore the data and remount the file system.

11.1.2. solution with lvm

Using **lvm** will create a virtual layer between the mounted file systems and the hardware devices. This virtual layer will allow for an administrator to enlarge a mounted file system in use. When **lvm** is properly used, then there is no need to unmount the file system to enlarge it.

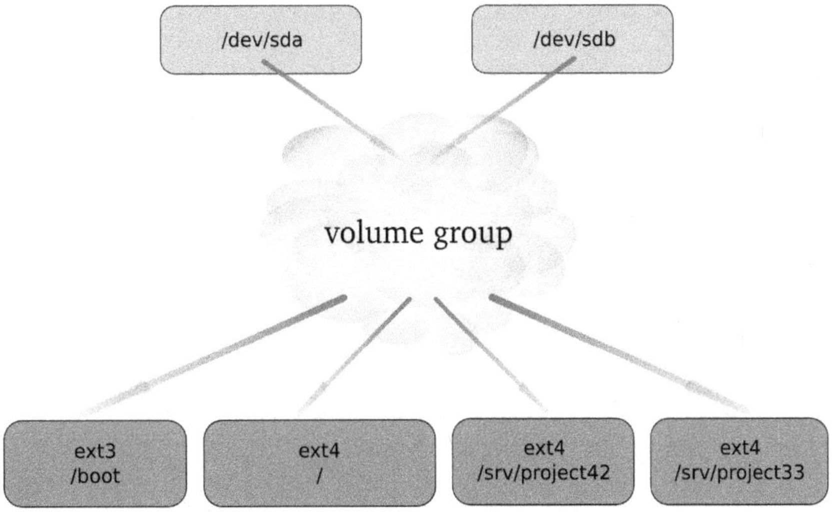

11.2. lvm terminology

11.2.1. physical volume (pv)

A **physical volume** is any block device (a disk, a partition, a RAID device or even an iSCSI device). All these devices can become a member of a **volume group**.

The commands used to manage a **physical volume** start with pv.

```
[root@centos65 ~]# pv
pvchange   pvck       pvcreate   pvdisplay  pvmove     pvremove
pvresize   pvs        pvscan
```

11.2.2. volume group (vg)

A **volume group** is an abstraction layer between **block devices** and **logical volumes**.

The commands used to manage a **volume group** start with vg.

```
[root@centos65 ~]# vg
vgcfgbackup    vgconvert      vgextend       vgmknodes      vgs
vgcfgrestore   vgcreate       vgimport       vgreduce       vgscan
vgchange       vgdisplay      vgimportclone  vgremove       vgsplit
vgck           vgexport       vgmerge        vgrename
```

11.2.3. logical volume (lv)

A **logical volume** is created in a **volume group**. Logical volumes that contain a file system can be mounted. The use of **logical volumes** is similar to the use of **partitions** and is accomplished with the same standard commands (mkfs, mount, fsck, df, ...).

The commands used to manage a **logical volume** start with lv.

```
[root@centos65 ~]# lv
lvchange     lvextend     lvmdiskscan  lvmsar       lvresize
lvconvert    lvm          lvmdump      lvreduce     lvs
lvcreate     lvmchange    lvmetad      lvremove     lvscan
lvdisplay    lvmconf      lvmsadc      lvrename
```

11.3. example: using lvm

This example shows how you can use a device (in this case /dev/sdc, but it could have been /dev/sdb or any other disk or partition) with lvm, how to create a volume group (vg) and how to create and use a logical volume (vg/lvol0).

First thing to do, is create physical volumes that can join the volume group with **pvcreate**. This command makes a disk or partition available for use in Volume Groups. The screenshot shows how to present the SCSI Disk device to LVM.

```
root@RHEL4:~# pvcreate /dev/sdc
Physical volume "/dev/sdc" successfully created
```

*Note: lvm **will** work fine when using the complete device, but another operating system on the same computer (or on the same SAN) will not recognize lvm and will mark the block device as being empty! You can avoid this by creating a partition that spans the whole device, then run **pvcreate** on the partition instead of the disk.*

Then **vgcreate** creates a volume group using one device. Note that more devices could be added to the volume group.

```
root@RHEL4:~# vgcreate vg /dev/sdc
Volume group "vg" successfully created
```

The last step **lvcreate** creates a logical volume.

```
root@RHEL4:~# lvcreate --size 500m vg
Logical volume "lvol0" created
```

The logical volume /dev/vg/lvol0 can now be formatted with ext3, and mounted for normal use.

```
root@RHELv4u2:~# mke2fs -m0 -j /dev/vg/lvol0
mke2fs 1.35 (28-Feb-2004)
Filesystem label=
OS type: Linux
Block size=1024 (log=0)
Fragment size=1024 (log=0)
128016 inodes, 512000 blocks
0 blocks (0.00%) reserved for the super user
First data block=1
Maximum filesystem blocks=67633152
63 block groups
8192 blocks per group, 8192 fragments per group
2032 inodes per group
Superblock backups stored on blocks:
8193, 24577, 40961, 57345, 73729, 204801, 221185, 401409

Writing inode tables: done
Creating journal (8192 blocks): done
Writing superblocks and filesystem accounting information: done

This filesystem will be automatically checked every 37 mounts or
180 days, whichever comes first.  Use tune2fs -c or -i to override.
root@RHELv4u2:~# mkdir /home/project10
root@RHELv4u2:~# mount /dev/vg/lvol0 /home/project10/
root@RHELv4u2:~# df -h | grep proj
/dev/mapper/vg-lvol0  485M   11M  474M   3% /home/project10
```

A logical volume is very similar to a partition, it can be formatted with a file system, and can be mounted so users can access it.

11.4. example: extend a logical volume

A logical volume can be extended without unmounting the file system. Whether or not a volume can be extended depends on the file system it uses. Volumes that are mounted as vfat or ext2 cannot be extended, so in the example here we use the ext3 file system.

The fdisk command shows us newly added scsi-disks that will serve our lvm volume. This volume will then be extended. First, take a look at these disks.

```
[root@RHEL5 ~]# fdisk -l | grep sd[bc]
Disk /dev/sdb doesn't contain a valid partition table
Disk /dev/sdc doesn't contain a valid partition table
Disk /dev/sdb: 1181 MB, 1181115904 bytes
Disk /dev/sdc: 429 MB, 429496320 bytes
```

You already know how to partition a disk, below the first disk is partitioned (in one big primary partition), the second disk is left untouched.

```
[root@RHEL5 ~]# fdisk -l | grep sd[bc]
Disk /dev/sdc doesn't contain a valid partition table
Disk /dev/sdb: 1181 MB, 1181115904 bytes
/dev/sdb1               1         143      1148616    83  Linux
Disk /dev/sdc: 429 MB, 429496320 bytes
```

You also know how to prepare disks for lvm with **pvcreate**, and how to create a volume group with **vgcreate**. This example adds both the partitioned disk and the untouched disk to the volume group named **vg2**.

```
[root@RHEL5 ~]# pvcreate /dev/sdb1
  Physical volume "/dev/sdb1" successfully created
[root@RHEL5 ~]# pvcreate /dev/sdc
  Physical volume "/dev/sdc" successfully created
[root@RHEL5 ~]# vgcreate vg2 /dev/sdb1 /dev/sdc
  Volume group "vg2" successfully created
```

You can use **pvdisplay** to verify that both the disk and the partition belong to the volume group.

```
[root@RHEL5 ~]# pvdisplay | grep -B1 vg2
  PV Name               /dev/sdb1
  VG Name               vg2
--
  PV Name               /dev/sdc
  VG Name               vg2
```

And you are familiar both with the **lvcreate** command to create a small logical volume and the **mke2fs** command to put ext3 on it.

```
[root@RHEL5 ~]# lvcreate --size 200m vg2
  Logical volume "lvol0" created
[root@RHEL5 ~]# mke2fs -m20 -j /dev/vg2/lvol0
...
```

As you see, we end up with a mounted logical volume that according to **df** is almost 200 megabyte in size.

```
[root@RHEL5 ~]# mkdir /home/resizetest
[root@RHEL5 ~]# mount /dev/vg2/lvol0 /home/resizetest/
[root@RHEL5 ~]# df -h | grep resizetest
                        194M  5.6M  149M   4% /home/resizetest
```

Extending the volume is easy with **lvextend**.

```
[root@RHEL5 ~]# lvextend -L +100 /dev/vg2/lvol0
  Extending logical volume lvol0 to 300.00 MB
  Logical volume lvol0 successfully resized
```

But as you can see, there is a small problem: it appears that df is not able to display the extended volume in its full size. This is because the filesystem is only set for the size of the volume before the extension was added.

```
[root@RHEL5 ~]# df -h | grep resizetest
                        194M  5.6M  149M   4% /home/resizetest
```

With **lvdisplay** however we can see that the volume is indeed extended.

```
[root@RHEL5 ~]# lvdisplay /dev/vg2/lvol0 | grep Size
  LV Size                300.00 MB
```

To finish the extension, you need **resize2fs** to span the filesystem over the full size of the logical volume.

```
[root@RHEL5 ~]# resize2fs /dev/vg2/lvol0
resize2fs 1.39 (29-May-2006)
Filesystem at /dev/vg2/lvol0 is mounted on /home/resizetest; on-line re\
sizing required
Performing an on-line resize of /dev/vg2/lvol0 to 307200 (1k) blocks.
The filesystem on /dev/vg2/lvol0 is now 307200 blocks long.
```

Congratulations, you just successfully expanded a logical volume.

```
[root@RHEL5 ~]# df -h | grep resizetest
                        291M  6.1M  225M   3% /home/resizetest
[root@RHEL5 ~]#
```

11.5. example: resize a physical Volume

This is a humble demonstration of how to resize a physical Volume with lvm (after you resize it with fdisk). The demonstration starts with a 100MB partition named /dev/sde1. We used fdisk to create it, and to verify the size.

```
[root@RHEL5 ~]# fdisk -l 2>/dev/null | grep sde1
/dev/sde1               1         100      102384   83  Linux
[root@RHEL5 ~]#
```

Now we can use pvcreate to create the Physical Volume, followed by pvs to verify the creation.

```
[root@RHEL5 ~]# pvcreate /dev/sde1
  Physical volume "/dev/sde1" successfully created
[root@RHEL5 ~]# pvs | grep sde1
  /dev/sde1             lvm2 --     99.98M  99.98M
[root@RHEL5 ~]#
```

The next step is to use fdisk to enlarge the partition (actually deleting it and then recreating /dev/sde1 with more cylinders).

```
[root@RHEL5 ~]# fdisk /dev/sde

Command (m for help): p

Disk /dev/sde: 858 MB, 858993152 bytes
64 heads, 32 sectors/track, 819 cylinders
Units = cylinders of 2048 * 512 = 1048576 bytes

   Device Boot      Start         End      Blocks   Id  System
/dev/sde1               1         100      102384   83  Linux

Command (m for help): d
Selected partition 1

Command (m for help): n
Command action
   e   extended
   p   primary partition (1-4)
p
Partition number (1-4):
Value out of range.
Partition number (1-4): 1
First cylinder (1-819, default 1):
Using default value 1
Last cylinder or +size or +sizeM or +sizeK (1-819, default 819): 200

Command (m for help): w
The partition table has been altered!

Calling ioctl() to re-read partition table.
Syncing disks.
[root@RHEL5 ~]#
```

When we now use fdisk and pvs to verify the size of the partition and the Physical Volume, then there is a size difference. LVM is still using the old size.

```
[root@RHEL5 ~]# fdisk -l 2>/dev/null | grep sde1
/dev/sde1               1         200      204784   83  Linux
[root@RHEL5 ~]# pvs | grep sde1
  /dev/sde1             lvm2 --     99.98M  99.98M
[root@RHEL5 ~]#
```

Executing pvresize on the Physical Volume will make lvm aware of the size change of the partition. The correct size can be displayed with pvs.

```
[root@RHEL5 ~]# pvresize /dev/sde1
  Physical volume "/dev/sde1" changed
  1 physical volume(s) resized / 0 physical volume(s) not resized
[root@RHEL5 ~]# pvs | grep sde1
  /dev/sde1             lvm2 --    199.98M 199.98M
[root@RHEL5 ~]#
```

11.6. example: mirror a logical volume

We start by creating three physical volumes for lvm. Then we verify the creation and the size with pvs. Three physical disks because lvm uses two disks for the mirror and a third disk for the mirror log!

```
[root@RHEL5 ~]# pvcreate /dev/sdb /dev/sdc /dev/sdd
  Physical volume "/dev/sdb" successfully created
  Physical volume "/dev/sdc" successfully created
  Physical volume "/dev/sdd" successfully created
[root@RHEL5 ~]# pvs
  PV         VG         Fmt  Attr PSize   PFree
  /dev/sdb              lvm2 --   409.60M 409.60M
  /dev/sdc              lvm2 --   409.60M 409.60M
  /dev/sdd              lvm2 --   409.60M 409.60M
```

Then we create the Volume Group and verify again with pvs. Notice how the three physical volumes now belong to vg33, and how the size is rounded down (in steps of the extent size, here 4MB).

```
[root@RHEL5 ~]# vgcreate vg33 /dev/sdb /dev/sdc /dev/sdd
  Volume group "vg33" successfully created
[root@RHEL5 ~]# pvs
  PV         VG         Fmt  Attr PSize   PFree
  /dev/sda2  VolGroup00 lvm2 a-    15.88G       0
  /dev/sdb   vg33       lvm2 a-   408.00M 408.00M
  /dev/sdc   vg33       lvm2 a-   408.00M 408.00M
  /dev/sdd   vg33       lvm2 a-   408.00M 408.00M
[root@RHEL5 ~]#
```

The last step is to create the Logical Volume with **lvcreate**. Notice the **-m 1** switch to create one mirror. Notice also the change in free space in all three Physical Volumes!

```
[root@RHEL5 ~]# lvcreate --size 300m -n lvmir -m 1 vg33
  Logical volume "lvmir" created
[root@RHEL5 ~]# pvs
  PV         VG         Fmt  Attr PSize   PFree
  /dev/sda2  VolGroup00 lvm2 a-    15.88G       0
  /dev/sdb   vg33       lvm2 a-   408.00M 108.00M
  /dev/sdc   vg33       lvm2 a-   408.00M 108.00M
  /dev/sdd   vg33       lvm2 a-   408.00M 404.00M
```

You can see the copy status of the mirror with lvs. It currently shows a 100 percent copy.

```
[root@RHEL5 ~]# lvs vg33/lvmir
  LV    VG   Attr   LSize   Origin Snap%  Move Log        Copy%
  lvmir vg33 mwi-ao 300.00M                    lvmir_mlog 100.00
```

11.7. example: snapshot a logical volume

A snapshot is a virtual copy of all the data at a point in time on a volume. A snapshot Logical Volume will retain a copy of all changed files of the snapshotted Logical Volume.

The example below creates a snapshot of the bigLV Logical Volume.

```
[root@RHEL5 ~]# lvcreate -L100M -s -n snapLV vg42/bigLV
  Logical volume "snapLV" created
[root@RHEL5 ~]#
```

You can see with lvs that the snapshot snapLV is indeed a snapshot of bigLV. Moments after taking the snapshot, there are few changes to bigLV (0.02 percent).

```
[root@RHEL5 ~]# lvs
  LV       VG        Attr   LSize   Origin Snap%  Move Log Copy%
  bigLV    vg42      owi-a- 200.00M
  snapLV   vg42      swi-a- 100.00M bigLV    0.02
[root@RHEL5 ~]#
```

But after using bigLV for a while, more changes are done. This means the snapshot volume has to keep more original data (10.22 percent).

```
[root@RHEL5 ~]# lvs | grep vg42
  bigLV    vg42      owi-ao 200.00M
  snapLV   vg42      swi-a- 100.00M bigLV   10.22
[root@RHEL5 ~]#
```

You can now use regular backup tools (dump, tar, cpio, ...) to take a backup of the snapshot Logical Volume. This backup will contain all data as it existed on bigLV at the time the snapshot was taken. When the backup is done, you can remove the snapshot.

```
[root@RHEL5 ~]# lvremove vg42/snapLV
Do you really want to remove active logical volume "snapLV"? [y/n]: y
  Logical volume "snapLV" successfully removed
[root@RHEL5 ~]#
```

11.8. verifying existing physical volumes

11.8.1. lvmdiskscan

To get a list of block devices that can be used with LVM, use **lvmdiskscan**. The example below uses grep to limit the result to SCSI devices.

```
[root@RHEL5 ~]# lvmdiskscan | grep sd
  /dev/sda1                [      101.94 MB]
  /dev/sda2                [       15.90 GB] LVM physical volume
  /dev/sdb                 [      409.60 MB]
  /dev/sdc                 [      409.60 MB]
  /dev/sdd                 [      409.60 MB] LVM physical volume
  /dev/sde1                [       95.98 MB]
  /dev/sde5                [      191.98 MB]
  /dev/sdf                 [      819.20 MB] LVM physical volume
  /dev/sdg1                [      818.98 MB]
[root@RHEL5 ~]#
```

11.8.2. pvs

The easiest way to verify whether devices are known to lvm is with the **pvs** command. The screenshot below shows that only /dev/sda2 is currently known for use with LVM. It shows that /dev/sda2 is part of Volgroup00 and is almost 16GB in size. It also shows /dev/sdc and /dev/sdd as part of vg33. The device /dev/sdb is knwon to lvm, but not linked to any Volume Group.

```
[root@RHEL5 ~]# pvs
  PV         VG         Fmt  Attr PSize   PFree
  /dev/sda2  VolGroup00 lvm2 a-    15.88G       0
  /dev/sdb              lvm2 --   409.60M 409.60M
  /dev/sdc   vg33       lvm2 a-   408.00M 408.00M
  /dev/sdd   vg33       lvm2 a-   408.00M 408.00M
[root@RHEL5 ~]#
```

11.8.3. pvscan

The **pvscan** command will scan all disks for existing Physical Volumes. The information is similar to pvs, plus you get a line with total sizes.

```
[root@RHEL5 ~]# pvscan
  PV /dev/sdc    VG vg33         lvm2 [408.00 MB / 408.00 MB free]
  PV /dev/sdd    VG vg33         lvm2 [408.00 MB / 408.00 MB free]
  PV /dev/sda2   VG VolGroup00   lvm2 [15.88 GB / 0    free]
  PV /dev/sdb                    lvm2 [409.60 MB]
  Total: 4 [17.07 GB] / in use: 3 [16.67 GB] / in no VG: 1 [409.60 MB]
[root@RHEL5 ~]#
```

11.8.4. pvdisplay

Use **pvdisplay** to get more information about physical volumes. You can also use **pvdisplay** without an argument to display information about all physical (lvm) volumes.

```
[root@RHEL5 ~]# pvdisplay /dev/sda2
  --- Physical volume ---
  PV Name               /dev/sda2
  VG Name               VolGroup00
  PV Size               15.90 GB / not usable 20.79 MB
  Allocatable           yes (but full)
  PE Size (KByte)       32768
  Total PE              508
  Free PE               0
  Allocated PE          508
  PV UUID               TobYfp-Ggg0-Rf8r-xtLd-5XgN-RSPc-8vkTHD

[root@RHEL5 ~]#
```

11.9. verifying existing volume groups

11.9.1. vgs

Similar to **pvs** is the use of **vgs** to display a quick overview of all volume groups. There is only one volume group in the screenshot below, it is named VolGroup00 and is almost 16GB in size.

```
[root@RHEL5 ~]# vgs
  VG         #PV #LV #SN Attr   VSize  VFree
  VolGroup00   1   2   0 wz--n- 15.88G    0
[root@RHEL5 ~]#
```

11.9.2. vgscan

The **vgscan** command will scan all disks for existing Volume Groups. It will also update the **/etc/lvm/.cache** file. This file contains a list of all current lvm devices.

```
[root@RHEL5 ~]# vgscan
  Reading all physical volumes.  This may take a while...
  Found volume group "VolGroup00" using metadata type lvm2
[root@RHEL5 ~]#
```

LVM will run the vgscan automatically at boot-up, so if you add hot swap devices, then you will need to run vgscan to update /etc/lvm/.cache with the new devices.

11.9.3. vgdisplay

The **vgdisplay** command will give you more detailed information about a volume group (or about all volume groups if you omit the argument).

```
[root@RHEL5 ~]# vgdisplay VolGroup00
  --- Volume group ---
  VG Name               VolGroup00
  System ID
  Format                lvm2
  Metadata Areas        1
  Metadata Sequence No  3
  VG Access             read/write
  VG Status             resizable
  MAX LV                0
  Cur LV                2
  Open LV               2
  Max PV                0
  Cur PV                1
  Act PV                1
  VG Size               15.88 GB
  PE Size               32.00 MB
  Total PE              508
  Alloc PE / Size       508 / 15.88 GB
  Free  PE / Size       0 / 0
  VG UUID               qsXvJb-71qV-917U-ishX-FobM-qptE-VXmKIg

[root@RHEL5 ~]#
```

11.10. verifying existing logical volumes

11.10.1. lvs

Use **lvs** for a quick look at all existing logical volumes. Below you can see two logical volumes named LogVol00 and LogVol01.

```
[root@RHEL5 ~]# lvs
  LV       VG         Attr   LSize  Origin Snap%  Move Log Copy%
  LogVol00 VolGroup00 -wi-ao 14.88G
  LogVol01 VolGroup00 -wi-ao  1.00G
[root@RHEL5 ~]#
```

11.10.2. lvscan

The **lvscan** command will scan all disks for existing Logical Volumes.

```
[root@RHEL5 ~]# lvscan
  ACTIVE            '/dev/VolGroup00/LogVol00' [14.88 GB] inherit
  ACTIVE            '/dev/VolGroup00/LogVol01' [1.00 GB] inherit
[root@RHEL5 ~]#
```

11.10.3. lvdisplay

More detailed information about logical volumes is available through the **lvdisplay(1)** command.

```
[root@RHEL5 ~]# lvdisplay VolGroup00/LogVol01
  --- Logical volume ---
  LV Name                /dev/VolGroup00/LogVol01
  VG Name                VolGroup00
  LV UUID                RnTGK6-xWsi-t530-ksJx-7cax-co5c-A1KlDp
  LV Write Access        read/write
  LV Status              available
  # open                 1
  LV Size                1.00 GB
  Current LE             32
  Segments               1
  Allocation             inherit
  Read ahead sectors     0
  Block device           253:1

[root@RHEL5 ~]#
```

11.11. manage physical volumes

11.11.1. pvcreate

Use the **pvcreate** command to add devices to lvm. This example shows how to add a disk (or hardware RAID device) to lvm.

```
[root@RHEL5 ~]# pvcreate /dev/sdb
  Physical volume "/dev/sdb" successfully created
[root@RHEL5 ~]#
```

This example shows how to add a partition to lvm.

```
[root@RHEL5 ~]# pvcreate /dev/sdc1
  Physical volume "/dev/sdc1" successfully created
[root@RHEL5 ~]#
```

You can also add multiple disks or partitions as target to pvcreate. This example adds three disks to lvm.

```
[root@RHEL5 ~]# pvcreate /dev/sde /dev/sdf /dev/sdg
  Physical volume "/dev/sde" successfully created
  Physical volume "/dev/sdf" successfully created
  Physical volume "/dev/sdg" successfully created
[root@RHEL5 ~]#
```

11.11.2. pvremove

Use the **pvremove** command to remove physical volumes from lvm. The devices may not be in use.

```
[root@RHEL5 ~]# pvremove /dev/sde /dev/sdf /dev/sdg
  Labels on physical volume "/dev/sde" successfully wiped
  Labels on physical volume "/dev/sdf" successfully wiped
  Labels on physical volume "/dev/sdg" successfully wiped
[root@RHEL5 ~]#
```

11.11.3. pvresize

When you used fdisk to resize a partition on a disk, then you must use **pvresize** to make lvm recognize the new size of the physical volume that represents this partition.

```
[root@RHEL5 ~]# pvresize /dev/sde1
  Physical volume "/dev/sde1" changed
  1 physical volume(s) resized / 0 physical volume(s) not resized
```

11.11.4. pvchange

With **pvchange** you can prevent the allocation of a Physical Volume in a new Volume Group or Logical Volume. This can be useful if you plan to remove a Physical Volume.

```
[root@RHEL5 ~]# pvchange -xn /dev/sdd
  Physical volume "/dev/sdd" changed
  1 physical volume changed / 0 physical volumes not changed
[root@RHEL5 ~]#
```

To revert your previous decision, this example shows you how te re-enable the Physical Volume to allow allocation.

```
[root@RHEL5 ~]# pvchange -xy /dev/sdd
  Physical volume "/dev/sdd" changed
  1 physical volume changed / 0 physical volumes not changed
[root@RHEL5 ~]#
```

11.11.5. pvmove

With **pvmove** you can move Logical Volumes from within a Volume Group to another Physical Volume. This must be done before removing a Physical Volume.

```
[root@RHEL5 ~]# pvs | grep vg1
  /dev/sdf   vg1        lvm2 a-   816.00M       0
  /dev/sdg   vg1        lvm2 a-   816.00M 816.00M
[root@RHEL5 ~]# pvmove /dev/sdf
  /dev/sdf: Moved: 70.1%
  /dev/sdf: Moved: 100.0%
[root@RHEL5 ~]# pvs | grep vg1
  /dev/sdf   vg1        lvm2 a-   816.00M 816.00M
  /dev/sdg   vg1        lvm2 a-   816.00M       0
```

11.12. manage volume groups

11.12.1. vgcreate

Use the **vgcreate** command to create a volume group. You can immediately name all the physical volumes that span the volume group.

```
[root@RHEL5 ~]# vgcreate vg42 /dev/sde /dev/sdf
  Volume group "vg42" successfully created
[root@RHEL5 ~]#
```

11.12.2. vgextend

Use the **vgextend** command to extend an existing volume group with a physical volume.

```
[root@RHEL5 ~]# vgextend vg42 /dev/sdg
  Volume group "vg42" successfully extended
[root@RHEL5 ~]#
```

11.12.3. vgremove

Use the **vgremove** command to remove volume groups from lvm. The volume groups may not be in use.

```
[root@RHEL5 ~]# vgremove vg42
  Volume group "vg42" successfully removed
[root@RHEL5 ~]#
```

11.12.4. vgreduce

Use the **vgreduce** command to remove a Physical Volume from the Volume Group.

The following example adds Physical Volume /dev/sdg to the vg1 Volume Group using vgextend. And then removes it again using vgreduce.

```
[root@RHEL5 ~]# pvs | grep sdg
  /dev/sdg              lvm2 --   819.20M 819.20M
[root@RHEL5 ~]# vgextend vg1 /dev/sdg
  Volume group "vg1" successfully extended
[root@RHEL5 ~]# pvs | grep sdg
  /dev/sdg   vg1        lvm2 a-   816.00M 816.00M
[root@RHEL5 ~]# vgreduce vg1 /dev/sdg
  Removed "/dev/sdg" from volume group "vg1"
[root@RHEL5 ~]# pvs | grep sdg
  /dev/sdg              lvm2 --   819.20M 819.20M
```

11.12.5. vgchange

Use the **vgchange** command to change parameters of a Volume Group.

This example shows how to prevent Physical Volumes from being added or removed to the Volume Group vg1.

```
[root@RHEL5 ~]# vgchange -xn vg1
  Volume group "vg1" successfully changed
[root@RHEL5 ~]# vgextend vg1 /dev/sdg
  Volume group vg1 is not resizable.
```

You can also use vgchange to change most other properties of a Volume Group. This example changes the maximum number of Logical Volumes and maximum number of Physical Volumes that vg1 can serve.

```
[root@RHEL5 ~]# vgdisplay vg1 | grep -i max
  MAX LV                0
  Max PV                0
[root@RHEL5 ~]# vgchange -l16 vg1
  Volume group "vg1" successfully changed
[root@RHEL5 ~]# vgchange -p8 vg1
  Volume group "vg1" successfully changed
[root@RHEL5 ~]# vgdisplay vg1 | grep -i max
  MAX LV                16
  Max PV                8
```

11.12.6. vgmerge

Merging two Volume Groups into one is done with **vgmerge**. The following example merges vg2 into vg1, keeping all the properties of vg1.

```
[root@RHEL5 ~]# vgmerge vg1 vg2
  Volume group "vg2" successfully merged into "vg1"
[root@RHEL5 ~]#
```

11.13. manage logical volumes

11.13.1. lvcreate

Use the **lvcreate** command to create Logical Volumes in a Volume Group. This example creates an 8GB Logical Volume in Volume Group vg42.

```
[root@RHEL5 ~]# lvcreate -L5G vg42
  Logical volume "lvol0" created
[root@RHEL5 ~]#
```

As you can see, lvm automatically names the Logical Volume **lvol0**. The next example creates a 200MB Logical Volume named MyLV in Volume Group vg42.

```
[root@RHEL5 ~]# lvcreate -L200M -nMyLV vg42
  Logical volume "MyLV" created
[root@RHEL5 ~]#
```

The next example does the same thing, but with different syntax.

```
[root@RHEL5 ~]# lvcreate --size 200M -n MyLV vg42
  Logical volume "MyLV" created
[root@RHEL5 ~]#
```

This example creates a Logical Volume that occupies 10 percent of the Volume Group.

```
[root@RHEL5 ~]# lvcreate -l 10%VG -n MyLV2 vg42
  Logical volume "MyLV2" created
[root@RHEL5 ~]#
```

This example creates a Logical Volume that occupies 30 percent of the remaining free space in the Volume Group.

```
[root@RHEL5 ~]# lvcreate -l 30%FREE -n MyLV3 vg42
  Logical volume "MyLV3" created
[root@RHEL5 ~]#
```

11.13.2. lvremove

Use the **lvremove** command to remove Logical Volumes from a Volume Group. Removing a Logical Volume requires the name of the Volume Group.

```
[root@RHEL5 ~]# lvremove vg42/MyLV
Do you really want to remove active logical volume "MyLV"? [y/n]: y
  Logical volume "MyLV" successfully removed
[root@RHEL5 ~]#
```

Removing multiple Logical Volumes will request confirmation for each individual volume.

```
[root@RHEL5 ~]# lvremove vg42/MyLV vg42/MyLV2 vg42/MyLV3
Do you really want to remove active logical volume "MyLV"? [y/n]: y
  Logical volume "MyLV" successfully removed
Do you really want to remove active logical volume "MyLV2"? [y/n]: y
  Logical volume "MyLV2" successfully removed
Do you really want to remove active logical volume "MyLV3"? [y/n]: y
  Logical volume "MyLV3" successfully removed
[root@RHEL5 ~]#
```

11.13.3. lvextend

Extending the volume is easy with **lvextend**. This example extends a 200MB Logical Volume with 100 MB.

```
[root@RHEL5 ~]# lvdisplay /dev/vg2/lvol0 | grep Size
  LV Size                200.00 MB
[root@RHEL5 ~]# lvextend -L +100 /dev/vg2/lvol0
  Extending logical volume lvol0 to 300.00 MB
  Logical volume lvol0 successfully resized
[root@RHEL5 ~]# lvdisplay /dev/vg2/lvol0 | grep Size
  LV Size                300.00 MB
```

The next example creates a 100MB Logical Volume, and then extends it to 500MB.

```
[root@RHEL5 ~]# lvcreate --size 100M -n extLV vg42
  Logical volume "extLV" created
[root@RHEL5 ~]# lvextend -L 500M vg42/extLV
  Extending logical volume extLV to 500.00 MB
  Logical volume extLV successfully resized
[root@RHEL5 ~]#
```

This example doubles the size of a Logical Volume.

```
[root@RHEL5 ~]# lvextend -l+100%LV vg42/extLV
  Extending logical volume extLV to 1000.00 MB
  Logical volume extLV successfully resized
[root@RHEL5 ~]#
```

11.13.4. lvrename

Renaming a Logical Volume is done with **lvrename**. This example renames extLV to bigLV in the vg42 Volume Group.

```
[root@RHEL5 ~]# lvrename vg42/extLV vg42/bigLV
  Renamed "extLV" to "bigLV" in volume group "vg42"
[root@RHEL5 ~]#
```

11.14. practice : lvm

1. Create a volume group that contains a complete disk and a partition on another disk.

2. Create two logical volumes (a small one and a bigger one) in this volumegroup. Format them wih ext3, mount them and copy some files to them.

3. Verify usage with fdisk, mount, pvs, vgs, lvs, pvdisplay, vgdisplay, lvdisplay and df. Does fdisk give you any information about lvm?

4. Enlarge the small logical volume by 50 percent, and verify your work!

5. Take a look at other commands that start with vg* , pv* or lv*.

6. Create a mirror and a striped Logical Volume.

7. Convert a linear logical volume to a mirror.

8. Convert a mirror logical volume to a linear.

9. Create a snapshot of a Logical Volume, take a backup of the snapshot. Then delete some files on the Logical Volume, then restore your backup.

10. Move your volume group to another disk (keep the Logical Volumes mounted).

11. If time permits, split a Volume Group with vgsplit, then merge it again with vgmerge.

11.15. solution : lvm

1. Create a volume group that contains a complete disk and a partition on another disk.

step 1: select disks:

```
root@rhel65:~# fdisk -l | grep Disk
Disk /dev/sda: 8589 MB, 8589934592 bytes
Disk identifier: 0x00055ca0
Disk /dev/sdb: 1073 MB, 1073741824 bytes
Disk identifier: 0x00000000
Disk /dev/sdc: 1073 MB, 1073741824 bytes
Disk identifier: 0x00000000
...
```

I choose /dev/sdb and /dev/sdc for now.

step 2: partition /dev/sdc

```
root@rhel65:~# fdisk /dev/sdc
Device contains neither a valid DOS partition table, nor Sun, SGI or OSF disk\
label
Building a new DOS disklabel with disk identifier 0x94c0e5d5.
Changes will remain in memory only, until you decide to write them.
After that, of course, the previous content won't be recoverable.

Warning: invalid flag 0x0000 of partition table 4 will be corrected by w(rite)

WARNING: DOS-compatible mode is deprecated. It's strongly recommended to
         switch off the mode (command 'c') and change display units to
         sectors (command 'u').

Command (m for help): n
Command action
   e   extended
   p   primary partition (1-4)
p
Partition number (1-4): 1
First cylinder (1-130, default 1):
Using default value 1
Last cylinder, +cylinders or +size{K,M,G} (1-130, default 130):
Using default value 130

Command (m for help): w
The partition table has been altered!

Calling ioctl() to re-read partition table.
Syncing disks.
```

step 3: pvcreate and vgcreate

```
root@rhel65:~# pvcreate /dev/sdb /dev/sdc1
  Physical volume "/dev/sdb" successfully created
  Physical volume "/dev/sdc1" successfully created
root@rhel65:~# vgcreate VG42 /dev/sdb /dev/sdc1
  Volume group "VG42" successfully created
```

2. Create two logical volumes (a small one and a bigger one) in this volumegroup. Format them wih ext3, mount them and copy some files to them.

```
root@rhel65:~# lvcreate --size 200m --name LVsmall VG42
  Logical volume "LVsmall" created
root@rhel65:~# lvcreate --size 600m --name LVbig VG42
  Logical volume "LVbig" created
root@rhel65:~# ls -l /dev/mapper/VG42-LVsmall
lrwxrwxrwx. 1 root root 7 Apr 20 20:41 /dev/mapper/VG42-LVsmall -> ../dm-2
root@rhel65:~# ls -l /dev/VG42/LVsmall
lrwxrwxrwx. 1 root root 7 Apr 20 20:41 /dev/VG42/LVsmall -> ../dm-2
root@rhel65:~# ls -l /dev/dm-2
brw-rw----. 1 root disk 253, 2 Apr 20 20:41 /dev/dm-2

root@rhel65:~# mkfs.ext3 /dev/mapper/VG42-LVsmall
mke2fs 1.41.12 (17-May-2010)
Filesystem label=
OS type: Linux
Block size=1024 (log=0)
Fragment size=1024 (log=0)
Stride=0 blocks, Stripe width=0 blocks
51200 inodes, 204800 blocks
10240 blocks (5.00%) reserved for the super user
First data block=1
Maximum filesystem blocks=67371008
25 block groups
8192 blocks per group, 8192 fragments per group
2048 inodes per group
Superblock backups stored on blocks:
 8193, 24577, 40961, 57345, 73729

Writing inode tables: done
Creating journal (4096 blocks): done
Writing superblocks and filesystem accounting information: done

This filesystem will be automatically checked every 39 mounts or
180 days, whichever comes first.  Use tune2fs -c or -i to override.

root@rhel65:~# mkfs.ext3 /dev/VG42/LVbig
mke2fs 1.41.12 (17-May-2010)
Filesystem label=
OS type: Linux
Block size=4096 (log=2)
Fragment size=4096 (log=2)
Stride=0 blocks, Stripe width=0 blocks
38400 inodes, 153600 blocks
7680 blocks (5.00%) reserved for the super user
First data block=0
Maximum filesystem blocks=159383552
5 block groups
32768 blocks per group, 32768 fragments per group
7680 inodes per group
Superblock backups stored on blocks:
 32768, 98304

Writing inode tables: done
Creating journal (4096 blocks): done
Writing superblocks and filesystem accounting information: done

This filesystem will be automatically checked every 25 mounts or
180 days, whichever comes first.  Use tune2fs -c or -i to override.
```

The mounting and copying of files.

```
root@rhel65:~# mkdir /srv/LVsmall
root@rhel65:~# mkdir /srv/LVbig
root@rhel65:~# mount /dev/mapper/VG42-LVsmall /srv/LVsmall
root@rhel65:~# mount /dev/VG42/LVbig /srv/LVbig
root@rhel65:~# cp -r /etc /srv/LVsmall/
root@rhel65:~# cp -r /var/log /srv/LVbig/
```

3. Verify usage with fdisk, mount, pvs, vgs, lvs, pvdisplay, vgdisplay, lvdisplay and df. Does fdisk give you any information about lvm?

Run all those commands (only two are shown below), then answer 'no'.

```
root@rhel65:~# df -h
Filesystem            Size  Used Avail Use% Mounted on
/dev/mapper/VolGroup-lv_root
                      6.7G  1.4G  5.0G  21% /
tmpfs                 246M     0  246M   0% /dev/shm
/dev/sda1             485M   77M  383M  17% /boot
/dev/mapper/VG42-LVsmall
                      194M   30M  154M  17% /srv/LVsmall
/dev/mapper/VG42-LVbig
                      591M   20M  541M   4% /srv/LVbig
root@rhel65:~# mount | grep VG42
/dev/mapper/VG42-LVsmall on /srv/LVsmall type ext3 (rw)
/dev/mapper/VG42-LVbig on /srv/LVbig type ext3 (rw)
```

4. Enlarge the small logical volume by 50 percent, and verify your work!

```
root@rhel65:~# lvextend VG42/LVsmall -l+50%LV
  Extending logical volume LVsmall to 300.00 MiB
  Logical volume LVsmall successfully resized
root@rhel65:~# resize2fs /dev/mapper/VG42-LVsmall
resize2fs 1.41.12 (17-May-2010)
Filesystem at /dev/mapper/VG42-LVsmall is mounted on /srv/LVsmall; on-line res\
izing required
old desc_blocks = 1, new_desc_blocks = 2
Performing an on-line resize of /dev/mapper/VG42-LVsmall to 307200 (1k) blocks.
The filesystem on /dev/mapper/VG42-LVsmall is now 307200 blocks long.

root@rhel65:~# df -h | grep small
/dev/mapper/VG42-LVsmall
                      291M   31M  246M  12% /srv/LVsmall
root@rhel65:~#
```

5. Take a look at other commands that start with vg* , pv* or lv*.

6. Create a mirror and a striped Logical Volume.

7. Convert a linear logical volume to a mirror.

8. Convert a mirror logical volume to a linear.

9. Create a snapshot of a Logical Volume, take a backup of the snapshot. Then delete some files on the Logical Volume, then restore your backup.

10. Move your volume group to another disk (keep the Logical Volumes mounted).

11. If time permits, split a Volume Group with vgsplit, then merge it again with vgmerge.

Chapter 12. iSCSI devices

This chapter teaches you how to setup an **iSCSI target server** and an **iSCSI initiator client**.

12.1. iSCSI terminology

iSCSI is a protocol that enables SCSI over IP. This means that you can have local SCSI devices (like /dev/sdb) without having the storage hardware in the local computer.

The computer holding the physical storage hardware is called the **iSCSI Target**. Each individual addressable iSCSI device on the target server will get a **LUN number**.

The iSCSI client computer that is connecting to the Target server is called an **Initiator**. An initiator will send SCSI commands over IP instead of directly to the hardware. The Initiator will connect to the Target.

12.2. iSCSI Target in RHEL/CentOS

This section will describe iSCSI Target setup on RHEL6, RHEL7 and CentOS.

Start with installing the **iSCSI Target** package.

```
yum install scsi-target-utils
```

We configure three local disks in **/etc/tgt/targets.conf** to become three LUN's.

```
<target iqn.2008-09.com.example:server.target2>
    direct-store /dev/sdb
    direct-store /dev/sdc
    direct-store /dev/sdd
    incominguser paul hunter2
</target>
```

Restart the service.

```
[root@centos65 ~]# service tgtd start
Starting SCSI target daemon:                                [  OK  ]
```

The standard local port for iSCSI Target is 3260, in case of doubt you can verify this with **netstat**.

```
[root@server1 tgt]# netstat -ntpl | grep tgt
tcp     0     0 0.0.0.0:3260          0.0.0.0:*             LISTEN      1670/tgtd
tcp     0     0 :::3260               :::*                  LISTEN      1670/tgtd
```

The **tgt-admin -s** command should now give you a nice overview of the three LUN's (and also LUN 0 for the controller).

```
[root@server1 tgt]# tgt-admin -s
Target 1: iqn.2014-04.be.linux-training:server1.target1
    System information:
        Driver: iscsi
        State: ready
    I_T nexus information:
    LUN information:
        LUN: 0
            Type: controller
            SCSI ID: IET     00010000
            SCSI SN: beaf10
            Size: 0 MB, Block size: 1
            Online: Yes
            Removable media: No
            Prevent removal: No
            Readonly: No
            Backing store type: null
            Backing store path: None
            Backing store flags:
        LUN: 1
            Type: disk
            SCSI ID: IET     00010001
            SCSI SN: VB9f23197b-af6cfb60
            Size: 1074 MB, Block size: 512
            Online: Yes
            Removable media: No
            Prevent removal: No
            Readonly: No
            Backing store type: rdwr
            Backing store path: /dev/sdb
            Backing store flags:
        LUN: 2
            Type: disk
            SCSI ID: IET     00010002
            SCSI SN: VB8f554351-a1410828
            Size: 1074 MB, Block size: 512
            Online: Yes
            Removable media: No
            Prevent removal: No
            Readonly: No
            Backing store type: rdwr
            Backing store path: /dev/sdc
            Backing store flags:
        LUN: 3
            Type: disk
            SCSI ID: IET     00010003
            SCSI SN: VB1035d2f0-7ae90b49
            Size: 1074 MB, Block size: 512
            Online: Yes
            Removable media: No
            Prevent removal: No
            Readonly: No
            Backing store type: rdwr
            Backing store path: /dev/sdd
            Backing store flags:
    Account information:
    ACL information:
        ALL
```

12.3. iSCSI Initiator in RHEL/CentOS

This section will describe iSCSI Initiator setup on RHEL6, RHEL7 and CentOS.

Start with installing the **iSCSI Initiator** package.

```
[root@server2 ~]# yum install iscsi-initiator-utils
```

Then ask the **iSCSI target server** to send you the target names.

```
[root@server2 ~]# iscsiadm -m discovery -t sendtargets -p 192.168.1.95:3260
Starting iscsid:                                           [  OK  ]
192.168.1.95:3260,1 iqn.2014-04.be.linux-training:centos65.target1
```

We received **iqn.2014-04.be.linux-training:centos65.target1**.

We use this iqn to configure the username and the password (paul and hunter2) that we set on the target server.

```
[root@server2 iscsi]# iscsiadm -m node --targetname iqn.2014-04.be.linux-tra\
ining:centos65.target1 --portal "192.168.1.95:3260" --op=update --name node.\
session.auth.username --value=paul
[root@server2 iscsi]# iscsiadm -m node --targetname iqn.2014-04.be.linux-tra\
ining:centos65.target1 --portal "192.168.1.95:3260" --op=update --name node.\
session.auth.password --value=hunter2
[root@server2 iscsi]# iscsiadm -m node --targetname iqn.2014-04.be.linux-tra\
ining:centos65.target1 --portal "192.168.1.95:3260" --op=update --name node.\
session.auth.authmethod --value=CHAP
```

RHEL and CentOS will store these in **/var/lib/iscsi/nodes/**.

```
[root@server2 iscsi]# grep auth /var/lib/iscsi/nodes/iqn.2014-04.be.linux-tr\
aining\:centos65.target1/192.168.1.95\,3260\,1/default
node.session.auth.authmethod = CHAP
node.session.auth.username = paul
node.session.auth.password = hunter2
node.conn[0].timeo.auth_timeout = 45
[root@server2 iscsi]#
```

A restart of the **iscsi** service will add three new devices to our system.

```
[root@server2 iscsi]# fdisk -l | grep Disk
Disk /dev/sda: 42.9 GB, 42949672960 bytes
Disk identifier: 0x0004f229
Disk /dev/sdb: 1073 MB, 1073741824 bytes
Disk identifier: 0x00000000
Disk /dev/sdc: 1073 MB, 1073741824 bytes
Disk identifier: 0x00000000
Disk /dev/sdd: 1073 MB, 1073741824 bytes
Disk identifier: 0x00000000
Disk /dev/sde: 2147 MB, 2147483648 bytes
Disk identifier: 0x00000000
Disk /dev/sdf: 2147 MB, 2147483648 bytes
Disk identifier: 0x00000000
Disk /dev/sdg: 2147 MB, 2147483648 bytes
Disk identifier: 0x00000000
Disk /dev/mapper/VolGroup-lv_root: 41.4 GB, 41448112128 bytes
Disk identifier: 0x00000000
Disk /dev/mapper/VolGroup-lv_swap: 973 MB, 973078528 bytes
Disk identifier: 0x00000000
[root@server2 iscsi]# service iscsi restart
Stopping iscsi:                                            [  OK  ]
Starting iscsi:                                            [  OK  ]
[root@server2 iscsi]# fdisk -l | grep Disk
Disk /dev/sda: 42.9 GB, 42949672960 bytes
Disk identifier: 0x0004f229
Disk /dev/sdb: 1073 MB, 1073741824 bytes
Disk identifier: 0x00000000
Disk /dev/sdc: 1073 MB, 1073741824 bytes
Disk identifier: 0x00000000
Disk /dev/sdd: 1073 MB, 1073741824 bytes
Disk identifier: 0x00000000
Disk /dev/sde: 2147 MB, 2147483648 bytes
Disk identifier: 0x00000000
Disk /dev/sdf: 2147 MB, 2147483648 bytes
Disk identifier: 0x00000000
Disk /dev/sdg: 2147 MB, 2147483648 bytes
Disk identifier: 0x00000000
Disk /dev/mapper/VolGroup-lv_root: 41.4 GB, 41448112128 bytes
Disk identifier: 0x00000000
Disk /dev/mapper/VolGroup-lv_swap: 973 MB, 973078528 bytes
Disk identifier: 0x00000000
Disk /dev/sdh: 1073 MB, 1073741824 bytes
Disk identifier: 0x00000000
Disk /dev/sdi: 1073 MB, 1073741824 bytes
Disk identifier: 0x00000000
Disk /dev/sdj: 1073 MB, 1073741824 bytes
Disk identifier: 0x00000000
```

You can verify iscsi status with:

```
service iscsi status
```

12.4. iSCSI target on Debian

Installing the software for the target server requires **iscsitarget** on Ubuntu and Debian, and an extra **iscsitarget-dkms** for the kernel modules only on Debian.

```
root@debby6:~# aptitude install iscsitarget
The following NEW packages will be installed:
  iscsitarget
0 packages upgraded, 1 newly installed, 0 to remove and 0 not upgraded.
Need to get 69.4 kB of archives. After unpacking 262 kB will be used.
Get:1 http://ftp.belnet.be/debian/ squeeze/main iscsitarget i386 1.4.20.2-1\
 [69.4 kB]
Fetched 69.4 kB in 0s (415 kB/s)
Selecting previously deselected package iscsitarget.
(Reading database ... 36441 files and directories currently installed.)
Unpacking iscsitarget (from .../iscsitarget_1.4.20.2-1_i386.deb) ...
Processing triggers for man-db ...
Setting up iscsitarget (1.4.20.2-1) ...
iscsitarget not enabled in "/etc/default/iscsitarget", not starting...(warning).
```

On Debian 6 you will also need **aptitude install iscsitarget-dkms** for the kernel modules, on Debian 5 this is **aptitude install iscsitarget-modules-`uname -a`**. Ubuntu includes the kernel modules in the main package.

The iSCSI target server is disabled by default, so we enable it.

```
root@debby6:~# cat /etc/default/iscsitarget
ISCSITARGET_ENABLE=false
root@debby6:~# vi /etc/default/iscsitarget
root@debby6:~# cat /etc/default/iscsitarget
ISCSITARGET_ENABLE=true
```

12.5. iSCSI target setup with dd files

You can use LVM volumes (/dev/md0/lvol0), physical partitions (/dev/sda) ,raid devices (/dev/md0) or just plain files for storage. In this demo, we use files created with **dd**.

This screenshot shows how to create three small files (100MB, 200MB and 300MB).

```
root@debby6:~# mkdir /iscsi
root@debby6:~# dd if=/dev/zero of=/iscsi/lun1.img bs=1M count=100
100+0 records in
100+0 records out
104857600 bytes (105 MB) copied, 0.315825 s, 332 MB/s
root@debby6:~# dd if=/dev/zero of=/iscsi/lun2.img bs=1M count=200
200+0 records in
200+0 records out
209715200 bytes (210 MB) copied, 1.08342 s, 194 MB/s
root@debby6:~# dd if=/dev/zero of=/iscsi/lun3.img bs=1M count=300
300+0 records in
300+0 records out
314572800 bytes (315 MB) copied, 1.36209 s, 231 MB/s
```

We need to declare these three files as iSCSI targets in **/etc/iet/ietd.conf** (used to be /etc/ietd.conf).

```
root@debby6:/etc/iet# cp ietd.conf ietd.conf.original
root@debby6:/etc/iet# > ietd.conf
root@debby6:/etc/iet# vi ietd.conf
root@debby6:/etc/iet# cat ietd.conf
Target iqn.2010-02.be.linux-training:storage.lun1
 IncomingUser isuser hunter2
 OutgoingUser
 Lun 0 Path=/iscsi/lun1.img,Type=fileio
 Alias LUN1

Target iqn.2010-02.be.linux-training:storage.lun2
 IncomingUser isuser hunter2
 OutgoingUser
 Lun 0 Path=/iscsi/lun2.img,Type=fileio
 Alias LUN2

Target iqn.2010-02.be.linux-training:storage.lun3
 IncomingUser isuser hunter2
 OutgoingUser
 Lun 0 Path=/iscsi/lun3.img,Type=fileio
 Alias LUN3
```

We also need to add our devices to the **/etc/initiators.allow** file.

```
root@debby6:/etc/iet# cp initiators.allow initiators.allow.original
root@debby6:/etc/iet# >initiators.allow
root@debby6:/etc/iet# vi initiators.allow
root@debby6:/etc/iet# cat initiators.allow
iqn.2010-02.be.linux-training:storage.lun1
iqn.2010-02.be.linux-training:storage.lun2
iqn.2010-02.be.linux-training:storage.lun3
```

Time to start the server now:

```
root@debby6:/etc/iet# /etc/init.d/iscsitarget start
Starting iSCSI enterprise target service:.
.
root@debby6:/etc/iet#
```

Verify activation of the storage devices in **/proc/net/iet**:

```
root@debby6:/etc/iet# cat /proc/net/iet/volume
tid:3 name:iqn.2010-02.be.linux-training:storage.lun3
 lun:0 state:0 iotype:fileio iomode:wt blocks:614400 blocksize:\
512 path:/iscsi/lun3.img
tid:2 name:iqn.2010-02.be.linux-training:storage.lun2
 lun:0 state:0 iotype:fileio iomode:wt blocks:409600 blocksize:\
512 path:/iscsi/lun2.img
tid:1 name:iqn.2010-02.be.linux-training:storage.lun1
 lun:0 state:0 iotype:fileio iomode:wt blocks:204800 blocksize:\
512 path:/iscsi/lun1.img
root@debby6:/etc/iet# cat /proc/net/iet/session
tid:3 name:iqn.2010-02.be.linux-training:storage.lun3
tid:2 name:iqn.2010-02.be.linux-training:storage.lun2
tid:1 name:iqn.2010-02.be.linux-training:storage.lun1
```

12.6. ISCSI initiator on ubuntu

First we install the iSCSi client software (on another computer than the target).

```
root@ubu1104:~# aptitude install open-iscsi
Reading package lists... Done
Building dependency tree
Reading state information... Done
Reading extended state information
Initializing package states... Done
The following NEW packages will be installed:
  open-iscsi open-iscsi-utils{a}
```

Then we set the iSCSI client to start automatically.

```
root@ubu1104:/etc/iscsi# cp iscsid.conf iscsid.conf.original
root@ubu1104:/etc/iscsi# vi iscsid.conf
root@ubu1104:/etc/iscsi# grep ^node.startup iscsid.conf
node.startup = automatic
```

Or you could start it manually.

```
root@ubu1104:/etc/iscsi/nodes# /etc/init.d/open-iscsi start
 * Starting iSCSI initiator service iscsid                          [ OK ]
 * Setting up iSCSI targets                                         [ OK ]
root@ubu1104:/etc/iscsi/nodes#
```

Now we can connect to the Target server and use **iscsiadm** to discover the devices it offers:

```
root@ubu1104:/etc/iscsi# iscsiadm  -m discovery -t st -p 192.168.1.31
192.168.1.31:3260,1 iqn.2010-02.be.linux-training:storage.lun2
192.168.1.31:3260,1 iqn.2010-02.be.linux-training:storage.lun1
192.168.1.31:3260,1 iqn.2010-02.be.linux-training:storage.lun3
```

We can use the same **iscsiadm** to edit the files in **/etc/iscsi/nodes/**.

```
root@ubu1104:/etc/iscsi# iscsiadm -m node --targetname "iqn.2010-02.be.linu\
x-training:storage.lun1" --portal "192.168.1.31:3260" --op=update --name no\
de.session.auth.authmethod --value=CHAP
root@ubu1104:/etc/iscsi# iscsiadm -m node --targetname "iqn.2010-02.be.linu\
x-training:storage.lun1" --portal "192.168.1.31:3260" --op=update --name no\
de.session.auth.username --value=isuser
root@ubu1104:/etc/iscsi# iscsiadm -m node --targetname "iqn.2010-02.be.linu\
x-training:storage.lun1" --portal "192.168.1.31:3260" --op=update --name no\
de.session.auth.password --value=hunter2
```

Repeat the above for the other two devices.

Restart the initiator service to log in to the target.

```
root@ubu1104:/etc/iscsi/nodes# /etc/init.d/open-iscsi restart
 * Disconnecting iSCSI targets                                      [ OK ]
 * Stopping iSCSI initiator service                                 [ OK ]
 * Starting iSCSI initiator service iscsid                          [ OK ]
 * Setting up iSCSI targets
```

Use **fdisk -l** to enjoy three new iSCSI devices.

```
root@ubu1104:/etc/iscsi/nodes# fdisk -l 2> /dev/null | grep Disk
Disk /dev/sda: 17.2 GB, 17179869184 bytes
Disk identifier: 0x0001983f
Disk /dev/sdb: 209 MB, 209715200 bytes
Disk identifier: 0x00000000
Disk /dev/sdd: 314 MB, 314572800 bytes
Disk identifier: 0x00000000
Disk /dev/sdc: 104 MB, 104857600 bytes
Disk identifier: 0x00000000
```

The Target (the server) now shows active sessions.

```
root@debby6:/etc/iet# cat /proc/net/iet/session
tid:3 name:iqn.2010-02.be.linux-training:storage.lun3
 sid:5348024611832320 initiator:iqn.1993-08.org.debian:01:8983ed2d770
  cid:0 ip:192.168.1.35 state:active hd:none dd:none
tid:2 name:iqn.2010-02.be.linux-training:storage.lun2
 sid:4785074624856576 initiator:iqn.1993-08.org.debian:01:8983ed2d770
  cid:0 ip:192.168.1.35 state:active hd:none dd:none
tid:1 name:iqn.2010-02.be.linux-training:storage.lun1
 sid:5066549618344448 initiator:iqn.1993-08.org.debian:01:8983ed2d770
  cid:0 ip:192.168.1.35 state:active hd:none dd:none
root@debby6:/etc/iet#
```

12.7. using iSCSI devices

There is no difference between using SCSI or iSCSI devices once they are connected : partition, make filesystem, mount.

```
root@ubu1104:/etc/iscsi/nodes# history | tail -13
   94  fdisk /dev/sdc
   95  fdisk /dev/sdd
   96  fdisk /dev/sdb
   97  mke2fs /dev/sdb1
   98  mke2fs -j /dev/sdc1
   99  mkfs.ext4 /dev/sdd1
  100  mkdir /mnt/is1
  101  mkdir /mnt/is2
  102  mkdir /mnt/is3
  103  mount /dev/sdb1 /mnt/is1
  104  mount /dev/sdc1 /mnt/is2
  105  mount /dev/sdd1 /mnt/is3
  106  history | tail -13
root@ubu1104:/etc/iscsi/nodes# mount | grep is
/dev/sdb1 on /mnt/is1 type ext2 (rw)
/dev/sdc1 on /mnt/is2 type ext3 (rw)
/dev/sdd1 on /mnt/is3 type ext4 (rw)
```

12.8. iSCSI Target RHEL7/CentOS7

The prefered tool to setup an iSCSI Target on RHEL is **targetcli**.

```
[root@centos7 ~]# yum install targetcli
Loaded plugins: fastestmirror
...
...
Installed:
  targetcli.noarch 0:2.1.fb37-3.el7

Complete!
[root@centos7 ~]#
```

The **targetcli** tool is interactive and represents the configuration fo the **target** in a structure that resembles a directory tree with several files. Although this is explorable inside **targetcli** with **ls**, **cd** and **pwd**, this are not files on the file system.

This tool also has tab-completion, which is very handy for the **iqn** names.

```
[root@centos7 ~]# targetcli
targetcli shell version 2.1.fb37
Copyright 2011-2013 by Datera, Inc and others.
For help on commands, type 'help'.

/> cd backstores/
/backstores> ls
o- backstores ......................................................... [...]
  o- block ............................................. [Storage Objects: 0]
  o- fileio ............................................ [Storage Objects: 0]
  o- pscsi ............................................. [Storage Objects: 0]
  o- ramdisk ........................................... [Storage Objects: 0]
/backstores> cd block
/backstores/block> ls
o- block ............................................... [Storage Objects: 0]
/backstores/block> create server1.disk1 /dev/sdb
Created block storage object server1.disk1 using /dev/sdb.
/backstores/block> ls
o- block ............................................... [Storage Objects: 1]
  o- server1.disk1 .................. [/dev/sdb (2.0GiB) write-thru deactivated]
/backstores/block> cd /iscsi
/iscsi> create iqn.2015-04.be.linux:iscsi1
Created target iqn.2015-04.be.linux:iscsi1.
Created TPG 1.
Global pref auto_add_default_portal=true
Created default portal listening on all IPs (0.0.0.0), port 3260.
/iscsi> cd /iscsi/iqn.2015-04.be.linux:iscsi1/tpg1/acls
/iscsi/iqn.20...si1/tpg1/acls> create iqn.2015-04.be.linux:server2
Created Node ACL for iqn.2015-04.be.linux:server2
/iscsi/iqn.20...si1/tpg1/acls> cd iqn.2015-04.be.linux:server2
/iscsi/iqn.20...linux:server2> set auth userid=paul
Parameter userid is now 'paul'.
/iscsi/iqn.20...linux:server2> set auth password=hunter2
Parameter password is now 'hunter2'.
/iscsi/iqn.20...linux:server2> cd /iscsi/iqn.2015-04.be.linux:iscsi1/tpg1/luns
/iscsi/iqn.20...si1/tpg1/luns> create /backstores/block/server1.disk1
Created LUN 0.
Created LUN 0->0 mapping in node ACL iqn.2015-04.be.linux:server2
s/scsi/iqn.20...si1/tpg1/luns> cd /iscsi/iqn.2015-04.be.linux:iscsi1/tpg1/portals
/iscsi/iqn.20.../tpg1/portals> create 192.168.1.128
Using default IP port 3260
Could not create NetworkPortal in configFS.
```

```
/iscsi/iqn.20.../tpg1/portals> cd /
/> ls
o- / ..................................................................... [...]
  o- backstores .......................................................... [...]
  | o- block .............................................. [Storage Objects: 1]
  | | o- server1.disk1 ............... [/dev/sdb (2.0GiB) write-thru activated]
  | o- fileio ............................................. [Storage Objects: 0]
  | o- pscsi .............................................. [Storage Objects: 0]
  | o- ramdisk ............................................ [Storage Objects: 0]
  o- iscsi ........................................................ [Targets: 1]
  | o- iqn.2015-04.be.linux:iscsi1 ................................... [TPGs: 1]
  |   o- tpg1 ........................................... [no-gen-acls, no-auth]
  |     o- acls ...................................................... [ACLs: 1]
  |     | o- iqn.2015-04.be.linux:server2 ..................... [Mapped LUNs: 1]
  |     |   o- mapped_lun0 .................... [lun0 block/server1.disk1 (rw)]
  |     o- luns ...................................................... [LUNs: 1]
  |     | o- lun0 ........................... [block/server1.disk1 (/dev/sdb)]
  |     o- portals ................................................ [Portals: 1]
  |       o- 0.0.0.0:3260 ................................................. [OK]
  o- loopback ..................................................... [Targets: 0]
/> saveconfig
Last 10 configs saved in /etc/target/backup.
Configuration saved to /etc/target/saveconfig.json
/> exit
Global pref auto_save_on_exit=true
Last 10 configs saved in /etc/target/backup.
Configuration saved to /etc/target/saveconfig.json
[root@centos7 ~]#
```

Use the **systemd** tools to manage the service:

```
[root@centos7 ~]# systemctl enable target
ln -s '/usr/lib/systemd/system/target.service' '/etc/systemd/system/multi-user.target.wants/t
[root@centos7 ~]# systemctl start target
[root@centos7 ~]#
```

Depending on your organisations policy, you may need to configure firewall and SELinux. The screenshot belows adds a firewall rule to allow all traffic over port 3260, and disables SELinux.

```
[root@centos7 ~]# firewall-cmd --permanent --add-port=3260/tcp
[root@centos7 ~]# firewall-cmd --reload
[root@centos7 ~]# setenforce 0
```

The total configuration is visible using **ls** from the root.

```
[root@centos7 ~]# targetcli
targetcli shell version 2.1.fb37
Copyright 2011-2013 by Datera, Inc and others.
For help on commands, type 'help'.

/> ls
o- / ..................................................................... [...]
  o- backstores .......................................................... [...]
  | o- block .............................................. [Storage Objects: 1]
  | | o- server1.disk1 ............... [/dev/sdb (2.0GiB) write-thru activated]
  | o- fileio ............................................. [Storage Objects: 0]
  | o- pscsi .............................................. [Storage Objects: 0]
  | o- ramdisk ............................................ [Storage Objects: 0]
  o- iscsi ........................................................ [Targets: 1]
  | o- iqn.2015-04.be.linux:iscsi1 ................................... [TPGs: 1]
  |   o- tpg1 ........................................... [no-gen-acls, no-auth]
  |     o- acls ...................................................... [ACLs: 1]
```

```
|     | o- iqn.2015-04.be.linux:server2 .................... [Mapped LUNs: 1]
|     |   o- mapped_lun0 .................... [lun0 block/server1.disk1 (rw)]
|     o- luns .............................................. [LUNs: 1]
|     | o- lun0 .......................... [block/server1.disk1 (/dev/sdb)]
|     o- portals ........................................... [Portals: 1]
|       o- 0.0.0.0:3260 ............................................. [OK]
  o- loopback .......................................... [Targets: 0]
/>
/> exit
Global pref auto_save_on_exit=true
Last 10 configs saved in /etc/target/backup.
Configuration saved to /etc/target/saveconfig.json
[root@centos7 ~]#
```

The iSCSI Target is now ready.

12.9. iSCSI Initiator RHEL7/CentOS7

This is identical to the RHEL6/CentOS6 procedure:

```
[root@centos7 ~]# yum install iscsi-initiator-utils
Loaded plugins: fastestmirror
...
...
Installed:
  iscsi-initiator-utils.x86_64 0:6.2.0.873-29.el7

Dependency Installed:
  iscsi-initiator-utils-iscsiuio.x86_64 0:6.2.0.873-29.el7

Complete!
```

Map your initiator name to the **targetcli** acl.

```
[root@centos7 ~]# cat /etc/iscsi/initiatorname.iscsi
InitiatorName=iqn.2015-04.be.linux:server2
[root@centos7 ~]#
```

Enter the CHAP authentication in **/etc/iscsi/iscsid.conf**.

```
[root@centos7 ~]# vi /etc/iscsi/iscsid.conf
...
[root@centos7 ~]# grep ^node.session.auth /etc/iscsi/iscsid.conf
node.session.auth.authmethod = CHAP
node.session.auth.username = paul
node.session.auth.password = hunter2
[root@centos7 ~]#
```

There are no extra devices yet...

```
[root@centos7 ~]# fdisk -l | grep sd
Disk /dev/sda: 22.0 GB, 22038806528 bytes, 43044544 sectors
/dev/sda1   *        2048     1026047      512000   83  Linux
/dev/sda2         1026048    43042815    21008384   8e  Linux LVM
Disk /dev/sdb: 2147 MB, 2147483648 bytes, 4194304 sectors
```

Enable the service and discover the target.

```
[root@centos7 ~]# systemctl enable iscsid
ln -s '/usr/lib/systemd/system/iscsid.service' '/etc/systemd/system/multi-user.target.wants/is
[root@centos7 ~]# iscsiadm -m discovery -t st -p 192.168.1.128
192.168.1.128:3260,1 iqn.2015-04.be.linux:iscsi1
```

Log into the target and see /dev/sdc appear.

```
[root@centos7 ~]# iscsiadm -m node -T iqn.2015-04.be.linux:iscsi1 -p 192.168.1.128 -l
Logging in to [iface: default, target: iqn.2015-04.be.linux:iscsi1, portal: 192.168.1.128,326
Login to [iface: default, target: iqn.2015-04.be.linux:iscsi1, portal: 192.168.1.128,3260] su
[root@centos7 ~]#
[root@centos7 ~]# fdisk -l | grep sd
Disk /dev/sda: 22.0 GB, 22038806528 bytes, 43044544 sectors
/dev/sda1   *        2048     1026047      512000   83  Linux
/dev/sda2         1026048    43042815    21008384   8e  Linux LVM
Disk /dev/sdb: 2147 MB, 2147483648 bytes, 4194304 sectors
Disk /dev/sdc: 2147 MB, 2147483648 bytes, 4194304 sectors
[root@centos7 ~]#
```

12.10. practice: iSCSI devices

1. Set up a target (using an LVM and a SCSI device) and an initiator that connects to both.

2. Set up an iSCSI Target and Initiator on two CentOS7/RHEL7 computers with the following information:

Table 12.1. iSCSI Target and Initiator practice

variable	value
Target Server IP	
shared devices on target	/dev/sd /dev/sd /dev/sd
shared device name sd	
shared device name sd	
shared device name sd	
target iqn	
initiator iqn	
username	
password	

12.11. solution: iSCSI devices

1. Set up a target (using an LVM and a SCSI device) and an initiator that connects to both.

This solution was done on **Debian/ubuntu/Mint**. For RHEL/CentOS check the theory.

Decide (with a partner) on a computer to be the Target and another computer to be the Initiator.

On the Target computer:

First install iscsitarget using the standard tools for installing software in your distribution. Then use your knowledge from the previous chapter to setup a logical volume (/dev/vg/lvol0) and use the RAID chapter to setup /dev/md0. Then perform the following step:

```
vi /etc/default/iscsitarget (set enable to true)
```

Add your devices to /etc/iet/ietf.conf

```
root@debby6:/etc/iet# cat ietd.conf
Target iqn.2010-02.be.linux-training:storage.lun1
 IncomingUser isuser hunter2
 OutgoingUser
 Lun 0 Path=/dev/vg/lvol0,Type=fileio
 Alias LUN1
Target iqn.2010-02.be.linux-training:storage.lun2
 IncomingUser isuser hunter2
 OutgoingUser
 Lun 0 Path=/dev/md0,Type=fileio
 Alias LUN2
```

Add both devices to /etc/iet/initiators.allow

```
root@debby6:/etc/iet# cat initiators.allow
iqn.2010-02.be.linux-training:storage.lun1
iqn.2010-02.be.linux-training:storage.lun2
```

Now start the iscsitarget daemon and move over to the Initiator.

On the Initiator computer:

Install open-iscsi and start the daemon.

Then use **iscsiadm -m discovery -t st -p 'target-ip'** to see the iscsi devices on the Target.

Edit the files **/etc/iscsi/nodes/** as shown in the book. Then restart the iSCSI daemon and rund **fdisk -l** to see the iSCSI devices.

2. Set up an iSCSI Target and Initiator on two CentOS7/RHEL7 computers with the following information:

Table 12.2. iSCSI Target and Initiator practice

variable	value
Target Server IP	192.168.1.143 (Adjust for your subnet!)
shared devices on target	/dev/sdb /dev/sdc /dev/sdd
shared device name sdb	target.disk1
shared device name sdc	target.disk2
shared device name sdd	target.disk3
target iqn	iqn.2015-04.be.linux:target
initiator iqn	iqn.2015-04.be.linux:initiator
username	paul
password	hunter2

On the iSCSI Target server:

```
[root@centos7 ~]# targetcli
targetcli shell version 2.1.fb37
Copyright 2011-2013 by Datera, Inc and others.
For help on commands, type 'help'.

/> cd /backstores/block
/backstores/block> ls
o- block ............................................... [Storage Objects: 0]
/backstores/block> create target.disk1 /dev/sdb
Created block storage object target.disk1 using /dev/sdb.
/backstores/block> create target.disk2 /dev/sdc
Created block storage object target.disk2 using /dev/sdc.
/backstores/block> create target.disk3 /dev/sdd
Created block storage object target.disk3 using /dev/sdd.
/backstores/block> ls
o- block ............................................... [Storage Objects: 3]
  o- target.disk1 .................. [/dev/sdb (8.0GiB) write-thru deactivated]
  o- target.disk2 .................. [/dev/sdc (8.0GiB) write-thru deactivated]
  o- target.disk3 .................. [/dev/sdd (8.0GiB) write-thru deactivated]
/backstores/block> cd /iscsi
/iscsi> create iqn.2015-04.be.linux:target
Created target iqn.2015-04.be.linux:target.
Created TPG 1.
Global pref auto_add_default_portal=true
Created default portal listening on all IPs (0.0.0.0), port 3260.
/iscsi> cd /iscsi/iqn.2015-04.be.linux:target/tpg1/acls
/iscsi/iqn.20...get/tpg1/acls> create iqn.2015-04.be.linux:initiator
Created Node ACL for iqn.2015-04.be.linux:initiator
/iscsi/iqn.20...get/tpg1/acls> cd iqn.2015-04.be.linux:initiator
/iscsi/iqn.20...nux:initiator> pwd
/iscsi/iqn.2015-04.be.linux:target/tpg1/acls/iqn.2015-04.be.linux:initiator
/iscsi/iqn.20...nux:initiator> set auth userid=paul
Parameter userid is now 'paul'.
/iscsi/iqn.20...nux:initiator> set auth password=hunter2
Parameter password is now 'hunter2'.
/iscsi/iqn.20...nux:initiator> cd /iscsi/iqn.2015-04.be.linux:target/tpg1/
/iscsi/iqn.20...x:target/tpg1> ls
o- tpg1 ............................................... [no-gen-acls, no-auth]
  o- acls .......................................................... [ACLs: 1]
  | o- iqn.2015-04.be.linux:initiator ....................... [Mapped LUNs: 0]
```

```
  o- luns ........................................................... [LUNs: 0]
  o- portals ..................................................... [Portals: 1]
    o- 0.0.0.0:3260 ...................................................... [OK]
/iscsi/iqn.20...x:target/tpg1> cd luns
/iscsi/iqn.20...get/tpg1/luns> create /backstores/block/target.disk1
Created LUN 0.
Created LUN 0->0 mapping in node ACL iqn.2015-04.be.linux:initiator
/iscsi/iqn.20...get/tpg1/luns> create /backstores/block/target.disk2
Created LUN 1.
Created LUN 1->1 mapping in node ACL iqn.2015-04.be.linux:initiator
/iscsi/iqn.20...get/tpg1/luns> create /backstores/block/target.disk3
Created LUN 2.
Created LUN 2->2 mapping in node ACL iqn.2015-04.be.linux:initiator
s/scsi/iqn.20...get/tpg1/luns> cd /iscsi/iqn.2015-04.be.linux:target/tpg1/portals
/iscsi/iqn.20.../tpg1/portals> create 192.168.1.143
Using default IP port 3260
Could not create NetworkPortal in configFS.
/iscsi/iqn.20.../tpg1/portals> cd /
/> ls
o- / ................................................................. [...]
  o- backstores ...................................................... [...]
  | o- block .......................................... [Storage Objects: 3]
  | | o- target.disk1 ................ [/dev/sdb (8.0GiB) write-thru activated]
  | | o- target.disk2 ................ [/dev/sdc (8.0GiB) write-thru activated]
  | | o- target.disk3 ................ [/dev/sdd (8.0GiB) write-thru activated]
  | o- fileio ......................................... [Storage Objects: 0]
  | o- pscsi .......................................... [Storage Objects: 0]
  | o- ramdisk ........................................ [Storage Objects: 0]
  o- iscsi ..................................................... [Targets: 1]
  | o- iqn.2015-04.be.linux:target ................................. [TPGs: 1]
  |   o- tpg1 ........................................ [no-gen-acls, no-auth]
  |     o- acls ................................................... [ACLs: 1]
  |     | o- iqn.2015-04.be.linux:initiator .................. [Mapped LUNs: 3]
  |     |   o- mapped_lun0 .................... [lun0 block/target.disk1 (rw)]
  |     |   o- mapped_lun1 .................... [lun1 block/target.disk2 (rw)]
  |     |   o- mapped_lun2 .................... [lun2 block/target.disk3 (rw)]
  |     o- luns ................................................... [LUNs: 3]
  |     | o- lun0 ......................... [block/target.disk1 (/dev/sdb)]
  |     | o- lun1 ......................... [block/target.disk2 (/dev/sdc)]
  |     | o- lun2 ......................... [block/target.disk3 (/dev/sdd)]
  |     o- portals ............................................. [Portals: 1]
  |       o- 0.0.0.0:3260 ................................................ [OK]
  o- loopback .................................................. [Targets: 0]
/> exit
Global pref auto_save_on_exit=true
Last 10 configs saved in /etc/target/backup.
Configuration saved to /etc/target/saveconfig.json
[root@centos7 ~]# systemctl enable target
ln -s '/usr/lib/systemd/system/target.service' '/etc/systemd/system/multi-user.target.wants/t
[root@centos7 ~]# systemctl start target
[root@centos7 ~]# setenforce 0
```

On the Initiator:

```
[root@centos7 ~]# cat /etc/iscsi/initiatorname.iscsi
InitiatorName=iqn.2015-04.be.linux:initiator
[root@centos7 ~]# vi /etc/iscsi/iscsid.conf
[root@centos7 ~]# grep ^node.session.au /etc/iscsi/iscsid.conf
node.session.auth.authmethod = CHAP
node.session.auth.username = paul
node.session.auth.password = hunter2
[root@centos7 ~]# fdisk -l 2>/dev/null | grep sd
Disk /dev/sda: 22.0 GB, 22038806528 bytes, 43044544 sectors
/dev/sda1   *        2048     1026047      512000   83  Linux
```

```
/dev/sda2         1026048    43042815    21008384   8e  Linux LVM
Disk /dev/sdb: 8589 MB, 8589934592 bytes, 16777216 sectors
/dev/sdb1            2048      821247      409600   83  Linux
/dev/sdb2          821248     1640447      409600   83  Linux
/dev/sdb3         1640448     2459647      409600   83  Linux
Disk /dev/sdc: 8589 MB, 8589934592 bytes, 16777216 sectors
Disk /dev/sdd: 8589 MB, 8589934592 bytes, 16777216 sectors
Disk /dev/sde: 2147 MB, 2147483648 bytes, 4194304 sectors
Disk /dev/sdf: 2147 MB, 2147483648 bytes, 4194304 sectors
[root@centos7 ~]# systemctl enable iscsid
ln -s '/usr/lib/systemd/system/iscsid.service' '/etc/systemd/system/multi-user.target.wants/is
[root@centos7 ~]# iscsiadm -m node -T iqn.2015-04.be.linux:target -p 192.168.1.143 -l
Logging in to [iface: default, target: iqn.2015-04.be.linux:target, portal: 192.168.1.143,3260
Login to [iface: default, target: iqn.2015-04.be.linux:target, portal: 192.168.1.143,3260] suc

[root@centos7 ~]# fdisk -l 2>/dev/null | grep sd
Disk /dev/sda: 22.0 GB, 22038806528 bytes, 43044544 sectors
/dev/sda1   *        2048     1026047      512000   83  Linux
/dev/sda2         1026048    43042815    21008384   8e  Linux LVM
Disk /dev/sdb: 8589 MB, 8589934592 bytes, 16777216 sectors
/dev/sdb1            2048      821247      409600   83  Linux
/dev/sdb2          821248     1640447      409600   83  Linux
/dev/sdb3         1640448     2459647      409600   83  Linux
Disk /dev/sdc: 8589 MB, 8589934592 bytes, 16777216 sectors
Disk /dev/sdd: 8589 MB, 8589934592 bytes, 16777216 sectors
Disk /dev/sde: 2147 MB, 2147483648 bytes, 4194304 sectors
Disk /dev/sdf: 2147 MB, 2147483648 bytes, 4194304 sectors
Disk /dev/sdg: 8589 MB, 8589934592 bytes, 16777216 sectors
Disk /dev/sdh: 8589 MB, 8589934592 bytes, 16777216 sectors
Disk /dev/sdi: 8589 MB, 8589934592 bytes, 16777216 sectors
[root@centos7 ~]#
```

Chapter 13. introduction to multipathing

13.1. install multipath

RHEL and CentOS need the **device-mapper-multipath** package.

```
yum install device-mapper-multipath
```

This will create a sample multipath.conf in **/usr/share/doc/device-mapper-multipath-0.4.9/multipath.conf**.

There is no **/etc/multipath.conf** until you initialize it with **mpathconf**.

```
[root@server2 ~]# mpathconf --enable --with_multipathd y
Starting multipathd daemon:                                    [  OK  ]
[root@server2 ~]# wc -l /etc/multipath.conf
99 /etc/multipath.conf
```

13.2. configure multipath

You can now choose to either edit **/etc/multipath.conf** or use **mpathconf** to change this file for you.

```
[root@server2 ~]# grep user_friendly_names /etc/multipath.conf
 user_friendly_names yes
# user_friendly_names yes
[root@server2 ~]# mpathconf --enable --user_friendly_names n
[root@server2 ~]# grep user_friendly_names /etc/multipath.conf
 user_friendly_names no
# user_friendly_names yes
[root@server2 ~]# mpathconf --enable --user_friendly_names y
[root@server2 ~]# grep user_friendly_names /etc/multipath.conf
 user_friendly_names yes
# user_friendly_names yes
```

13.3. network

This example uses three networks, make sure the iSCSI Target is connected to all three networks.

```
[root@server1 tgt]# ifconfig | grep -B1 192.168
eth1      Link encap:Ethernet  HWaddr 08:00:27:4E:AB:8E
          inet addr:192.168.1.98  Bcast:192.168.1.255  Mask:255.255.255.0
--
eth2      Link encap:Ethernet  HWaddr 08:00:27:3F:A9:D1
          inet addr:192.168.2.98  Bcast:192.168.2.255  Mask:255.255.255.0
--
eth3      Link encap:Ethernet  HWaddr 08:00:27:94:52:26
          inet addr:192.168.3.98  Bcast:192.168.3.255  Mask:255.255.255.0
```

The same must be true for the multipath Initiator:

```
[root@server2 ~]# ifconfig | grep -B1 192.168
eth1      Link encap:Ethernet  HWaddr 08:00:27:A1:43:41
          inet addr:192.168.1.99  Bcast:192.168.1.255  Mask:255.255.255.0
--
eth2      Link encap:Ethernet  HWaddr 08:00:27:12:A8:70
          inet addr:192.168.2.99  Bcast:192.168.2.255  Mask:255.255.255.0
--
eth3      Link encap:Ethernet  HWaddr 08:00:27:6E:99:9B
          inet addr:192.168.3.99  Bcast:192.168.3.255  Mask:255.255.255.0
```

Test the triple discovery in three networks (screenshot newer than above).

```
[root@centos7 ~]# iscsiadm -m discovery -t st -p 192.168.1.150
192.168.1.150:3260,1 iqn.2015-04.be.linux:target1
[root@centos7 ~]# iscsiadm -m discovery -t st -p 192.168.2.150
192.168.2.150:3260,1 iqn.2015-04.be.linux:target1
[root@centos7 ~]# iscsiadm -m discovery -t st -p 192.168.3.150
192.168.3.150:3260,1 iqn.2015-04.be.linux:target1
```

13.4. start multipathd and iscsi

Time to start (or restart) both the multipathd and iscsi services:

```
[root@server2 ~]# service multipathd restart
Stopping multipathd daemon:                                [  OK  ]
Starting multipathd daemon:                                [  OK  ]
[root@server2 ~]# service iscsi restart
Stopping iscsi:                                            [  OK  ]
Starting iscsi:                                            [  OK  ]
```

This shows **fdisk** output when leaving the default friendly_names option to yes. The bottom three are the multipath devices to use.

```
[root@server2 ~]# fdisk -l | grep Disk
Disk /dev/sda: 42.9 GB, 42949672960 bytes
Disk identifier: 0x0004f229
Disk /dev/sdb: 1073 MB, 1073741824 bytes
Disk identifier: 0x00000000
Disk /dev/sdc: 1073 MB, 1073741824 bytes
Disk identifier: 0x00000000
Disk /dev/sdd: 1073 MB, 1073741824 bytes
Disk identifier: 0x00000000
Disk /dev/sde: 2147 MB, 2147483648 bytes
Disk identifier: 0x00000000
Disk /dev/sdf: 2147 MB, 2147483648 bytes
Disk identifier: 0x00000000
Disk /dev/sdg: 2147 MB, 2147483648 bytes
Disk identifier: 0x00000000
Disk /dev/mapper/VolGroup-lv_root: 41.4 GB, 41448112128 bytes
Disk identifier: 0x00000000
Disk /dev/mapper/VolGroup-lv_swap: 973 MB, 973078528 bytes
Disk identifier: 0x00000000
Disk /dev/sdh: 1073 MB, 1073741824 bytes
Disk identifier: 0x00000000
Disk /dev/sdi: 1073 MB, 1073741824 bytes
Disk identifier: 0x00000000
Disk /dev/sdj: 1073 MB, 1073741824 bytes
Disk identifier: 0x00000000
Disk /dev/sdl: 1073 MB, 1073741824 bytes
Disk identifier: 0x00000000
Disk /dev/sdn: 1073 MB, 1073741824 bytes
Disk identifier: 0x00000000
Disk /dev/sdk: 1073 MB, 1073741824 bytes
Disk identifier: 0x00000000
Disk /dev/sdm: 1073 MB, 1073741824 bytes
Disk identifier: 0x00000000
Disk /dev/sdp: 1073 MB, 1073741824 bytes
Disk identifier: 0x00000000
Disk /dev/sdo: 1073 MB, 1073741824 bytes
Disk identifier: 0x00000000
Disk /dev/mapper/mpathh: 1073 MB, 1073741824 bytes
Disk identifier: 0x00000000
Disk /dev/mapper/mpathi: 1073 MB, 1073741824 bytes
Disk identifier: 0x00000000
Disk /dev/mapper/mpathj: 1073 MB, 1073741824 bytes
Disk identifier: 0x00000000
[root@server2 ~]#
```

13.5. multipath list

You can list the multipath connections and devices with **multipath -ll**.

```
[root@server2 ~]# multipath -ll
mpathj (1IET     00010001) dm-4 Reddy,VBOX HARDDISK
size=1.0G features='0' hwhandler='0' wp=rw
|-+- policy='round-robin 0' prio=1 status=active
| `- 13:0:0:1 sdh 8:112 active ready running
|-+- policy='round-robin 0' prio=1 status=enabled
| `- 12:0:0:1 sdi 8:128 active ready running
`-+- policy='round-robin 0' prio=1 status=enabled
  `- 14:0:0:1 sdm 8:192 active ready running
mpathi (1IET     00010003) dm-3 Reddy,VBOX HARDDISK
size=1.0G features='0' hwhandler='0' wp=rw
|-+- policy='round-robin 0' prio=1 status=active
| `- 13:0:0:3 sdk 8:160 active ready running
|-+- policy='round-robin 0' prio=1 status=enabled
| `- 12:0:0:3 sdn 8:208 active ready running
`-+- policy='round-robin 0' prio=1 status=enabled
  `- 14:0:0:3 sdp 8:240 active ready running
mpathh (1IET     00010002) dm-2 Reddy,VBOX HARDDISK
size=1.0G features='0' hwhandler='0' wp=rw
|-+- policy='round-robin 0' prio=1 status=active
| `- 12:0:0:2 sdl 8:176 active ready running
|-+- policy='round-robin 0' prio=1 status=enabled
| `- 13:0:0:2 sdj 8:144 active ready running
`-+- policy='round-robin 0' prio=1 status=enabled
  `- 14:0:0:2 sdo 8:224 active ready running
[root@server2 ~]#
```

The IET (iSCSI Enterprise Target) ID should match the ones you see on the Target server.

```
[root@server1 ~]# tgt-admin -s | grep -e LUN -e IET -e dev
    LUN information:
        LUN: 0
            SCSI ID: IET     00010000
        LUN: 1
            SCSI ID: IET     00010001
            Backing store path: /dev/sdb
        LUN: 2
            SCSI ID: IET     00010002
            Backing store path: /dev/sdc
        LUN: 3
            SCSI ID: IET     00010003
            Backing store path: /dev/sdd
```

13.6. using the device

The rest is standard mkfs, mkdir, mount:

```
[root@server2 ~]# mkfs.ext4 /dev/mapper/mpathi
mke2fs 1.41.12 (17-May-2010)
Filesystem label=
OS type: Linux
Block size=4096 (log=2)
Fragment size=4096 (log=2)
Stride=0 blocks, Stripe width=0 blocks
65536 inodes, 262144 blocks
13107 blocks (5.00%) reserved for the super user
First data block=0
Maximum filesystem blocks=268435456
8 block groups
32768 blocks per group, 32768 fragments per group
8192 inodes per group
Superblock backups stored on blocks:
 32768, 98304, 163840, 229376

Writing inode tables: done
Creating journal (8192 blocks): done
Writing superblocks and filesystem accounting information: done

This filesystem will be automatically checked every 38 mounts or
180 days, whichever comes first.  Use tune2fs -c or -i to override.
[root@server2 ~]# mkdir /srv/multipath
[root@server2 ~]# mount /dev/mapper/mpathi /srv/multipath/
[root@server2 ~]# df -h /srv/multipath/
Filesystem            Size  Used Avail Use% Mounted on
/dev/mapper/mpathi 1008M   34M  924M   4% /srv/multipath
```

13.7. practice: multipathing

1. Find a partner and decide who will be iSCSI Target and who will be iSCSI Initiator and Multipather. Set up Multipath as we did in the theory.

2. Uncomment the big 'defaults' section in /etc/multipath.conf and disable friendly names. Verify that multipath can work. You may need to check the manual for **/lib/dev/scsi_id** and for **multipath.conf**.

13.8. solution: multipathing

1. Find a partner and decide who will be iSCSI Target and who will be iSCSI Initiator and Multipather. Set up Multipath as we did in the theory.

```
Look in the theory...
```

2. Uncomment the big 'defaults' section in /etc/multipath.conf and disable friendly names. Verify that multipath can work. You may need to check the manual for **/lib/dev/scsi_id** and for **multipath.conf**.

```
vi multipath.conf
```

```
remove # for the big defaults section
add # for the very small one with friendly_names active
add the --replace-whitespace option to scsi_id.

defaults {
        udev_dir                /dev
        polling_interval        10
        path_selector           "round-robin 0"
        path_grouping_policy    multibus
        getuid_callout          "/lib/udev/scsi_id --whitelisted --replace\
-whitespace --device=/dev/%n"
        prio                    const
        path_checker            readsector0
        rr_min_io               100
        max_fds                 8192
        rr_weight               priorities
        failback                immediate
        no_path_retry           fail
        user_friendly_names     no
}
```

The names now (after service restart) look like:

```
root@server2 etc]# multipath -ll
1IET_00010001 dm-8 Reddy,VBOX HARDDISK
size=1.0G features='0' hwhandler='0' wp=rw
`-+- policy='round-robin 0' prio=1 status=active
  |- 17:0:0:1 sdh 8:112 active ready running
  |- 16:0:0:1 sdi 8:128 active ready running
  `- 15:0:0:1 sdn 8:208 active ready running
1IET_00010003 dm-10 Reddy,VBOX HARDDISK
size=1.0G features='0' hwhandler='0' wp=rw
`-+- policy='round-robin 0' prio=1 status=active
  |- 17:0:0:3 sdl 8:176 active ready running
  |- 16:0:0:3 sdm 8:192 active ready running
  `- 15:0:0:3 sdp 8:240 active ready running
1IET_00010002 dm-9 Reddy,VBOX HARDDISK
size=1.0G features='0' hwhandler='0' wp=rw
`-+- policy='round-robin 0' prio=1 status=active
  |- 17:0:0:2 sdj 8:144 active ready running
  |- 16:0:0:2 sdk 8:160 active ready running
  `- 15:0:0:2 sdo 8:224 active ready running
```

Did you blacklist your own devices ?

```
 vi multipath.conf
--> search for blacklist:
add
        devnode "^sd[a-g]"
```

Part III. boot management

Table of Contents

Chapter 14. bootloader

This chapter briefly discusses the boot sequence of an (Intel 32-bit or 64-bit) Linux computer.

Systems booting with **lilo** are rare nowadays, so this section is brief.

The most common bootloader on Linux systems today is **grub**, yet this is not a Linux project. Distributions like **FreeBSD** and **Solaris** also use **grub**.

Likewise, **grub** is not limited to Intel architecture. It can also load kernels on PowerPC.

Note that **grub**, while still the default in Debian, is slowly being replaced in most distributions with **grub2**.

14.1. boot terminology

The exact order of things that happen when starting a computer system, depends on the hardware architecture (**Intel x86** is different from **Sun Sparc** etc), on the boot loader (**grub** is different from **lilo**) and on the operating system (**Linux**, **Solaris**, **BSD** etc). Most of this chapter is focused on booting **Linux** on **Intel x86** with **grub**.

14.1.1. post

A computer starts booting the moment you turn on the power (no kidding). This first process is called **post** or **power on self test**. If all goes well then this leads to the **bios**. If all goes not so well, then you might hear nothing, or hear beeping, or see an error message on the screen, or maybe see smoke coming out of the computer (burning hardware smells bad!).

14.1.2. bios

All **Intel x86** computers will have a **basic input/output system** or **bios** to detect, identify and initialize hardware. The **bios** then goes looking for a **boot device**. This can be a floppy, hard disk, cdrom, network card or usb drive.

During the **bios** you can see a message on the screen telling you which key (often **Del** or **F2**) to press to enter the **bios** setup.

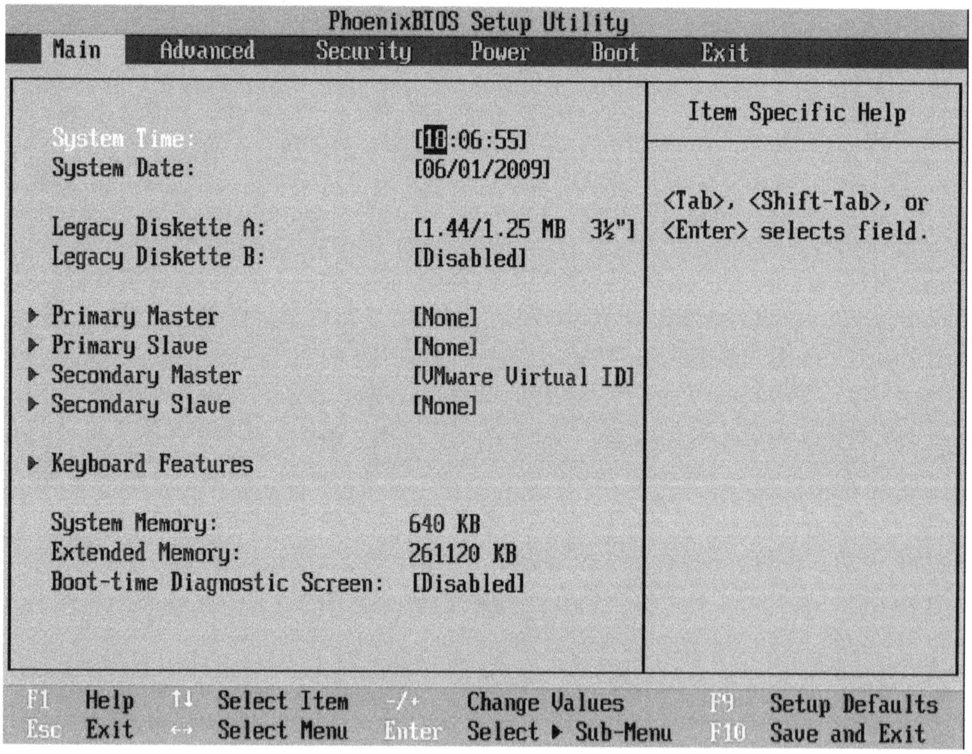

14.1.3. openboot

Sun **sparc** systems start with **openboot** to test the hardware and to boot the operating system. **Bill Callkins** explains **openboot** in his Solaris System Administration books. The details of **openboot** are not the focus of this course.

14.1.4. boot password

The **bios** allows you to set a password. Do not forget this password, or you will have to open up the hardware to reset it. You can sometimes set a password to boot the system, and another password to protect the **bios** from being modified.

14.1.5. boot device

The **bios** will look for a **boot device** in the order configured in the bios setup. Usually an operating system on a production server boots of a hard disk.

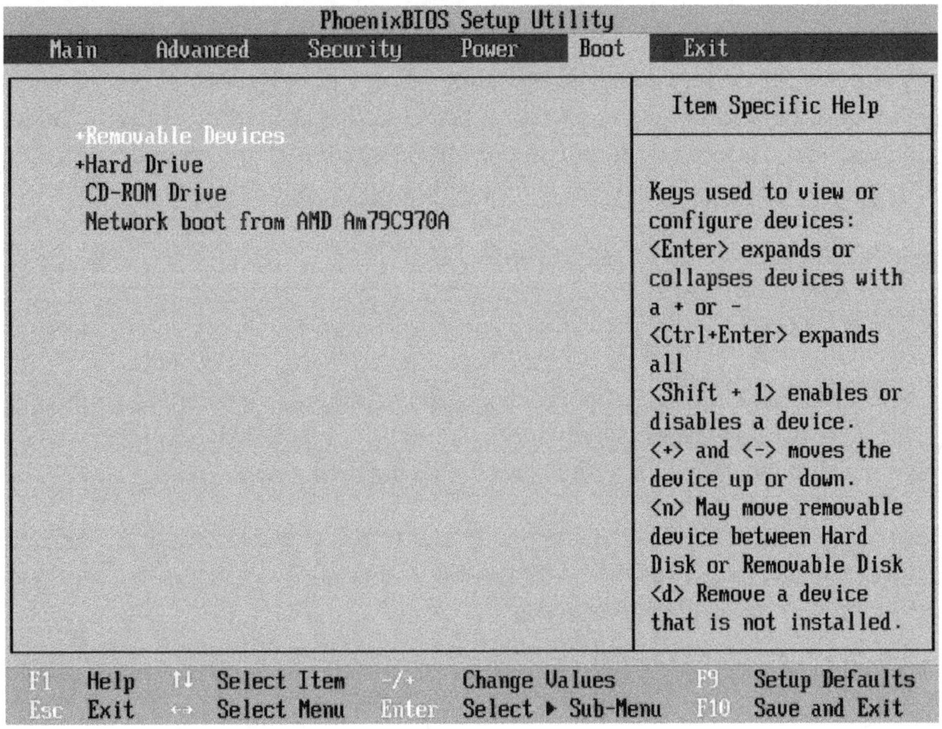

14.1.6. master boot record

The **master boot record** or **mbr** is the first sector of a hard disk. The partitioning of a disk in **primary** partitions, and the active partition are defined in the **mbr**.

The **mbr** is 512 bytes long and can be copied with **dd**.

```
dd if=/dev/sda of=bootsect.mbr count=1 bs=512
```

14.1.7. bootloader

The **mbr** is executed by the **bios** and contains either (a small) **bootloader** or code to load a **bootloader**.

Looking at the **mbr** with **od** can reveal information about the **bootloader**.

```
paul@laika:~$ sudo dd if=/dev/sda count=1 bs=16 skip=24 2>/dev/null|od -c
0000000 376   G   R   U   B      \0   G   e   o   m  \0   H   a   r   d
0000020
```

There are a variety of bootloaders available, most common on **Intel** architecture is **grub**, which is replacing **lilo** in many places. When installing **Linux** on **sparc** architecture, you can choose **silo**, **Itanium** systems can use **elilo**, **IBM S/390** and **zSeries** use **z/IPL**, **Alpha** uses **milo** and **PowerPC** architectures use **yaboot** (yet another boot loader).

Bootable cd's and dvd's often use **syslinux**.

14.1.8. kernel

The goal of all this is to load an operating system, or rather the **kernel** of an operating system. A typical bootloader like **grub** will copy a kernel from hard disk to memory, and will then hand control of the computer to the kernel (execute the kernel).

Once the Linux kernel is loaded, the bootloader turns control over to it. From that moment on, the kernel is in control of the system. After discussing bootloaders, we continue with the **init system** that starts all the daemons.

14.2. grub

14.2.1. /boot/grub/grub.cfg

Debian switched to **grub2**, which will be discussed in the next section. The main boot menu configuration file for **grub2** is **grub.cfg**.

```
root@debian7:~# ls -l /boot/grub/grub.cfg
-r--r--r-- 1 root root 2453 May 13 17:22 /boot/grub/grub.cfg
root@debian7:~#
```

14.2.2. /boot/grub/grub.conf

Distributions like Red Hat Enterprise Linux 6 use **grub.conf** and provide a symbolic link from **/boot/grub/menu.lst** and from **/etc/grub.conf** to this file.

```
[root@centos65 ~]# ls -l /boot/grub/menu.lst
lrwxrwxrwx. 1 root root 11 Mar  7 11:53 /boot/grub/menu.lst -> ./grub.conf
[root@centos65 ~]# ls -l /boot/grub/grub.conf
-rw-------. 1 root root 1189 May  5 11:47 /boot/grub/grub.conf
[root@centos65 ~]#
```

The file currently (RHEL 6.5) looks like this:

```
[root@centos65 ~]# more /boot/grub/grub.conf
# grub.conf generated by anaconda
#
# Note that you do not have to rerun grub after making changes to this file
# NOTICE:  You have a /boot partition.  This means that
#          all kernel and initrd paths are relative to /boot/, eg.
#          root (hd0,0)
#          kernel /vmlinuz-version ro root=/dev/mapper/VolGroup-lv_root
#          initrd /initrd-[generic-]version.img
#boot=/dev/sda
default=0
timeout=5
splashimage=(hd0,0)/grub/splash.xpm.gz
hiddenmenu
title CentOS (2.6.32-431.11.2.el6.x86_64)
        root (hd0,0)
        kernel /vmlinuz-2.6.32-431.11.2.el6.x86_64 ro root=/dev/mapper/VolGr\
oup-lv_root rd_NO_LUKS LANG=en_US.UTF-8 rd_NO_MD rd_LVM_LV=VolGroup/lv_swap \
SYSFONT=latarcyrheb-sun16 crashkernel=auto rd_LVM_LV=VolGroup/lv_root  KEYBO\
ARDTYPE=pc KEYTABLE=us rd_NO_DM rhgb quiet
        initrd /initramfs-2.6.32-431.11.2.el6.x86_64.img
title CentOS (2.6.32-431.el6.x86_64)
        root (hd0,0)
        kernel /vmlinuz-2.6.32-431.el6.x86_64 ro root=/dev/mapper/VolGroup-l\
v_root rd_NO_LUKS LANG=en_US.UTF-8 rd_NO_MD rd_LVM_LV=VolGroup/lv_swap SYSFO\
NT=latarcyrheb-sun16 crashkernel=auto rd_LVM_LV=VolGroup/lv_root  KEYBOARDTY\
PE=pc KEYTABLE=us rd_NO_DM rhgb quiet
        initrd /initramfs-2.6.32-431.el6.x86_64.img
[root@centos65 ~]#
```

14.2.3. menu commands

The **menu commands** must be at the top of **grub**'s configuration file.

default

The **default** command sets a default **entry** to start. The first **entry** has number 0.

```
default=0
```

Each entry or **stanza** starts with a **title** directive.

fallback

In case the **default** does not boot, use the **fallback** entry instead.

```
fallback=1
```

timeout

The **timeout** will wait a number of seconds before booting the **default** entry.

```
timeout=5
```

hiddenmenu

The **hiddenmenu** will hide the **grub** menu unless the user presses **Esc** before the **timeout** expires.

```
hiddenmenu
```

title

With **title** we can start a new **entry** or **stanza**.

```
title CentOS (2.6.32-431.11.2.el6.x86_64)
```

password

You can add a **password** to prevent interactive selection of a boot environment while **grub** is running.

```
password --md5 $1$Ec.id/$T2C2ahI/EG3WRRsmmu/HN/
```

Use the **grub** interactive shell to create the password hash.

```
grub> md5crypt

Password: ********
Encrypted: $1$Ec.id/$T2C2ahI/EG3WRRsmmu/HN/
```

14.2.4. stanza commands

Every **operating system** or **kernel** that you want to boot with **grub** will have a **stanza** aka an **entry** of a couple of lines. Listed here are some of the common **stanza** commands.

boot

Technically the **boot** command is only mandatory when running the **grub command line**. This command does not have any parameters and can only be set as the last command of a stanza.

```
boot
```

kernel

The **kernel** command points to the location of the kernel. To boot Linux this means booting a **gzip** compressed **zImage** or **bzip2** compressed **bzImage**.

This screenshot shows a **kernel** command used to load a Debian kernel.

```
kernel  /boot/vmlinuz-2.6.17-2-686 root=/dev/hda1 ro
```

And this is how RHEL 5 uses the **kernel** command.

```
kernel /vmlinuz-2.6.18-128.el5 ro root=/dev/VolGroup00/LogVol00 rhgb quiet
```

All parameters in the kernel line can be read by the kernel itself or by any other program (which are started later) by reading **/proc/cmdline**

initrd

Many **Linux** installations will need an **initial ramdisk** at boot time. This can be set in **grub** with the **initrd** command.

Here a screenshot of Debian 4.0

```
initrd /boot/initrd.img-2.6.17-2-686
```

And the same for Red Hat Enterprise Linux 5

```
initrd /initrd-2.6.18-128.el5.img
```

root

The **root** command accepts the root device as a parameter.

The **root** command will point to the hard disk and partition to use, with **hd0** as the first hard disk device and **hd1** as the second hard disk device. The same numbering is used for partitions, so **hd0,0** is the first partition on the first disk and **hd0,1** is the second partition on that disk.

```
root (hd0,0)
```

savedefault

The **savedefault** command can be used together with **default saved** as a menu command. This combination will set the currently booted stanza as the next default stanza to boot.

```
default saved
timeout 10

title Linux
root (hd0,0)
kernel /boot/vmlinuz
savedefault

title DOS
root (hd0,1)
makeactive
chainloader +1
savedefault
```

14.2.5. chainloading

With **grub** booting, there are two choices: loading an operating system or **chainloading** another bootloader. The **chainloading** feature of grub loads the bootsector of a partition (that contains an operating system).

Some older operating systems require a **primary partition** that is set as **active**. Only one partition can be set **active** so **grub** can do this on the fly just before **chainloading**.

This screenshot shows how to set the first primary partition **active** with **grub**.

```
root  (hd0,0)
makeactive
```

Chainloading refers to grub loading another operating system's bootloader. The **chainloader** switch receives one option: the number of sectors to read and boot. For **DOS** and **OS/2** one sector is enough. Note that **DOS** requires the boot/root partition to be active!

Here is a complete example to **chainload** an old operating system.

```
title MS-DOS 6.22
root  (hd0,1)
makeactive
chainloader +1
```

14.2.6. simple stanza examples

This is a screenshot of a **Debian 4** stanza.

```
title   Debian GNU/Linux, kernel 2.6.17-2-686
root    (hd0,0)
kernel  /boot/vmlinuz-2.6.17-2-686 root=/dev/hda1 ro
initrd  /boot/initrd.img-2.6.17-2-686
```

Here a screenshot of a **Red Hat Enterprise Linux 5** stanza.

```
title Red Hat Enterprise Linux Server (2.6.18-128.el5)
 root (hd0,0)
 kernel /vmlinuz-2.6.18-98.el5 ro root=/dev/VolGroup00/LogVol00 rhgb quiet
 initrd /initrd-2.6.18-98.el5.img
```

14.2.7. editing grub at boot time

At boot time, when the **grub** menu is displayed, you can type **e** to edit the current stanza. This enables you to add parameters to the kernel.

One such parameter, useful when you lost the root password, is **single**. This will boot the kernel in single user mode (although some distributions will still require you to type the root password.

```
kernel  /boot/vmlinuz-2.6.17-2-686 root=/dev/hda1 ro single
```

Another option to reset a root password is to use an **init=/bin/bash** parameter.

```
kernel  /boot/vmlinuz-2.6.17-2-686 root=/dev/hda1 ro init=/bin/bash
```

Note that some distributions will disable this option at kernel compile time.

14.2.8. installing grub

Run the **grub-install** command to install **grub**. The command requires a destination for overwriting the **boot sector** or **mbr**.

```
# grub-install /dev/hda
```

You will rarely have to do this manually, since grub is installed when installing the operating system and does not need any re-install when changing configuration (as is the case for **lilo**).

14.3. grub2

14.3.1. grub 2.0 ?

The main configuration file is now **/boot/grub/grub.cfg**. And while this file may look familiar, one should never edit this file directly (because it is generated!).

```
root@debian7:~# ls -l /boot/grub/grub.cfg
-r--r--r-- 1 root root 2453 May 13 17:22 /boot/grub/grub.cfg
root@debian7:~# head -3 /boot/grub/grub.cfg
#
# DO NOT EDIT THIS FILE
#
```

14.3.2. /etc/grub.d/40_custom

The **/etc/grub.d/40_custom** file can be changed to include custom entries. These entries are automatically added to grub.

```
root@debian7:~# ls -l /etc/grub.d/40_custom
-rwxr-xr-x 1 root root 214 Jul  3  2013 /etc/grub.d/40_custom
root@debian7:~# cat /etc/grub.d/40_custom
#!/bin/sh
exec tail -n +3 $0
# This file provides an easy way to add custom menu entries.  Simply type the
# menu entries you want to add after this comment.  Be careful not to change
# the 'exec tail' line above.
```

14.3.3. /etc/default/grub

The new configuration file for changing grub is now **/etc/default/grub**.

```
root@debian7:~# head /etc/default/grub
# If you change this file, run 'update-grub' afterwards to update
# /boot/grub/grub.cfg.
# For full documentation of the options in this file, see:
#   info -f grub -n 'Simple configuration'

GRUB_DEFAULT=0
GRUB_TIMEOUT=5
GRUB_DISTRIBUTOR=`lsb_release -i -s 2> /dev/null || echo Debian`
GRUB_CMDLINE_LINUX_DEFAULT="quiet"
GRUB_CMDLINE_LINUX="debian-installer=en_US"
```

14.3.4. update-grub

Whenever the **/etc/default/grub** file is changed, you will need to run **update-grub** to apply the changes.

```
root@debian7:~# vi /etc/default/grub
root@debian7:~# update-grub
Generating grub.cfg ...
Found linux image: /boot/vmlinuz-3.2.0-4-amd64
Found initrd image: /boot/initrd.img-3.2.0-4-amd64
done
```

14.4. lilo

14.4.1. Linux loader

lilo used to be the most used Linux bootloader, but is steadily being replaced with **grub** and recently **grub2**.

14.4.2. lilo.conf

Here is an example of a **lilo.conf** file. The **delay** switch receives a number in tenths of a second. So the delay below is three seconds, not thirty!

```
boot = /dev/hda
delay = 30

image = /boot/vmlinuz
  root = /dev/hda1
  label = Red Hat 5.2

image = /boot/vmlinuz
  root = /dev/hda2
  label = S.U.S.E. 8.0

other = /dev/hda4
  table = /dev/hda
  label = MS-DOS 6.22
```

The configration file shows three example stanzas. The first one boots Red Hat from the first partition on the first disk (hda1). The second stanza boots Suse 8.0 from the next partition. The last one loads MS-DOS.

14.5. practice: bootloader

0. Find out whether your system is using lilo, grub or grub2. Only do the practices that are appropriate for your system.

1. Make a copy of the kernel, initrd and System.map files in /boot. Put the copies also in /boot but replace 2.x or 3.x with 4.0 (just imagine that Linux 4.0 is out.).

2. Add a stanza in grub for the 4.0 files. Make sure the title is different.

3. Set the boot menu timeout to 30 seconds.

4. Reboot and test the new stanza.

14.6. solution: bootloader

0. Find out whether your system is using lilo, grub or grub2. Only do the practices that are appropriate for your system.

1. Make a copy of the kernel, initrd and System.map files in /boot. Put the copies also in / boot but replace 2.x or 3.x with 4.0 (just imagine that Linux 4.0 is out.).

```
[root@centos65 boot]# uname -r
2.6.32-431.11.2.el6.x86_64
[root@centos65 boot]# cp System.map-2.6.32-431.11.2.el6.x86_64 System.map-4.0
[root@centos65 boot]# cp vmlinuz-2.6.32-431.11.2.el6.x86_64 vmlinuz-4.0
[root@centos65 boot]# cp initramfs-2.6.32-431.11.2.el6.x86_64.img initramfs-4.0\
.img
```

Do not forget that the initrd (or initramfs) file ends in **.img** .

2. Add a stanza in grub for the 4.0 files. Make sure the title is different.

```
[root@centos65 grub]# cut -c1-70 menu.lst | tail -12
title CentOS (4.0)
        root (hd0,0)
        kernel /vmlinuz-4.0 ro root=/dev/mapper/VolGroup-lv_root rd_NO_LUKS L
        initrd /initramfs-4.0.img
title CentOS (2.6.32-431.11.2.el6.x86_64)
        root (hd0,0)
        kernel /vmlinuz-2.6.32-431.11.2.el6.x86_64 ro root=/dev/mapper/VolGro
        initrd /initramfs-2.6.32-431.11.2.el6.x86_64.img
title CentOS (2.6.32-431.el6.x86_64)
        root (hd0,0)
        kernel /vmlinuz-2.6.32-431.el6.x86_64 ro root=/dev/mapper/VolGroup-lv
        initrd /initramfs-2.6.32-431.el6.x86_64.img
[root@centos65 grub]#
```

3. Set the boot menu timeout to 30 seconds.

```
[root@centos65 grub]# vi menu.lst
[root@centos65 grub]# grep timeout /boot/grub/grub.conf
timeout=30
```

4. Reboot and test the new stanza.

```
[root@centos65 grub]# reboot
```

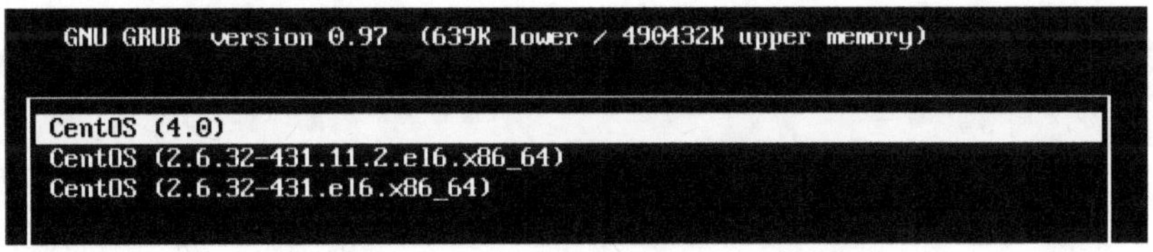

Select your stanza and if it boots then you did it correct.

Chapter 15. init and runlevels

Many Unix and Linux distributions use **init** scripts to start daemons in the same way that **Unix System V** did. This chapter will explain in detail how that works.

Init starts daemons by using scripts, where each script starts one daemon, and where each script waits for the previous script to finish. This serial process of starting daemons is slow, and although slow booting is not a problem on servers where uptime is measured in years, the recent uptake of Linux on the desktop results in user complaints.

To improve Linux startup speed, **Canonical** has developed **upstart**, which was first used in Ubuntu. Solaris also used **init** up to Solaris 9, for Solaris 10 **Sun** developed **Service Management Facility**. Both systems start daemons in parallel and can replace the SysV init scripts. There is also an ongoing effort to create **initng** (init next generation).

In 2014 the **systemd** initiative has taken a lead when after Fedora, RHEL7 and CentOS7 also Debian has chosen this to be the prefered replacement for init. The end of this module contains an introduction to **systemd**.

15.1. system init(ialization)

15.1.1. process id 1

The kernel receives system control from the bootloader. After a while the kernel starts the **init daemon**. The **init** daemon (**/sbin/init**) is the first daemon that is started and receives **process id 1** (PID 1). **Init** never dies.

15.1.2. configuration in /etc/inittab

When **/sbin/init** is started, it will first read its configuration file **/etc/inittab**. In that file, it will look for the value of initdefault (3 in the screenshot below).

```
[paul@rhel4 ~]$ grep ^id /etc/inittab
id:3:initdefault:
```

15.1.3. initdefault

The value found in **initdefault** indicates the default **runlevel**. Some Linux distributions have a brief description of runlevels in /etc/inittab, like here on Red Hat Enterprise Linux 4.

```
# Default runlevel. The runlevels used by RHS are:
#   0 - halt (Do NOT set initdefault to this)
#   1 - Single user mode
#   2 - Multiuser, without NFS (The same as 3, if you don't have network)
#   3 - Full multiuser mode
#   4 - unused
#   5 - X11
#   6 - reboot (Do NOT set initdefault to this)
```

Runlevel 0 means the system is shutting down. **Runlevel 1** is used for troubleshooting, only the root user can log on, and only at the console. **Runlevel 3** is typical for servers, whereas **runlevel 5** is typical for desktops (graphical logon). Besides runlevels 0, 1 and 6, the use may vary depending on the distribution. Debian and derived Linux systems have full network and GUI logon on runlevels 2 to 5. So always verify the proper meaning of runlevels on your system.

15.1.4. sysinit script

/etc/rc.d/rc.sysinit

The next line in **/etc/inittab** in Red Hat and derivatives is the following.

```
si::sysinit:/etc/rc.d/rc.sysinit
```

This means that independent of the selected runlevel, **init** will run the **/etc/rc.d/rc.sysinit** script. This script initializes hardware, sets some basic environment, populates **/etc/mtab** while mounting file systems, starts swap and more.

```
[paul@rhel ~]$ egrep -e"^# Ini" -e"^# Sta" -e"^# Che" /etc/rc.d/rc.sysinit
# Check SELinux status
# Initialize hardware
# Start the graphical boot, if necessary; /usr may not be mounted yet...
# Initialiaze ACPI bits
# Check filesystems
# Start the graphical boot, if necessary and not done yet.
# Check to see if SELinux requires a relabel
# Initialize pseudo-random number generator
# Start up swapping.
# Initialize the serial ports.
```

*That **egrep** command could also have been written with **grep** like this :*

```
grep "^# \(Ini\|Sta\|Che\)".
```

/etc/init.d/rcS

Debian has the following line after **initdefault**.

```
si::sysinit:/etc/init.d/rcS
```

The **/etc/init.d/rcS** script will always run on Debian (independent of the selected runlevel). The script is actually running all scripts in the **/etc/rcS.d/** directory in alphabetical order.

```
root@barry:~# cat /etc/init.d/rcS
#! /bin/sh
#
# rcS
#
# Call all S??* scripts in /etc/rcS.d/ in numerical/alphabetical order
#

exec /etc/init.d/rc S
```

15.1.5. rc scripts

Init will continue to read **/etc/inittab** and meets this section on Debian Linux.

```
l0:0:wait:/etc/init.d/rc 0
l1:1:wait:/etc/init.d/rc 1
l2:2:wait:/etc/init.d/rc 2
l3:3:wait:/etc/init.d/rc 3
l4:4:wait:/etc/init.d/rc 4
l5:5:wait:/etc/init.d/rc 5
l6:6:wait:/etc/init.d/rc 6
```

On Red Hat Enterprise Linux it is identical except **init.d** is **rc.d**.

```
l0:0:wait:/etc/rc.d/rc 0
l1:1:wait:/etc/rc.d/rc 1
l2:2:wait:/etc/rc.d/rc 2
l3:3:wait:/etc/rc.d/rc 3
l4:4:wait:/etc/rc.d/rc 4
l5:5:wait:/etc/rc.d/rc 5
l6:6:wait:/etc/rc.d/rc 6
```

In both cases, this means that **init** will start the rc script with the runlevel as the only parameter. Actually **/etc/inittab** has fields separated by colons. The second field determines the runlevel in which this line should be executed. So in both cases, only one line of the seven will be executed, depending on the runlevel set by **initdefault**.

15.1.6. rc directories

When you take a look any of the **/etc/rcX.d/** directories, then you will see a lot of (links to) scripts who's name start with either uppercase K or uppercase S.

```
[root@RHEL52 rc3.d]# ls -l | tail -4
lrwxrwxrwx 1 root root 19 Oct 11  2008 S98haldaemon -> ../init.d/haldaemon
lrwxrwxrwx 1 root root 19 Oct 11  2008 S99firstboot -> ../init.d/firstboot
lrwxrwxrwx 1 root root 11 Jan 21 04:16 S99local -> ../rc.local
lrwxrwxrwx 1 root root 16 Jan 21 04:17 S99smartd -> ../init.d/smartd
```

The **/etc/rcX.d/** directories only contain links to scripts in **/etc/init.d/**. Links allow for the script to have a different name. When entering a runlevel, all scripts that start with uppercase K or uppercase S will be started in alphabetical order. Those that start with K will be started first, with **stop** as the only parameter. The remaining scripts with S will be started with **start** as the only parameter.

All this is done by the **/etc/rc.d/rc** script on Red Hat and by the **/etc/init.d/rc** script on Debian.

15.1.7. mingetty

mingetty in /etc/inittab

Almost at the end of **/etc/inittab** there is a section to start and **respawn** several **mingetty** daemons.

```
[root@RHEL4b ~]# grep getty /etc/inittab
# Run gettys in standard runlevels
1:2345:respawn:/sbin/mingetty tty1
2:2345:respawn:/sbin/mingetty tty2
3:2345:respawn:/sbin/mingetty tty3
4:2345:respawn:/sbin/mingetty tty4
5:2345:respawn:/sbin/mingetty tty5
6:2345:respawn:/sbin/mingetty tty6
```

mingetty and /bin/login

This **/sbin/mingetty** will display a message on a virtual console and allow you to type a userid. Then it executes the **/bin/login** command with that userid. The **/bin/login** program will verify whether that user exists in **/etc/passwd** and prompt for (and verify) a password. If the password is correct, **/bin/login** passes control to the shell listed in **/etc/passwd.**

respawning mingetty

The mingetty daemons are started by **init** and watched until they die (user exits the shell and is logged out). When this happens, the **init** daemon will **respawn** a new mingetty. So even if you **kill** a mingetty daemon, it will be restarted automatically.

This example shows that init respawns mingetty daemons. Look at the PID's of the last two mingetty processes.

```
[root@RHEL52 ~]# ps -C mingetty
  PID TTY          TIME CMD
 2407 tty1     00:00:00 mingetty
 2408 tty2     00:00:00 mingetty
 2409 tty3     00:00:00 mingetty
 2410 tty4     00:00:00 mingetty
 2411 tty5     00:00:00 mingetty
 2412 tty6     00:00:00 mingetty
```

When we **kill** the last two mingettys, then **init** will notice this and start them again (with a different PID).

```
[root@RHEL52 ~]# kill 2411 2412
[root@RHEL52 ~]# ps -C mingetty
  PID TTY          TIME CMD
 2407 tty1     00:00:00 mingetty
 2408 tty2     00:00:00 mingetty
 2409 tty3     00:00:00 mingetty
 2410 tty4     00:00:00 mingetty
 2821 tty5     00:00:00 mingetty
 2824 tty6     00:00:00 mingetty
```

disabling a mingetty

You can disable a mingetty for a certain tty by removing the runlevel from the second field in its line in /etc/inittab. Don't forget to tell init about the change of its configuration file with **kill -1 1**.

The example below shows how to disable mingetty on tty3 to tty6 in runlevels 4 and 5.

```
[root@RHEL52 ~]# grep getty /etc/inittab
# Run gettys in standard runlevels
1:2345:respawn:/sbin/mingetty tty1
2:2345:respawn:/sbin/mingetty tty2
3:23:respawn:/sbin/mingetty tty3
4:23:respawn:/sbin/mingetty tty4
5:23:respawn:/sbin/mingetty tty5
6:23:respawn:/sbin/mingetty tty6
```

15.2. daemon or demon ?

A **daemon** is a process that runs in background, without a link to a GUI or terminal. Daemons are usually started at system boot, and stay alive until the system shuts down. In more recent technical writings, daemons are often refered to as **services**.

Unix **daemons** are not to be confused with demons. **Evi Nemeth**, co-author of the UNIX System Administration Handbook has the following to say about daemons:

Many people equate the word "daemon" with the word "demon", implying some kind of satanic connection between UNIX and the underworld. This is an egregious misunderstanding. "Daemon" is actually a much older form of "demon"; daemons have no particular bias towards good or evil, but rather serve to help define a person's character or personality. The ancient Greeks' concept of a "personal daemon" was similar to the modern concept of a "guardian angel" ....

15.3. starting and stopping daemons

The K and S scripts are links to the real scripts in **/etc/init.d/**. These can also be used when the system is running to start and stop daemons (or services). Most of them accept the following parameters: start, stop, restart, status.

For example in this screenshot we restart the samba daemon.

```
root@laika:~# /etc/init.d/samba restart
 * Stopping Samba daemons...                                 [ OK ]
 * Starting Samba daemons...                                 [ OK ]
```

You can achieve the same result on RHEL/Fedora with the **service** command.

```
[root@RHEL4b ~]# service smb restart
Shutting down SMB services:                                  [  OK  ]
Shutting down NMB services:                                  [  OK  ]
Starting SMB services:                                       [  OK  ]
Starting NMB services:                                       [  OK  ]
```

You might also want to take a look at **chkconfig**, **update-rc.d**.

15.4. chkconfig

The purpose of **chkconfig** is to relieve system administrators of manually managing all the links and scripts in **/etc/init.d** and **/etc/rcX.d/**.

15.4.1. chkconfig --list

Here we use **chkconfig** to list the status of a service in the different runlevels. You can see that the **crond** daemon (or service) is only activated in runlevels 2 to 5.

```
[root@RHEL52 ~]# chkconfig --list crond
crond           0:off 1:off 2:on 3:on 4:on 5:on 6:off
```

When you compare the screenshot above with the one below, you can see that **off** equals to a K link to the script, whereas **on** equals to an S link.

```
[root@RHEL52 etc]# find ./rc?.d/ -name \*crond -exec ls -l {} \;|cut -b40-
./rc0.d/K60crond -> ../init.d/crond
./rc1.d/K60crond -> ../init.d/crond
./rc2.d/S90crond -> ../init.d/crond
./rc3.d/S90crond -> ../init.d/crond
./rc4.d/S90crond -> ../init.d/crond
./rc5.d/S90crond -> ../init.d/crond
./rc6.d/K60crond -> ../init.d/crond
```

15.4.2. runlevel configuration

Here you see how to use chkconfig to disable (or enable) a service in a certain runlevel.

This screenshot shows how to disable **crond** in runlevel 3.

```
[root@RHEL52 ~]# chkconfig --level 3 crond off
[root@RHEL52 ~]# chkconfig --list crond
crond           0:off 1:off 2:on 3:off 4:on 5:on 6:off
```

This screenshot shows how to enable **crond** in runlevels 3 and 4.

```
[root@RHEL52 ~]# chkconfig --level 34 crond on
[root@RHEL52 ~]# chkconfig --list crond
crond           0:off 1:off 2:on 3:on 4:on 5:on 6:off
```

15.4.3. chkconfig configuration

Every script in **/etc/init.d/** can have (comment) lines to tell chkconfig what to do with the service. The line with # **chkconfig:** contains the runlevels in which the service should be started (2345), followed by the priority for start (90) and stop (60).

```
[root@RHEL52 ~]# head -9 /etc/init.d/crond | tail -5
# chkconfig: 2345 90 60
# description: cron is a standard UNIX program that runs user-specified
#              programs at periodic scheduled times. vixie cron adds a
#              number of features to the basic UNIX cron, including better
#              security and more powerful configuration options.
```

15.4.4. enable and disable services

Services can be enabled or disabled in all runlevels with one command. Runlevels 0, 1 and 6 are always stopping services (or calling the scripts with **stop**) even when their name starts with uppercase S.

```
[root@RHEL52 ~]# chkconfig crond off
[root@RHEL52 ~]# chkconfig --list crond
crond           0:off   1:off   2:off   3:off   4:off   5:off   6:off
[root@RHEL52 ~]# chkconfig crond on
[root@RHEL52 ~]# chkconfig --list crond
crond           0:off   1:off   2:on    3:on    4:on    5:on    6:off
```

15.5. update-rc.d

15.5.1. about update-rc.d

The Debian equivalent of **chkconfig** is called **update-rc.d**. This tool is designed for use in scripts, if you prefer a graphical tool then look at **bum**.

When there are existing links in **/etc/rcX.d/** then **update-rc.d** does not do anything. This is to avoid that post installation scripts using **update-rc.d** are overwriting changes made by a system administrator.

```
root@barry:~# update-rc.d cron remove
update-rc.d: /etc/init.d/cron exists during rc.d purge (use -f to force)
```

As you can see in the next screenshot, nothing changed for the cron daemon.

```
root@barry:~# find /etc/rc?.d/ -name '*cron' -exec ls -l {} \;|cut -b44-
/etc/rc0.d/K11cron -> ../init.d/cron
/etc/rc1.d/K11cron -> ../init.d/cron
/etc/rc2.d/S89cron -> ../init.d/cron
/etc/rc3.d/S89cron -> ../init.d/cron
/etc/rc4.d/S89cron -> ../init.d/cron
/etc/rc5.d/S89cron -> ../init.d/cron
/etc/rc6.d/K11cron -> ../init.d/cron
```

15.5.2. removing a service

Here we remove **cron** from all runlevels. Remember that the proper way to disable a service is to put K scripts oin all runlevels!

```
root@barry:~# update-rc.d -f cron remove
 Removing any system startup links for /etc/init.d/cron ...
   /etc/rc0.d/K11cron
   /etc/rc1.d/K11cron
   /etc/rc2.d/S89cron
   /etc/rc3.d/S89cron
   /etc/rc4.d/S89cron
   /etc/rc5.d/S89cron
   /etc/rc6.d/K11cron
root@barry:~# find /etc/rc?.d/ -name '*cron' -exec ls -l {} \;|cut -b44-
root@barry:~#
```

15.5.3. enable a service

This screenshot shows how to use **update-rc.d** to enable a service in runlevels 2, 3, 4 and 5 and disable the service in runlevels 0, 1 and 6.

```
root@barry:~# update-rc.d cron defaults
 Adding system startup for /etc/init.d/cron ...
   /etc/rc0.d/K20cron -> ../init.d/cron
   /etc/rc1.d/K20cron -> ../init.d/cron
   /etc/rc6.d/K20cron -> ../init.d/cron
   /etc/rc2.d/S20cron -> ../init.d/cron
   /etc/rc3.d/S20cron -> ../init.d/cron
   /etc/rc4.d/S20cron -> ../init.d/cron
   /etc/rc5.d/S20cron -> ../init.d/cron
```

15.5.4. customize a service

And here is an example on how to set your custom configuration for the cron daemon.

```
root@barry:~# update-rc.d -n cron start 11 2 3 4 5 . stop 89 0 1 6 .
 Adding system startup for /etc/init.d/cron ...
   /etc/rc0.d/K89cron -> ../init.d/cron
   /etc/rc1.d/K89cron -> ../init.d/cron
   /etc/rc6.d/K89cron -> ../init.d/cron
   /etc/rc2.d/S11cron -> ../init.d/cron
   /etc/rc3.d/S11cron -> ../init.d/cron
   /etc/rc4.d/S11cron -> ../init.d/cron
   /etc/rc5.d/S11cron -> ../init.d/cron
```

15.6. bum

This screenshot shows **bum** in advanced mode.

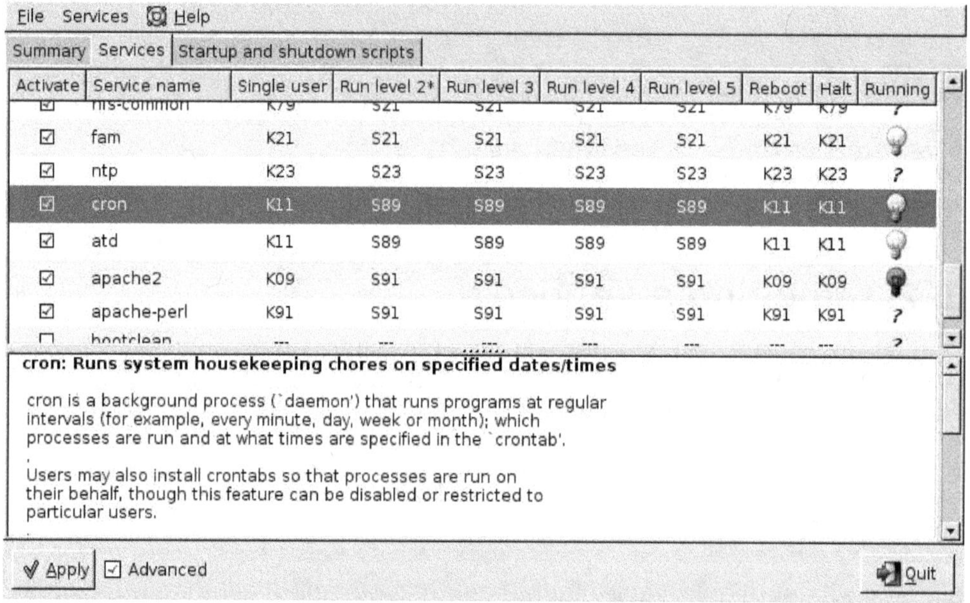

15.7. runlevels

15.7.1. display the runlevel

You can see your current runlevel with the **runlevel** or **who -r** commands.

The runlevel command is typical Linux and will output the previous and the current runlevel. If there was no previous runlevel, then it will mark it with the letter N.

```
[root@RHEL4b ~]# runlevel
N 3
```

The history of **who -r** dates back to Seventies Unix, it still works on Linux.

```
[root@RHEL4b ~]# who -r
         run-level 3  Jul 28 09:15                   last=S
```

15.7.2. changing the runlevel

You can switch to another runlevel with the **telinit** command. On Linux **/sbin/telinit** is usually a (hard) link to **/sbin/init**.

This screenshot shows how to switch from runlevel 2 to runlevel 3 without reboot.

```
root@barry:~# runlevel
N 2
root@barry:~# init 3
root@barry:~# runlevel
2 3
```

15.7.3. /sbin/shutdown

The **shutdown** command is used to properly shut down a system.

Common switches used with **shutdown** are **-a**, **-t**, **-h** and **-r**.

The **-a** switch forces **/sbin/shutdown** to use **/etc/shutdown.allow**. The **-t** switch is used to define the number of seconds between the sending of the **TERM** signal and the **KILL** signal. The **-h** switch halts the system instead of changing to runlevel 1. The **-r** switch tells **/sbin/shutdown** to reboot after shutting down.

This screenshot shows how to use **shutdown** with five seconds between TERM and KILL signals.

```
root@barry:~# shutdown -t5 -h now
```

The **now** is the time argument. This can be **+m** for the number of minutes to wait before shutting down (with **now** as an alias for **+0**. The command will also accept hh:mm instead of **+m**.

15.7.4. halt, reboot and poweroff

The binary **/sbin/reboot** is the same as **/sbin/halt** and **/sbin/poweroff**. Depending on the name we use to call the command, it can behave differently.

When in runlevel 0 or 6 **halt**, **reboot** and **poweroff** will tell the kernel to **halt**, **reboot** or **poweroff** the system.

When not in runlevel 0 or 6, typing **reboot** as root actually calls the **shutdown** command with the **-r** switch and typing **poweroff** will switch off the power when halting the system.

15.7.5. /var/log/wtmp

halt, **reboot** and **poweroff** all write to **/var/log/wtmp**. To look at **/var/log/wtmp**, we need to use th **last**.

```
[root@RHEL52 ~]# last | grep reboot
reboot   system boot  2.6.18-128.el5   Fri May 29 11:44    (192+05:01)
reboot   system boot  2.6.18-128.el5   Wed May 27 12:10     (06:49)
reboot   system boot  2.6.18-128.el5   Mon May 25 19:34    (1+15:59)
reboot   system boot  2.6.18-128.el5   Mon Feb  9 13:20    (106+21:13)
```

15.7.6. Ctrl-Alt-Del

When **rc** is finished starting all those scripts, **init** will continue to read /etc/inittab. The next line is about what to do when the user hits **Ctrl-Alt-Delete** on the keyboard.

Here is what Debian 4.0 does.

```
root@barry:~# grep -i ctrl /etc/inittab
# What to do when CTRL-ALT-DEL is pressed.
ca:12345:ctrlaltdel:/sbin/shutdown -t1 -a -r now
```

Which is very similar to the default Red Hat Enterprise Linux 5.2 action.

```
[root@RHEL52 ~]# grep -i ctrl /etc/inittab
# Trap CTRL-ALT-DELETE
ca::ctrlaltdel:/sbin/shutdown -t3 -r now
```

One noticable difference is that Debian forces shutdown to use **/etc/shutdown.allow**, where Red Hat allows everyone to invoke **shutdown** pressing **Ctrl-Alt-Delete**.

15.7.7. UPS and loss of power

```
[root@RHEL52 ~]# grep ^p /etc/inittab
pf::powerfail:/sbin/shutdown -f -h +2 "Power Failure; System Shutting Down"
pr:12345:powerokwait:/sbin/shutdown -c "Power Restored; Shutdown Cancelled"
```

It will read commands on what to execute in case of **powerfailure**, **powerok** and **Ctrl-Alt-Delete**. The init process never stops keeping an eye on power failures and that triple key combo.

```
root@barry:~# grep ^p /etc/inittab
pf::powerwait:/etc/init.d/powerfail start
pn::powerfailnow:/etc/init.d/powerfail now
po::powerokwait:/etc/init.d/powerfail stop
```

15.8. systemd

It is likely that **systemd** will replace all the standard init/runlevel/rc functionality. Both Red Hat and Debian have decided in 2014 that **systemd** will be replacing **init** in future releases (RHEL7/CentOS7 and Debian 8).

The screenshot below shows **systemd** running as **pid 1** on RHEL7.

```
[root@rhel7 ~]# ps fax | grep systemd | cut -c1-76
    1 ?        Ss     0:01 /usr/lib/systemd/systemd --switched-root --system
  505 ?        Ss     0:00 /usr/lib/systemd/systemd-journald
  545 ?        Ss     0:00 /usr/lib/systemd/systemd-udevd
  670 ?        Ss     0:00 /usr/lib/systemd/systemd-logind
  677 ?        Ssl    0:00 /bin/dbus-daemon --system --address=systemd: --no
 2662 pts/1    S+     0:00          \_ grep --color=auto systemd
[root@rhel7 ~]#
```

Debian 8 (not yet released in September 2014) uses parts of **systemd**, but still has **init** as **pid 1**.

```
root@debian8:~# ps fax | grep systemd
 2042 ?        S      0:00 /sbin/cgmanager --daemon -m name=systemd
10127 pts/4    S+     0:00          |                   \_ grep systemd
 2777 ?        S      0:00 /lib/systemd/systemd-logind
root@debian8:~#
```

15.8.1. systemd targets

The first command to learn is **systemctl list-units --type=target** (or the shorter version **systemctl -t target**). It will show you the different targets on the system.

```
[root@rhel7 ~]# systemctl list-units --type=target
UNIT                 LOAD   ACTIVE SUB    DESCRIPTION
basic.target         loaded active active Basic System
cryptsetup.target    loaded active active Encrypted Volumes
getty.target         loaded active active Login Prompts
graphical.target     loaded active active Graphical Interface
local-fs-pre.target  loaded active active Local File Systems (Pre)
local-fs.target      loaded active active Local File Systems
multi-user.target    loaded active active Multi-User System
network.target       loaded active active Network
nfs.target           loaded active active Network File System Server
paths.target         loaded active active Paths
remote-fs.target     loaded active active Remote File Systems
slices.target        loaded active active Slices
sockets.target       loaded active active Sockets
swap.target          loaded active active Swap
sysinit.target       loaded active active System Initialization
timers.target        loaded active active Timers

LOAD   = Reflects whether the unit definition was properly loaded.
ACTIVE = The high-level unit activation state, i.e. generalization of SUB.
SUB    = The low-level unit activation state, values depend on unit type.

16 loaded units listed. Pass --all to see loaded but inactive units, too.
To show all installed unit files use 'systemctl list-unit-files'.
[root@rhel7 ~]#
```

Targets are the replacement of runlevels and define specific points to reach when booting the system. For example the **graphical.target** is reached when you get a graphical interface, and the **nfs.target** requires a running nfs server.

To switch to a target (for example **multi-user.target**), we now use **systemctl isolate** (instead of the equivalent **init 3** to change the runlevel).

```
[root@rhel7 ~]# ps fax | wc -l
169
[root@rhel7 ~]# systemctl isolate multi-user.target
[root@rhel7 ~]# ps fax | wc -l
129
[root@rhel7 ~]#
```

To change the default target, we again use this **systemctl** command (instead of editing the **/etc/inittab** file).

```
[root@rhel7 ~]# systemctl enable multi-user.target --force
rm '/etc/systemd/system/default.target'
ln -s '/usr/lib/systemd/system/multi-user.target' '/etc/systemd/system/default\
.target'
[root@rhel7 ~]#
```

This command removed the file **/etc/systemd/system/default.target** and replaced it with a symbolic link to the **multi-user-.target** target.

15.8.2. systemd dependencies

Dependencies are no longer defined by alfabetical order of running scripts, but by configuration in **/etc/systemd/system/**. For example here are the required services for the **multi-user.target** on Red Hat Enterprise 7.

```
[root@rhel7 ~]# ls /etc/systemd/system/multi-user.target.wants/
abrt-ccpp.service      hypervkvpd.service      postfix.service
abrtd.service          hypervvssd.service      remote-fs.target
abrt-oops.service      irqbalance.service      rhsmcertd.service
abrt-vmcore.service    ksm.service             rngd.service
abrt-xorg.service      ksmtuned.service        rpcbind.service
atd.service            libstoragemgmt.service  rsyslog.service
auditd.service         libvirtd.service        smartd.service
avahi-daemon.service   mdmonitor.service       sshd.service
chronyd.service        ModemManager.service    sysstat.service
crond.service          NetworkManager.service  tuned.service
cups.path              nfs.target              vmtoolsd.service
[root@rhel7 ~]#
```

Debian8 is not fully migrated yet.

```
root@debian8:~# ls /etc/systemd/system/multi-user.target.wants/
anacron.service        binfmt-support.service  pppd-dns.service  ssh.service
atd.service            fancontrol.service      remote-fs.target
avahi-daemon.service   lm-sensors.service      rsyslog.service
```

Typical **rc scripts** are replaced with services. Issue the **systemctl list-units -t service --all** (or **systemctl -at service**) to get a list of all services on your system.

```
[root@rhel7 ~]# systemctl -at service | head -5 | column -t | cut -c1-78
UNIT                 LOAD    ACTIVE    SUB      DESCRIPTION
abrt-ccpp.service    loaded  active    exited   Install      ABRT     coredump
abrt-oops.service    loaded  active    running  ABRT         kernel   log
abrt-vmcore.service  loaded  inactive  dead     Harvest      vmcores  for
abrt-xorg.service    loaded  active    running  ABRT         Xorg     log
[root@rhel7 ~]#
```

And here an example on how to see the status of the **sshd** service.

```
[root@rhel7 ~]# systemctl status sshd.service
sshd.service - OpenSSH server daemon
   Loaded: loaded (/usr/lib/systemd/system/sshd.service; enabled)
   Active: active (running) since Wed 2014-09-10 13:42:21 CEST; 55min ago
 Main PID: 1400 (sshd)
   CGroup: /system.slice/sshd.service
           --1400 /usr/sbin/sshd -D

Sep 10 13:42:21 rhel7 systemd[1]: Started OpenSSH server daemon.
Sep 10 13:42:21 rhel7 sshd[1400]: Server listening on 0.0.0.0 port 22.
Sep 10 13:42:21 rhel7 sshd[1400]: Server listening on :: port 22.
[root@rhel7 ~]#
```

15.8.3. systemd services

The **chkconfig** and **service** commands are considered 'legacy'. They are replaced with **systemctl**.

This screenshot shows the new way to start and stop a service.

```
[root@rhel7 ~]# systemctl start crond.service
[root@rhel7 ~]# systemctl show crond.service | grep State
LoadState=loaded
ActiveState=active
SubState=running
UnitFileState=enabled
[root@rhel7 ~]# systemctl stop crond.service
[root@rhel7 ~]# systemctl show crond.service | grep State
LoadState=loaded
ActiveState=inactive
SubState=dead
UnitFileState=enabled
[root@rhel7 ~]#
```

And here is the new way to stop and disable a service.

```
[root@rhel7 ~]# systemctl stop crond.service
[root@rhel7 ~]# systemctl disable crond.service
rm '/etc/systemd/system/multi-user.target.wants/crond.service'
[root@rhel7 ~]# systemctl show crond.service | grep State
LoadState=loaded
ActiveState=inactive
SubState=dead
UnitFileState=disabled
[root@rhel7 ~]#
```

This screenshot shows how to enable and start the service again.

```
[root@rhel7 ~]# systemctl enable crond.service
ln -s '/usr/lib/systemd/system/crond.service' '/etc/systemd/system/multi-user.\
target.wants/crond.service'
[root@rhel7 ~]# systemctl start crond.service
[root@rhel7 ~]# systemctl show crond.service | grep State
LoadState=loaded
ActiveState=active
SubState=running
UnitFileState=enabled
[root@rhel7 ~]#
```

15.8.4. systemd signalling

You can also use **systemd** to **kill** problematic services.

```
[root@rhel7 ~]# systemctl show crond.service | grep State
LoadState=loaded
ActiveState=active
SubState=running
UnitFileState=enabled
[root@rhel7 ~]# systemctl kill -s SIGKILL crond.service
[root@rhel7 ~]# systemctl show crond.service | grep State
LoadState=loaded
ActiveState=failed
SubState=failed
UnitFileState=enabled
[root@rhel7 ~]#
```

15.8.5. systemd shutdown

The **poweroff**, **halt** and **reboot** commands are considered legacy now and are handeld by **systemctl**. The table below shows the legacy commands on the left and their new **systemd** equivalent on the right.

Table 15.1. systemd power management

legacy command	systemd command
poweroff	systemctl poweroff
reboot	systemctl reboot
halt	systemctl halt
pm-suspend	systemctl suspend
pm-hibernate	systemctl hibernate

15.8.6. remote systemd

The **systemctl** utility has a buil-in remote control providing there is an **ssh daemon** running on the remote system.

This screenshot shows how to use **systemctl** to verify a service on an other RHEL server.

```
[root@rhel7 ~]# systemctl -H root@192.168.1.65 status sshd
root@192.168.1.65's password:
sshd.service - OpenSSH server daemon
   Loaded: loaded (/usr/lib/systemd/system/sshd.service; enabled)
   Active: active (running) since Thu 2014-09-11 13:04:10 CEST; 16min ago
  Process: 1328 ExecStartPre=/usr/sbin/sshd-keygen (code=exited, status=0/SUCCE\
SS)
 Main PID: 1363 (sshd)
   CGroup: /system.slice/sshd.service
[root@rhel7 ~]#
```

15.8.7. there is more systemd

There are other tools...

```
systemd-analyze              systemd-loginctl
systemd-ask-password         systemd-machine-id-setup
systemd-cat                  systemd-notify
systemd-cgls                 systemd-nspawn
systemd-cgtop                systemd-run
systemd-coredumpctl          systemd-stdio-bridge
systemd-delta                systemd-sysv-convert
systemd-detect-virt          systemd-tmpfiles
systemd-inhibit              systemd-tty-ask-password-agent
```

For example **systemd-analyze blame** will give you an overview of the time it took for each service to boot.

```
[root@rhel7 ~]# systemd-analyze blame | head
          1.977s firewalld.service
          1.096s tuned.service
           993ms postfix.service
           939ms iprinit.service
           925ms vboxadd-x11.service
           880ms firstboot-graphical.service
           839ms accounts-daemon.service
           829ms network.service
           822ms iprupdate.service
           795ms boot.mount
[root@rhel7 ~]#
```

15.9. practice: init

1. Change **/etc/inittab** so that only two mingetty's are respawned. Kill the other **mingetty's** and verify that they don't come back.

2. Use the Red Hat Enterprise Linux virtual machine. Go to runlevel 5, display the current and previous runlevel, then go back to runlevel 3.

3. Is the sysinit script on your computers setting or changing the PATH environment variable ?

4. List all init.d scripts that are started in runlevel 2.

5. Write a script that acts like a daemon script in **/etc/init.d/**. It should have a case statement to act on start/stop/restart and status. Test the script!

6. Use **chkconfig** to setup your script to start in runlevels 3,4 and 5, and to stop in any other runlevel.

15.10. solution : init

1. Change **/etc/inittab** so that only two mingetty's are respawned. Kill the other **mingetty's** and verify that they don't come back.

Killing the mingetty's will result in init respawning them. You can edit **/etc/inittab** so it looks like the screenshot below. Don't forget to also run **kill -1 1**.

```
[root@RHEL5 ~]# grep tty /etc/inittab
# Run gettys in standard runlevels
1:2345:respawn:/sbin/mingetty tty1
2:2345:respawn:/sbin/mingetty tty2
3:2:respawn:/sbin/mingetty tty3
4:2:respawn:/sbin/mingetty tty4
5:2:respawn:/sbin/mingetty tty5
6:2:respawn:/sbin/mingetty tty6
[root@RHEL5 ~]#
```

2. Use the Red Hat Enterprise Linux virtual machine. Go to runlevel 5, display the current and previous runlevel, then go back to runlevel 3.

```
init 5 (watch the console for the change taking place)
runlevel
init 3 (again you can follow this on the console)
```

3. Is the sysinit script on your computers setting or changing the PATH environment variable ?

On Red Hat, grep for PATH in **/etc/rc.sysinit**, on Debian/Ubuntu check **/etc/rc.local** and **/etc/ini.t/rc.local**. The answer is probably no, but on RHEL5 the **rc.sysinit** script does set the HOSTNAME variable.

```
[root@RHEL5 etc]# grep HOSTNAME rc.sysinit
```

4. List all init.d scripts that are started in runlevel 2.

```
root@RHEL5 ~# chkconfig --list | grep '2:on'
```

5. Write a script that acts like a daemon script in **/etc/init.d/**. It should have a case statement to act on start/stop/restart and status. Test the script!

The script could look something like this.

```
#!/bin/bash
#
# chkconfig: 345 99 01
# description: pold demo script
#
# /etc/init.d/pold
```

```
#

case "$1" in
  start)
      echo -n "Starting pold..."
      sleep 1;
      touch /var/lock/subsys/pold
      echo "done."
      echo pold started >> /var/log/messages
      ;;
  stop)
      echo -n "Stopping pold..."
      sleep 1;
      rm -rf /var/lock/subsys/pold
      echo "done."
      echo pold stopped >> /var/log/messages
      ;;
  *)
      echo "Usage: /etc/init.d/pold {start|stop}"
      exit 1
      ;;
esac
exit 0
```

The **touch /var/lock/subsys/pold** is mandatory and must be the same filename as the script name, if you want the stop sequence (the K01pold link) to be run.

6. Use **chkconfig** to setup your script to start in runlevels 3,4 and 5, and to stop in any other runlevel.

```
chkconfig --add pold
```

The command above will only work when the # **chkconfig:** and # **description:** lines in the pold script are there.

Part IV. system management

Table of Contents

Chapter 16. scheduling

Linux administrators use the **at** to schedule one time jobs. Recurring jobs are better scheduled with **cron**. The next two sections will discuss both tools.

16.1. one time jobs with at

16.1.1. at

Simple scheduling can be done with the **at** command. This screenshot shows the scheduling of the date command at 22:01 and the sleep command at 22:03.

```
root@laika:~# at 22:01
at> date
at> <EOT>
job 1 at Wed Aug  1 22:01:00 2007
root@laika:~# at 22:03
at> sleep 10
at> <EOT>
job 2 at Wed Aug  1 22:03:00 2007
root@laika:~#
```

In real life you will hopefully be scheduling more useful commands ;-)

16.1.2. atq

It is easy to check when jobs are scheduled with the **atq** or **at -l** commands.

```
root@laika:~# atq
1       Wed Aug  1 22:01:00 2007 a root
2       Wed Aug  1 22:03:00 2007 a root
root@laika:~# at -l
1       Wed Aug  1 22:01:00 2007 a root
2       Wed Aug  1 22:03:00 2007 a root
root@laika:~#
```

The at command understands English words like tomorrow and teatime to schedule commands the next day and at four in the afternoon.

```
root@laika:~# at 10:05 tomorrow
at> sleep 100
at> <EOT>
job 5 at Thu Aug  2 10:05:00 2007
root@laika:~# at teatime tomorrow
at> tea
at> <EOT>
job 6 at Thu Aug  2 16:00:00 2007
root@laika:~# atq
6       Thu Aug  2 16:00:00 2007 a root
5       Thu Aug  2 10:05:00 2007 a root
root@laika:~#
```

16.1.3. atrm

Jobs in the at queue can be removed with **atrm**.

```
root@laika:~# atq
6       Thu Aug  2 16:00:00 2007 a root
5       Thu Aug  2 10:05:00 2007 a root
root@laika:~# atrm 5
root@laika:~# atq
6       Thu Aug  2 16:00:00 2007 a root
root@laika:~#
```

16.1.4. at.allow and at.deny

You can also use the **/etc/at.allow** and **/etc/at.deny** files to manage who can schedule jobs with at.

The **/etc/at.allow** file can contain a list of users that are allowed to schedule **at** jobs. When **/etc/at.allow** does not exist, then everyone can use **at** unless their username is listed in **/etc/at.deny**.

If none of these files exist, then everyone can use **at**.

16.2. cron

16.2.1. crontab file

The **crontab(1)** command can be used to maintain the **crontab(5)** file. Each user can have their own crontab file to schedule jobs at a specific time. This time can be specified with five fields in this order: minute, hour, day of the month, month and day of the week. If a field contains an asterisk (*), then this means all values of that field.

The following example means : run script42 eight minutes after two, every day of the month, every month and every day of the week.

```
8 14 * * * script42
```

Run script8472 every month on the first of the month at 25 past midnight.

```
25 0 1 * * script8472
```

Run this script33 every two minutes on Sunday (both 0 and 7 refer to Sunday).

```
*/2 * * * 0
```

Instead of these five fields, you can also type one of these: @reboot, @yearly or @annually, @monthly, @weekly, @daily or @midnight, and @hourly.

16.2.2. crontab command

Users should not edit the crontab file directly, instead they should type **crontab -e** which will use the editor defined in the EDITOR or VISUAL environment variable. Users can display their cron table with **crontab -l**.

16.2.3. cron.allow and cron.deny

The **cron daemon crond** is reading the cron tables, taking into account the **/etc/cron.allow** and **/etc/cron.deny** files.

These files work in the same way as **at.allow** and **at.deny**. When the **cron.allow** file exists, then your username has to be in it, otherwise you cannot use **cron**. When the **cron.allow** file does not exists, then your username cannot be in the **cron.deny** file if you want to use **cron**.

16.2.4. /etc/crontab

The **/etc/crontab** file contains entries for when to run hourly/daily/weekly/monthly tasks. It will look similar to this output.

```
SHELL=/bin/sh
PATH=/usr/local/sbin:/usr/local/bin:/sbin:/bin:/usr/sbin:/usr/bin

20 3 * * *          root    run-parts --report /etc/cron.daily
40 3 * * 7          root    run-parts --report /etc/cron.weekly
55 3 1 * *          root    run-parts --report /etc/cron.monthly
```

16.2.5. /etc/cron.*

The directories shown in the next screenshot contain the tasks that are run at the times scheduled in **/etc/crontab**. The **/etc/cron.d** directory is for special cases, to schedule jobs that require finer control than hourly/daily/weekly/monthly.

```
paul@laika:~$ ls -ld /etc/cron.*
drwxr-xr-x 2 root root 4096 2008-04-11 09:14 /etc/cron.d
drwxr-xr-x 2 root root 4096 2008-04-19 15:04 /etc/cron.daily
drwxr-xr-x 2 root root 4096 2008-04-11 09:14 /etc/cron.hourly
drwxr-xr-x 2 root root 4096 2008-04-11 09:14 /etc/cron.monthly
drwxr-xr-x 2 root root 4096 2008-04-11 09:14 /etc/cron.weekly
```

16.2.6. /etc/cron.*

Note that Red Hat uses **anacron** to schedule daily, weekly and monthly cron jobs.

```
root@rhel65:/etc# cat anacrontab
# /etc/anacrontab: configuration file for anacron

# See anacron(8) and anacrontab(5) for details.

SHELL=/bin/sh
PATH=/sbin:/bin:/usr/sbin:/usr/bin
MAILTO=root
# the maximal random delay added to the base delay of the jobs
RANDOM_DELAY=45
# the jobs will be started during the following hours only
START_HOURS_RANGE=3-22

#period in days   delay in minutes   job-identifier   command
1         5       cron.daily              nice run-parts /etc/cron.daily
7         25      cron.weekly             nice run-parts /etc/cron.weekly
@monthly 45       cron.monthly            nice run-parts /etc/cron.monthly
root@rhel65:/etc#
```

16.3. practice : scheduling

1. Schedule two jobs with **at**, display the **at queue** and remove a job.

2. As normal user, use **crontab -e** to schedule a script to run every four minutes.

3. As root, display the **crontab** file of your normal user.

4. As the normal user again, remove your **crontab** file.

5. Take a look at the **cron** files and directories in **/etc** and understand them. What is the **run-parts** command doing ?

16.4. solution : scheduling

1. Schedule two jobs with **at**, display the **at queue** and remove a job.

```
root@rhel55 ~# at 9pm today
at> echo go to bed >> /root/todo.txt
at> <EOT>
job 1 at 2010-11-14 21:00
root@rhel55 ~# at 17h31 today
at> echo go to lunch >> /root/todo.txt
at> <EOT>
job 2 at 2010-11-14 17:31
root@rhel55 ~# atq
2 2010-11-14 17:31 a root
1 2010-11-14 21:00 a root
root@rhel55 ~# atrm 1
root@rhel55 ~# atq
2 2010-11-14 17:31 a root
root@rhel55 ~# date
Sun Nov 14 17:31:01 CET 2010
root@rhel55 ~# cat /root/todo.txt
go to lunch
```

2. As normal user, use **crontab -e** to schedule a script to run every four minutes.

```
paul@rhel55 ~$ crontab -e
no crontab for paul - using an empty one
crontab: installing new crontab
```

3. As root, display the **crontab** file of your normal user.

```
root@rhel55 ~# crontab -l -u paul
*/4 * * * * echo `date` >> /home/paul/crontest.txt
```

4. As the normal user again, remove your **crontab** file.

```
paul@rhel55 ~$ crontab -r
paul@rhel55 ~$ crontab -l
no crontab for paul
```

5. Take a look at the **cron** files and directories in **/etc** and understand them. What is the **run-parts** command doing ?

```
run-parts runs a script in a directory
```

Chapter 17. logging

This chapter has three distinct subjects.

First we look at login logging ; how can we find out who is logging in to the system, when and from where. And who is not logging in, who fails at **su** or **ssh**.

Second we discuss how to configure the syslog daemon, and how to test it with **logger**.

The last part is mostly about **rotating logs** and mentions the **tail -f** and **watch** commands for **watching logs**.

17.1. login logging

To keep track of who is logging into the system, Linux can maintain the **/var/log/wtmp**, **/var/log/btmp**, **/var/run/utmp** and **/var/log/lastlog** files.

17.1.1. /var/run/utmp (who)

Use the **who** command to see the /var/run/utmp file. This command is showing you all the **currently** logged in users. Notice that the utmp file is in /var/run and not in /var/log .

```
[root@rhel4 ~]# who
paul     pts/1        Feb 14 18:21 (192.168.1.45)
sandra   pts/2        Feb 14 18:11 (192.168.1.42)
inge     pts/3        Feb 14 12:01 (192.168.1.33)
els      pts/4        Feb 14 14:33 (192.168.1.19)
```

17.1.2. /var/log/wtmp (last)

The /var/log/wtmp file is updated by the **login program**. Use **last** to see the /var/run/wtmp file.

```
[root@rhel4a ~]# last | head
paul     pts/1        192.168.1.45     Wed Feb 14 18:39   still logged in
reboot   system boot  2.6.9-42.0.8.ELs Wed Feb 14 18:21          (01:15)
nicolas  pts/5        pc-dss.telematic Wed Feb 14 12:32 - 13:06  (00:33)
stefaan  pts/3        pc-sde.telematic Wed Feb 14 12:28 - 12:40  (00:12)
nicolas  pts/3        pc-nae.telematic Wed Feb 14 11:36 - 12:21  (00:45)
nicolas  pts/3        pc-nae.telematic Wed Feb 14 11:34 - 11:36  (00:01)
dirk     pts/5        pc-dss.telematic Wed Feb 14 10:03 - 12:31  (02:28)
nicolas  pts/3        pc-nae.telematic Wed Feb 14 09:45 - 11:34  (01:48)
dimitri  pts/5        rhel4            Wed Feb 14 07:57 - 08:38  (00:40)
stefaan  pts/4        pc-sde.telematic Wed Feb 14 07:16 - down   (05:50)
[root@rhel4a ~]#
```

The last command can also be used to get a list of last reboots.

```
[paul@rekkie ~]$ last reboot
reboot   system boot  2.6.16-rekkie   Mon Jul 30 05:13     (370+08:42)

wtmp begins Tue May 30 23:11:45 2006
[paul@rekkie ~]
```

17.1.3. /var/log/lastlog (lastlog)

Use **lastlog** to see the /var/log/lastlog file.

```
[root@rhel4a ~]# lastlog | tail
tim              pts/5   10.170.1.122     Tue Feb 13 09:36:54 +0100 2007
rm               pts/6   rhel4            Tue Feb 13 10:06:56 +0100 2007
henk                                      **Never logged in**
stefaan          pts/3   pc-sde.telematic Wed Feb 14 12:28:38 +0100 2007
dirk             pts/5   pc-dss.telematic Wed Feb 14 10:03:11 +0100 2007
arsene                                    **Never logged in**
nicolas          pts/5   pc-dss.telematic Wed Feb 14 12:32:18 +0100 2007
dimitri          pts/5   rhel4            Wed Feb 14 07:57:19 +0100 2007
bashuserrm       pts/7   rhel4            Tue Feb 13 10:35:40 +0100 2007
kornuserrm       pts/5   rhel4            Tue Feb 13 10:06:17 +0100 2007
[root@rhel4a ~]#
```

17.1.4. /var/log/btmp (lastb)

There is also the **lastb** command to display the **/var/log/btmp** file. This file is updated by the login program when entering the wrong password, so it contains failed login attempts. Many computers will not have this file, resulting in no logging of failed login attempts.

```
[root@RHEL4b ~]# lastb
lastb: /var/log/btmp: No such file or directory
Perhaps this file was removed by the operator to prevent logging lastb\
 info.
[root@RHEL4b ~]#
```

The reason given for this is that users sometimes type their password by mistake instead of their login, so this world readable file poses a security risk. You can enable bad login logging by simply creating the file. Doing a chmod o-r /var/log/btmp improves security.

```
[root@RHEL4b ~]# touch /var/log/btmp
[root@RHEL4b ~]# ll /var/log/btmp
-rw-r--r--  1 root root 0 Jul 30 06:12 /var/log/btmp
[root@RHEL4b ~]# chmod o-r /var/log/btmp
[root@RHEL4b ~]# lastb

btmp begins Mon Jul 30 06:12:19 2007
[root@RHEL4b ~]#
```

Failed logins via ssh, rlogin or su are not registered in /var/log/btmp. Failed logins via tty are.

```
[root@RHEL4b ~]# lastb
HalvarFl tty3                  Mon Jul 30 07:10 - 07:10  (00:00)
Maria    tty1                  Mon Jul 30 07:09 - 07:09  (00:00)
Roberto  tty1                  Mon Jul 30 07:09 - 07:09  (00:00)

btmp begins Mon Jul 30 07:09:32 2007
[root@RHEL4b ~]#
```

17.1.5. su and ssh logins

Depending on the distribution, you may also have the **/var/log/secure** file being filled with messages from the auth and/or authpriv syslog facilities. This log will include su and/or ssh failed login attempts. Some distributions put this in **/var/log/auth.log**, verify the syslog configuration.

```
[root@RHEL4b ~]# cat /var/log/secure
Jul 30 07:09:03 sshd[4387]: Accepted publickey for paul from ::ffff:19\
2.168.1.52 port 33188 ssh2
Jul 30 05:09:03 sshd[4388]: Accepted publickey for paul from ::ffff:19\
2.168.1.52 port 33188 ssh2
Jul 30 07:22:27 sshd[4655]: Failed password for Hermione from ::ffff:1\
92.168.1.52 port 38752 ssh2
Jul 30 05:22:27 sshd[4656]: Failed password for Hermione from ::ffff:1\
92.168.1.52 port 38752 ssh2
Jul 30 07:22:30 sshd[4655]: Failed password for Hermione from ::ffff:1\
92.168.1.52 port 38752 ssh2
Jul 30 05:22:30 sshd[4656]: Failed password for Hermione from ::ffff:1\
92.168.1.52 port 38752 ssh2
Jul 30 07:22:33 sshd[4655]: Failed password for Hermione from ::ffff:1\
92.168.1.52 port 38752 ssh2
Jul 30 05:22:33 sshd[4656]: Failed password for Hermione from ::ffff:1\
92.168.1.52 port 38752 ssh2
Jul 30 08:27:33 sshd[5018]: Invalid user roberto from ::ffff:192.168.1\
.52
Jul 30 06:27:33 sshd[5019]: input_userauth_request: invalid user rober\
to
Jul 30 06:27:33 sshd[5019]: Failed none for invalid user roberto from \
::ffff:192.168.1.52 port 41064 ssh2
Jul 30 06:27:33 sshd[5019]: Failed publickey for invalid user roberto \
from ::ffff:192.168.1.52 port 41064 ssh2
Jul 30 08:27:36 sshd[5018]: Failed password for invalid user roberto f\
rom ::ffff:192.168.1.52 port 41064 ssh2
Jul 30 06:27:36 sshd[5019]: Failed password for invalid user roberto f\
rom ::ffff:192.168.1.52 port 41064 ssh2
[root@RHEL4b ~]#
```

You can enable this yourself, with a custom log file by adding the following line tot syslog.conf.

```
auth.*,authpriv.*                /var/log/customsec.log
```

17.2. syslogd

17.2.1. about syslog

The standard method of logging on Linux was through the **syslogd** daemon. Syslog was developed by **Eric Allman** for sendmail, but quickly became a standard among many Unix applications and was much later written as rfc 3164. The syslog daemon can receive messages on udp **port 514** from many applications (and appliances), and can append to log files, print, display messages on terminals and forward logs to other syslogd daemons on other machines. The syslogd daemon is configured in **/etc/syslog.conf**.

17.2.2. about rsyslog

The new method is called **reliable and extended syslogd** and uses the **rsyslogd** daemon and the **/etc/rsyslogd.conf** configuration file. The syntax is backwards compatible.

Each line in the configuration file uses a **facility** to determine where the message is coming from. It also contains a **priority** for the severity of the message, and an **action** to decide on what to do with the message.

17.2.3. modules

The new **rsyslog** has many more features that can be expanded by using modules. Modules allow for example exporting of syslog logging to a database.

Se the manuals for more information (when you are done with this chapter).

```
root@rhel65:/etc# man rsyslog.conf
root@rhel65:/etc# man rsyslogd
root@rhel65:/etc#
```

17.2.4. facilities

The **man rsyslog.conf** command will explain the different default facilities for certain daemons, such as mail, lpr, news and kern(el) messages. The local0 to local7 facility can be used for appliances (or any networked device that supports syslog). Here is a list of all facilities for rsyslog.conf version 1.3. The security keyword is deprecated.

```
auth (security)
authpriv
cron
daemon
ftp
kern
lpr mail
mark (internal use only)
news
syslog
user
uucp
local0-7
```

17.2.5. priorities

The worst severity a message can have is **emerg** followed by **alert** and **crit**. Lowest priority should go to **info** and **debug** messages. Specifying a severity will also log all messages with a higher severity. You can prefix the severity with = to obtain only messages that match that severity. You can also specify **.none** to prevent a specific action from any message from a certain facility.

Here is a list of all priorities, in ascending order. The keywords warn, error and panic are deprecated.

```
debug
info
notice
warning (warn)
err (error)
crit
alert
emerg (panic)
```

17.2.6. actions

The default action is to send a message to the username listed as action. When the action is prefixed with a / then rsyslog will send the message to the file (which can be a regular file, but also a printer or terminal). The @ sign prefix will send the message on to another syslog server. Here is a list of all possible actions.

```
root,user1      list of users, separated by comma's
*               message to all logged on users
/               file (can be a printer, a console, a tty, ...)
-/              file, but don't sync after every write
|               named pipe
@               other syslog hostname
```

In addition, you can prefix actions with a - to omit syncing the file after every logging.

17.2.7. configuration

Below a sample configuration of custom local4 messages in **/etc/rsyslog.conf**.

```
local4.crit                     /var/log/critandabove
local4.=crit                    /var/log/onlycrit
local4.*                        /var/log/alllocal4
```

17.2.8. restarting rsyslogd

Don't forget to restart the server after changing its configuration.

```
root@rhel65:/etc# service rsyslog restart
Shutting down system logger:                               [  OK  ]
Starting system logger:                                    [  OK  ]
root@rhel65:/etc#
```

17.3. logger

The logger command can be used to generate syslog test messages. You can aslo use it in scripts. An example of testing syslogd with the **logger** tool.

```
[root@rhel4a ~]# logger -p local4.debug "l4 debug"
[root@rhel4a ~]# logger -p local4.crit "l4 crit"
[root@rhel4a ~]# logger -p local4.emerg "l4 emerg"
[root@rhel4a ~]#
```

The results of the tests with logger.

```
[root@rhel4a ~]# cat /var/log/critandabove
Feb 14 19:55:19 rhel4a paul: l4 crit
Feb 14 19:55:28 rhel4a paul: l4 emerg
[root@rhel4a ~]# cat /var/log/onlycrit
Feb 14 19:55:19 rhel4a paul: l4 crit
[root@rhel4a ~]# cat /var/log/alllocal4
Feb 14 19:55:11 rhel4a paul: l4 debug
Feb 14 19:55:19 rhel4a paul: l4 crit
Feb 14 19:55:28 rhel4a paul: l4 emerg
[root@rhel4a ~]#
```

17.4. watching logs

You might want to use the **tail -f** command to look at the last lines of a log file. The **-f** option will dynamically display lines that are appended to the log.

```
paul@ubu1010:~$ tail -f /var/log/udev
SEQNUM=1741
SOUND_INITIALIZED=1
ID_VENDOR_FROM_DATABASE=nVidia Corporation
ID_MODEL_FROM_DATABASE=MCP79 High Definition Audio
ID_BUS=pci
ID_VENDOR_ID=0x10de
ID_MODEL_ID=0x0ac0
ID_PATH=pci-0000:00:08.0
SOUND_FORM_FACTOR=internal
```

You can automatically repeat commands by preceding them with the **watch** command. When executing the following:

```
[root@rhel6 ~]# watch who
```

Something similar to this, repeating the output of the **who** command every two seconds, will appear on the screen.

```
Every 2.0s: who                     Sun Jul 17 15:31:03 2011

root      tty1        2011-07-17 13:28
paul      pts/0       2011-07-17 13:31 (192.168.1.30)
paul      pts/1       2011-07-17 15:19 (192.168.1.30)
```

17.5. rotating logs

A lot of log files are always growing in size. To keep this within bounds, you may want to use **logrotate** to rotate, compress, remove and mail log files. More info on the logrotate command in **/etc/logrotate.conf.**. Individual configurations can be found in the / **etc/logrotate.d/** directory.

Below a screenshot of the default Red Hat logrotate.conf file.

```
root@rhel65:/etc# cat logrotate.conf
# see "man logrotate" for details
# rotate log files weekly
weekly

# keep 4 weeks worth of backlogs
rotate 4

# create new (empty) log files after rotating old ones
create

# use date as a suffix of the rotated file
dateext

# uncomment this if you want your log files compressed
#compress

# RPM packages drop log rotation information into this directory
include /etc/logrotate.d

# no packages own wtmp and btmp -- we'll rotate them here
/var/log/wtmp {
    monthly
    create 0664 root utmp
        minsize 1M
    rotate 1
}

/var/log/btmp {
    missingok
    monthly
    create 0600 root utmp
    rotate 1
}

# system-specific logs may be also be configured here.
root@rhel65:/etc#
```

17.6. practice : logging

1. Display the /var/run/utmp file with the proper command (not with cat or vi).

2. Display the /var/log/wtmp file.

3. Use the lastlog and lastb commands, understand the difference.

4. Examine syslog to find the location of the log file containing ssh failed logins.

5. Configure syslog to put local4.error and above messages in /var/log/l4e.log and local4.info only .info in /var/log/l4i.log. Test that it works with the logger tool!

6. Configure /var/log/Mysu.log, all the su to root messages should go in that log. Test that it works!

7. Send the local5 messages to the syslog server of your neighbour. Test that it works.

8. Write a script that executes logger to local4 every 15 seconds (different message). Use tail -f and watch on your local4 log files.

17.7. solution : logging

1. Display the /var/run/utmp file.

```
who
```

2. Display the /var/log/wtmp file.

```
last
```

3. Use the lastlog and lastb commands, understand the difference.

```
lastlog : when users last logged on
```

```
lastb: failed (bad) login attempts
```

4. Examine syslog to find the location of the log file containing ssh failed logins.

Answer depends on whether you machine uses **syslog** or **rsyslog** (newer).

```
[root@rhel53 ~]# grep authpriv /etc/syslog.conf
authpriv.*                                              /var/log/secure
```

```
[root@rhel71 ~]# grep ^authpriv /etc/rsyslog.conf
authpriv.*                                              /var/log/secure
```

```
paul@debian8:~$ grep ^auth /etc/rsyslog.conf
auth,authpriv.*                         /var/log/auth.log
```

5. Configure syslog to put local4.error and above messages in /var/log/l4e.log and local4.info only .info in /var/log/l4i.log. Test that it works with the logger tool!

With **syslog:**

```
echo local4.error /var/log/l4e.log >> /etc/syslog.conf
echo local4.=info /var/log/l4i.log >> /etc/syslog.conf
service syslog restart
```

With **rsyslog:**

```
echo local4.error /var/log/l4e.log >> /etc/rsyslog.conf
echo local4.=info /var/log/l4i.log >> /etc/rsyslog.conf
service rsyslog restart
```

On both:

```
logger -p local4.error "l4 error test"
logger -p local4.alert "l4 alert test"
logger -p local4.info "l4 info test"
cat /var/log/l4e.log
cat /var/log/l4i.log
```

6. Configure /var/log/Mysu.log, all the su to root messages should go in that log. Test that it works!

```
echo authpriv.*  /var/log/Mysu.log >> /etc/syslog.conf
```

This will log more than just the **su** usage.

7. Send the local5 messages to the syslog server of your neighbour. Test that it works.

On RHEL5, edit **/etc/sysconfig/syslog** to enable remote listening on the server.

On RHEL7, uncomment these two lines in **/etc/rsyslog.conf** to enable 'UDP syslog reception'.

```
# Provides UDP syslog reception
$ModLoad imudp
$UDPServerRun 514
```

On Debian/Ubuntu edit **/etc/default/syslog** or **/etc/default/rsyslog**.

```
on the client: logger -p local5.info "test local5 to neighbour"
```

8. Write a script that executes logger to local4 every 15 seconds (different message). Use tail -f and watch on your local4 log files.

```
root@rhel53 scripts# cat logloop
#!/bin/bash

for i in `seq 1 10`
do
logger -p local4.info "local4.info test number $i"
sleep 15
done

root@rhel53 scripts# chmod +x logloop
root@rhel53 scripts# ./logloop &
[1] 8264
root@rhel53 scripts# tail -f /var/log/local4.all.log
Mar 28 13:13:36 rhel53 root: local4.info test number 1
Mar 28 13:13:51 rhel53 root: local4.info test number 2
...
```

Chapter 18. memory management

This chapter will tell you how to manage RAM memory and cache.

We start with some simple tools to display information about memory: **free -om**, **top** and **cat /proc/meminfo**.

We continue with managing swap space, using terms like **swapping**, **paging** and **virtual memory**.

The last part is about using **vmstat** to monitor swap usage.

18.1. displaying memory and cache

18.1.1. /proc/meminfo

Displaying **/proc/meminfo** will tell you a lot about the memory on your Linux computer.

```
paul@ubu1010:~$ cat /proc/meminfo
MemTotal:        3830176 kB
MemFree:          244060 kB
Buffers:           41020 kB
Cached:          2035292 kB
SwapCached:         9892 kB
...
```

The first line contains the total amount of physical RAM, the second line is the unused RAM. **Buffers** is RAM used for buffering files, **cached** is the amount of RAM used as cache and **SwapCached** is the amount of swap used as cache. The file gives us much more information outside of the scope of this course.

18.1.2. free

The **free** tool can display the information provided by **/proc/meminfo** in a more readable format. The example below displays brief memory information in megabytes.

```
paul@ubu1010:~$ free -om
             total       used       free     shared    buffers     cached
Mem:          3740       3519        221          0         42       1994
Swap:         6234         82       6152
```

18.1.3. top

The **top** tool is often used to look at processes consuming most of the cpu, but it also displays memory information on line four and five (which can be toggled by pressing **m**).

Below a screenshot of top on the same ubu1010 from above.

```
top - 10:44:34 up 16 days, 9:56, 6 users, load average: 0.13, 0.09, 0.12
Tasks: 166 total,   1 running, 165 sleeping,   0 stopped,   0 zombie
Cpu(s):  5.1%us, 4.6%sy, 0.6%ni, 88.7%id, 0.8%wa, 0.0%hi, 0.3%si, 0.0%st
Mem:   3830176k total,  3613720k used,   216456k free,    45452k buffers
Swap:  6384636k total,    84988k used,  6299648k free,  2050948k cached
```

18.2. managing swap space

18.2.1. about swap space

When the operating system needs more memory than physically present in RAM, it can use **swap space**. Swap space is located on slower but cheaper memory. Notice that, although hard disks are commonly used for swap space, their access times are one hundred thousand times slower.

The swap space can be a file, a partition, or a combination of files and partitions. You can see the swap space with the **free** command, or with **cat /proc/swaps**.

```
paul@ubu1010:~$ free -o | grep -v Mem
             total       used       free     shared    buffers     cached
Swap:      6384636      84988    6299648
paul@ubu1010:~$ cat /proc/swaps
Filename                   Type            Size     Used    Priority
/dev/sda3                  partition       6384636  84988   -1
```

The amount of swap space that you need depends heavily on the services that the computer provides.

18.2.2. creating a swap partition

You can activate or deactivate swap space with the **swapon** and **swapoff** commands. New swap space can be created with the **mkswap** command. The screenshot below shows the creation and activation of a swap partition.

```
root@RHELv4u4:~# fdisk -l 2> /dev/null | grep hda
Disk /dev/hda: 536 MB, 536870912 bytes
/dev/hda1                  1          1040        524128+  83  Linux
root@RHELv4u4:~# mkswap /dev/hda1
Setting up swapspace version 1, size = 536702 kB
root@RHELv4u4:~# swapon /dev/hda1
```

Now you can see that **/proc/swaps** displays all swap spaces separately, whereas the **free -om** command only makes a human readable summary.

```
root@RHELv4u4:~# cat /proc/swaps
Filename                            Type          Size     Used    Priority
/dev/mapper/VolGroup00-LogVol01     partition     1048568  0       -1
/dev/hda1                           partition     524120   0       -2
root@RHELv4u4:~# free -om
          total     used    free   shared   buffers    cached
Mem:        249      245       4        0       125        54
Swap:      1535        0    1535
```

18.2.3. creating a swap file

Here is one more example showing you how to create a **swap file**. On Solaris you can use **mkfile** instead of **dd**.

```
root@RHELv4u4:~# dd if=/dev/zero of=/smallswapfile bs=1024 count=4096
4096+0 records in
4096+0 records out
root@RHELv4u4:~# mkswap /smallswapfile
Setting up swapspace version 1, size = 4190 kB
root@RHELv4u4:~# swapon /smallswapfile
root@RHELv4u4:~# cat /proc/swaps
Filename                           Type          Size      Used    Priority
/dev/mapper/VolGroup00-LogVol01    partition     1048568   0       -1
/dev/hda1                          partition     524120    0       -2
/smallswapfile                     file          4088      0       -3
```

18.2.4. swap space in /etc/fstab

If you like these swaps to be permanent, then don't forget to add them to **/etc/fstab**. The lines in /etc/fstab will be similar to the following.

```
/dev/hda1         swap        swap      defaults       0 0
/smallswapfile    swap        swap      defaults       0 0
```

18.3. monitoring memory with vmstat

You can find information about **swap usage** using **vmstat**.

Below a simple **vmstat** displaying information in megabytes.

```
paul@ubu1010:~$ vmstat -S m
procs ---------memory-------- ---swap-- -----io---- -system- ----cpu----
 r  b  swpd  free  buff cache   si    so    bi     bo     in    cs us sy id wa
 0  0    87   225    46  2097    0     0     2      5     14     8  6  5 89  1
```

Below a sample **vmstat** when (in another terminal) root launches a **find** /. It generates a lot of disk i/o (bi and bo are disk blocks in and out). There is no need for swapping here.

```
paul@ubu1010:~$ vmstat 2 100
procs ----------memory---------- ---swap-- -----io---- -system-- ----cpu----
 r  b   swpd    free   buff   cache   si    so     bi     bo   in    cs us sy id wa
 0  0  84984 1999436 53416 269536   0     0      2      5    2    10  6  5 89  1
 0  0  84984 1999428 53416 269564   0     0      0      0 1713 2748  4  4 92  0
 0  0  84984 1999552 53416 269564   0     0      0      0 1672 1838  4  6 90  0
 0  0  84984 1999552 53424 269560   0     0      0     14 1587 2526  5  7 87  2
 0  0  84984 1999180 53424 269580   0     0      0    100 1748 2193  4  6 91  0
 1  0  84984 1997800 54508 269760   0     0    610      0 1836 3890 17 10 68  4
 1  0  84984 1994620 55040 269748   0     0    250    168 1724 4365 19 17 56  9
 0  1  84984 1978508 55292 269704   0     0    126      0 1957 2897 19 18 58  4
 0  0  84984 1974608 58964 269784   0     0   1826    478 2605 4355  7  7 44 41
 0  2  84984 1971260 62268 269728   0     0   1634    756 2257 3865  7  7 47 39
```

Below a sample **vmstat** when executing (on RHEL6) a simple memory leaking program. Now you see a lot of memory being swapped (si is 'swapped in').

```
[paul@rhel6c ~]$ vmstat 2 100

procs ----------memory-------- ---swap-- ----io---- --system-- -----cpu-----
 r  b   swpd  free   buff cache     si    so  bi    bo   in    cs us sy id wa st
 0  3 245208  5280    232  1916    261     0   0    42   27    21  0  1 98  1  0
 0  2 263372  4800     72   908 143840   128   0  1138  462   191  2 10  0 88  0
 1  3 350672  4792     56   992 169280   256   0  1092  360   142  1 13  0 86  0
 1  4 449584  4788     56  1024 95880     64   0   606  471   191  2 13  0 85  0
 0  4 471968  4828     56  1140 44832     80   0   390  235    90  2 12  0 87  0
 3  5 505960  4764     56  1136 68008     16   0   538  286   109  1 12  0 87  0
```

The code below was used to simulate a memory leak (and force swapping). This code was found on wikipedia without author.

```
paul@mac:~$ cat memleak.c
#include <stdlib.h>

int main(void)
{
     while (malloc(50));
     return 0;
}
```

18.4. practice : memory

1. Use **dmesg** to find the total amount of memory in your computer.

2. Use **free** to display memory usage in kilobytes (then in megabytes).

3. On a virtual machine, create a swap partition (you might need an extra virtual disk for this).

4. Add a 20 megabyte swap file to the system.

5. Put all swap spaces in **/etc/fstab** and activate them. Test with a reboot that they are mounted.

6. Use **free** to verify usage of current swap.

7. (optional) Display the usage of swap with **vmstat** and **free -s** during a memory leak.

18.5. solution : memory

1. Use **dmesg** to find the total amount of memory in your computer.

```
dmesg | grep Memory
```

2. Use **free** to display memory usage in kilobytes (then in megabytes).

```
free ; free -m
```

3. On a virtual machine, create a swap partition (you might need an extra virtual disk for this).

```
mkswap /dev/sdd1 ; swapon /dev/sdd1
```

4. Add a 20 megabyte swap file to the system.

```
dd if=/dev/zero of=/swapfile20mb bs=1024 count=20000
mkswap /swapfile20mb
swapon /swapfile20mb
```

5. Put all swap spaces in **/etc/fstab** and activate them. Test with a reboot that they are mounted.

```
root@computer# tail -2 /etc/fstab
/dev/sdd1      swap swap defaults 0 0
/swapfile20mb swap swap defaults 0 0
```

6. Use **free** to verify usage of current swap.

```
free -om
```

7. (optional) Display the usage of swap with **vmstat** and **free -s** during a memory leak.

Chapter 19. resource monitoring

Monitoring is the process of obtaining information about the utilization of memory, cpu, bandwidth and storage. You should start monitoring your system as soon as possible, to be able to create a **baseline**. Make sure that you get to know your system! This baseline is important because it allows you to see a steady or sudden growth in **resource utilization** and likewise steady (or sudden) decline in **resource availability**. It will allow you to plan for scaling up or scaling out.

Let us look at some tools that go beyond **ps fax**, **df -h**, **free -om** and **du -sh**.

19.1. four basic resources

The four basic resources to monitor are:

- cpu
- network
- ram memory
- storage

19.2. top

To start monitoring, you can use **top**. This tool will monitor ram memory, cpu and swap. Top will automatically refresh. Inside **top** you can use many commands, like **k** to kill processes, or **t** and **m** to toggle displaying task and memory information, or the number **1** to have one line per cpu, or one summary line for all cpu's.

```
top - 12:23:16 up 2 days,  4:01, 2 users, load average: 0.00, 0.00, 0.00
Tasks:  61 total,   1 running,  60 sleeping,   0 stopped,   0 zombie
Cpu(s):  0.3% us,  0.5% sy, 0.0% ni, 98.9% id, 0.2% wa, 0.0% hi, 0.0% si
Mem:    255972k total,   240952k used,    15020k free,    59024k buffers
Swap:   524280k total,      144k used,   524136k free,   112356k cached

PID USER       PR  NI  VIRT  RES  SHR S %CPU %MEM    TIME+  COMMAND
  1 root       16   0  2816  560  480 S  0.0  0.2   0:00.91 init
  2 root       34  19     0    0    0 S  0.0  0.0   0:00.01 ksoftirqd/0
  3 root        5 -10     0    0    0 S  0.0  0.0   0:00.57 events/0
  4 root        5 -10     0    0    0 S  0.0  0.0   0:00.00 khelper
  5 root       15 -10     0    0    0 S  0.0  0.0   0:00.00 kacpid
 16 root        5 -10     0    0    0 S  0.0  0.0   0:00.08 kblockd/0
 26 root       15   0     0    0    0 S  0.0  0.0   0:02.86 pdflush
...
```

You can customize top to display the columns of your choice, or to display only the processes that you find interesting.

```
[paul@RHELv4u3 ~]$ top p 3456 p 8732 p 9654
```

19.3. free

The **free** command is common on Linux to monitor free memory. You can use free to display information every x seconds, but the output is not ideal.

```
[paul@RHELv4u3 gen]$ free -om -s 10
total       used       free     shared    buffers     cached
Mem:        249        222          27          0         50        109
Swap:       511          0         511

total       used       free     shared    buffers     cached
Mem:        249        222          27          0         50        109
Swap:       511          0         511

[paul@RHELv4u3 gen]$
```

19.4. watch

It might be more interesting to combine free with the **watch** program. This program can run commands with a delay, and can highlight changes (with the -d switch).

```
[paul@RHELv4u3 ~]$ watch -d -n 3 free -om
...
Every 3.0s: free -om                                   Sat Jan 27 12:13:03 2007

total          used        free      shared    buffers       cached
Mem:             249         230          19           0          56        109
Swap:            511           0         511
```

19.5. vmstat

To monitor CPU, disk and memory statistics in one line there is **vmstat**. The screenshot below shows vmstat running every two seconds 100 times (or until the Ctrl-C). Below the r, you see the number of processes waiting for the CPU, sleeping processes go below b. Swap usage (swpd) stayed constant at 144 kilobytes, free memory dropped from 16.7MB to 12.9MB. See man vmstat for the rest.

```
[paul@RHELv4u3 ~]$ vmstat 2 100
procs ----------memory--------- --swap-- ---io--- --system-- ---cpu----
r  b  swpd   free   buff  cache  si  so  bi   bo   in    cs us sy id wa
0  0   144  16708  58212 111612   0   0   3    4   75    62  0  1 99  0
0  0   144  16708  58212 111612   0   0   0    0  976    22  0  0 100 0
0  0   144  16708  58212 111612   0   0   0    0  958    14  0  1 99  0
1  0   144  16528  58212 111612   0   0   0   18 1432  7417  1 32 66  0
1  0   144  16468  58212 111612   0   0   0    0 2910 20048  4 95  1  0
1  0   144  16408  58212 111612   0   0   0    0 3210 19509  4 97  0  0
1  0   144  15568  58816 111612   0   0 300 1632 2423 10189  2 62  0 36
0  1   144  13648  60324 111612   0   0 754    0 1910  2843  1 27  0 72
0  0   144  12928  60948 111612   0   0 312  418 1346  1258  0 14 57 29
0  0   144  12928  60948 111612   0   0   0    0  977    19  0  0 100 0
0  0   144  12988  60948 111612   0   0   0    0  977    15  0  0 100 0
0  0   144  12988  60948 111612   0   0   0    0  978    18  0  0 100 0

[paul@RHELv4u3 ~]$
```

19.6. iostat

The **iostat** tool can display disk and cpu statistics. The -d switch below makes iostat only display disk information (500 times every two seconds). The first block displays statistics since the last reboot.

```
[paul@RHELv4u3 ~]$ iostat -d 2 500
Linux 2.6.9-34.EL (RHELv4u3.localdomain)          01/27/2007

Device:          tps   Blk_read/s   Blk_wrtn/s   Blk_read   Blk_wrtn
hdc             0.00         0.01         0.00       1080          0
sda             0.52         5.07         7.78     941798    1445148
sda1            0.00         0.01         0.00        968          4
sda2            1.13         5.06         7.78     939862    1445144
dm-0            1.13         5.05         7.77     939034    1444856
dm-1            0.00         0.00         0.00        360        288

Device:          tps   Blk_read/s   Blk_wrtn/s   Blk_read   Blk_wrtn
hdc             0.00         0.00         0.00          0          0
sda             0.00         0.00         0.00          0          0
sda1            0.00         0.00         0.00          0          0
sda2            0.00         0.00         0.00          0          0
dm-0            0.00         0.00         0.00          0          0
dm-1            0.00         0.00         0.00          0          0
...
[paul@RHELv4u3 ~]$
```

You can have more statistics using **iostat -d -x**, or display only cpu statistics with **iostat -c**.

```
[paul@RHELv4u3 ~]$ iostat -c 5 500
Linux 2.6.9-34.EL (RHELv4u3.localdomain)          01/27/2007

avg-cpu:  %user   %nice    %sys %iowait   %idle
0.31    0.02    0.52    0.23   98.92

avg-cpu:  %user   %nice    %sys %iowait   %idle
0.62    0.00   52.16   47.23    0.00

avg-cpu:  %user   %nice    %sys %iowait   %idle
2.92    0.00   36.95   60.13    0.00

avg-cpu:  %user   %nice    %sys %iowait   %idle
0.63    0.00   36.63   62.32    0.42

avg-cpu:  %user   %nice    %sys %iowait   %idle
0.00    0.00    0.20    0.20   99.59

[paul@RHELv4u3 ~]$
```

19.7. mpstat

On multi-processor machines, **mpstat** can display statistics for all, or for a selected cpu.

```
paul@laika:~$ mpstat -P ALL
Linux 2.6.20-3-generic (laika)   02/09/2007

CPU %user  %nice   %sys %iowait   %irq   %soft  %steal   %idle   intr/s
all  1.77   0.03   1.37    1.03   0.02    0.39    0.00   95.40  1304.91
  0  1.73   0.02   1.47    1.93   0.04    0.77    0.00   94.04  1304.91
  1  1.81   0.03   1.27    0.13   0.00    0.00    0.00   96.76     0.00
paul@laika:~$
```

19.8. sadc and sar

The **sadc** tool writes system utilization data to **/var/log/sa/sa??**, where ?? is replaced with the current day of the month. By default, cron runs the **sal** script every 10 minutes, the sal script runs sadc for one second. Just before midnight every day, cron runs the **sa2** script, which in turn invokes **sar**. The sar tool will read the daily data generated by sadc and put it in /var/log/sa/sar??. These **sar reports** contain a lot of statistics.

You can also use sar to display a portion of the statistics that were gathered. Like this example for cpu statistics.

```
[paul@RHELv4u3 sa]$ sar -u | head
Linux 2.6.9-34.EL (RHELv4u3.localdomain)          01/27/2007

12:00:01 AM       CPU     %user     %nice   %system   %iowait     %idle
12:10:01 AM       all      0.48      0.01      0.60      0.04     98.87
12:20:01 AM       all      0.49      0.01      0.60      0.06     98.84
12:30:01 AM       all      0.49      0.01      0.64      0.25     98.62
12:40:02 AM       all      0.44      0.01      0.62      0.07     98.86
12:50:01 AM       all      0.42      0.01      0.60      0.10     98.87
01:00:01 AM       all      0.47      0.01      0.65      0.08     98.80
01:10:01 AM       all      0.45      0.01      0.68      0.08     98.78
[paul@RHELv4u3 sa]$
```

There are other useful sar options, like **sar -I PROC** to display interrupt activity per interrupt and per CPU, or **sar -r** for memory related statistics. Check the manual page of sar for more.

19.9. ntop

The **ntop** tool is not present in default Red Hat installs. Once run, it will generate a very extensive analysis of network traffic in html on http://localhost:3000 .

19.10. iftop

The **iftop** tool will display bandwidth by socket statistics for a specific network device. Not available on default Red Hat servers.

```
1.91Mb          3.81Mb           5.72Mb          7.63Mb    9.54Mb
--------------|-------------|--------------|-------------|--------|----
laika.local          => barry                         4.94Kb  6.65Kb  69.9Kb
                     <=                               7.41Kb  16.4Kb   766Kb
laika.local          => ik-in-f19.google.com              0b  1.58Kb  14.4Kb
                     <=                                   0b    292b  41.0Kb
laika.local          => ik-in-f99.google.com              0b     83b  4.01Kb
                     <=                                   0b     83b  39.8Kb
laika.local          => ug-in-f189.google.com             0b     42b    664b
                     <=                                   0b     42b    406b
laika.local          => 10.0.0.138                        0b      0b    149b
                     <=                                   0b      0b    256b
laika.local          => 224.0.0.251                       0b      0b     86b
                     <=                                   0b      0b      0b
laika.local          => ik-in-f83.google.com              0b      0b     39b
                     <=                                   0b      0b     21b
```

19.11. iptraf

Use **iptraf** for a colourful display of ip traffic over the network cards.

```
[root@centos65 ~]# iptraf
[root@centos65 ~]# iptraf -i eth0
```

19.12. nmon

Another popular and all round tool is **nmon**.

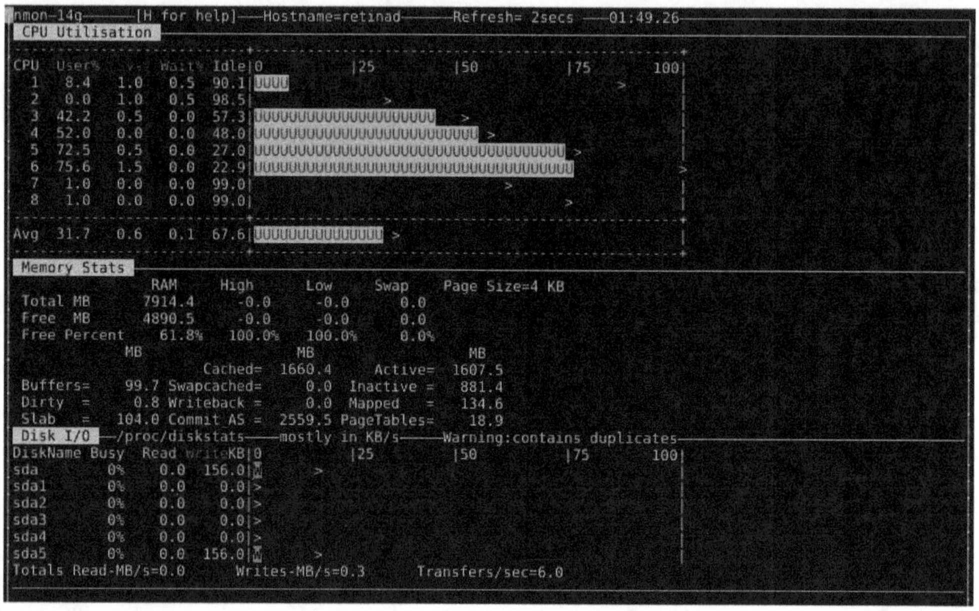

19.13. htop

You can use **htop** instead of top.

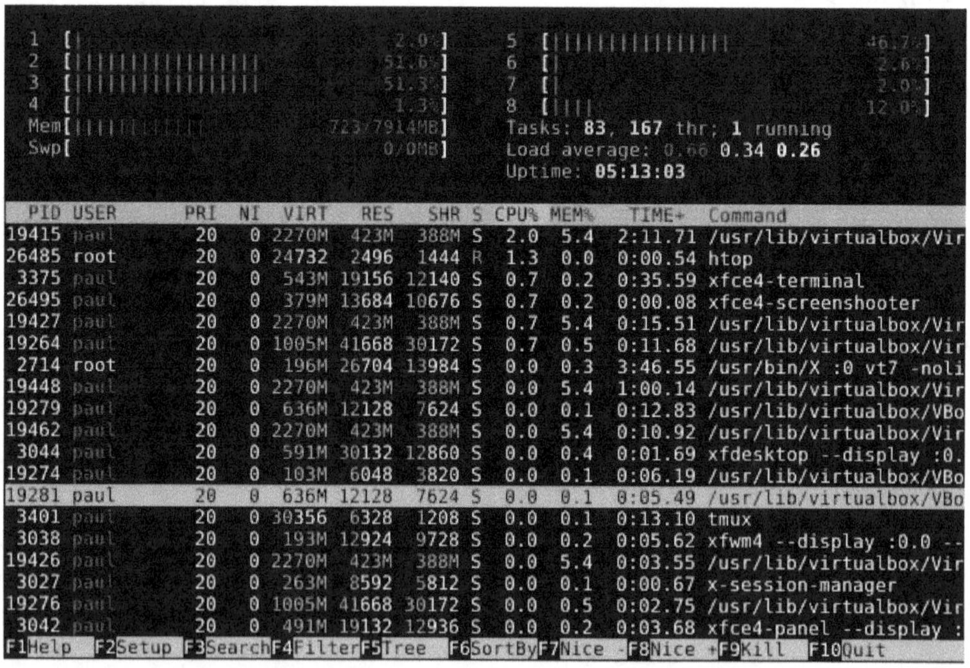

Chapter 20. package management

Most Linux distributions have a **package management** system with online **repositories** containing thousands of packages. This makes it very easy to install and remove applications, operating system components, documentation and much more.

We first discuss the Debian package format **.deb** and its tools **dpkg**, **apt-get** and **aptitude**. This should be similar on Debian, Ubuntu, Mint and all derived distributions.

Then we look at the Red Hat package format **.rpm** and its tools **rpm** and **yum**. This should be similar on Red Hat, Fedora, CentOS and all derived distributions.

20.1. package terminology

20.1.1. repository

A lot of software and documentation for your Linux distribution is available as **packages** in one or more centrally distributed **repositories**. These **packages** in such a **repository** are tested and very easy to install (or remove) with a graphical or command line installer.

20.1.2. .deb packages

Debian, Ubuntu, Mint and all derivatives from Debian and Ubuntu use **.deb** packages. To manage software on these systems, you can use **aptitude** or **apt-get**, both these tools are a front end for **dpkg**.

20.1.3. .rpm packages

Red Hat, Fedora, CentOS, OpenSUSE, Mandriva, Red Flag and others use **.rpm** packages. The tools to manage software packages on these systems are **yum** and **rpm**.

20.1.4. dependency

Some packages need other packages to function. Tools like **apt-get**, **aptitude** and **yum** will install all **dependencies** you need. When using **dpkg** or **rpm**, or when building from **source**, you will need to install dependencies yourself.

20.1.5. open source

These repositories contain a lot of independent **open source software**. Often the source code is customized to integrate better with your distribution. Most distributions also offer this modified source code as a **package** in one or more **source repositories**.

You are free to go to the project website itself (samba.org, apache.org, github.com, ...) an download the **vanilla** (= without the custom distribution changes) source code.

20.1.6. GUI software management

End users have several graphical applications available via the desktop (look for 'add/remove software' or something similar).

Below a screenshot of Ubuntu Software Center running on Ubuntu 12.04. Graphical tools are not discussed in this book.

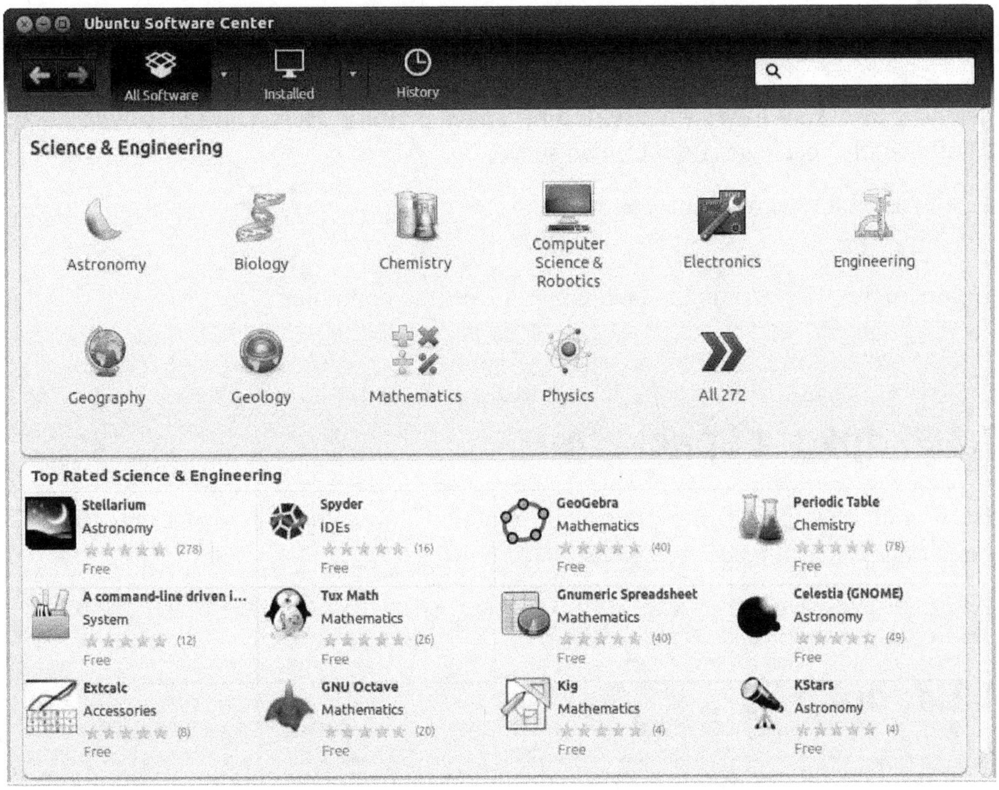

20.2. deb package management

20.2.1. about deb

Most people use **aptitude** or **apt-get** to manage their Debian/Ubuntu family of Linux distributions. Both are a front end for **dpkg** and are themselves a back end for **synaptic** and other graphical tools.

20.2.2. dpkg -l

The low level tool to work with **.deb** packages is **dpkg**. Here you see how to obtain a list of all installed packages on a Debian server.

```
root@debian6:~# dpkg -l | wc -l
265
```

Compare this to the same list on a Ubuntu Desktop computer.

```
root@ubu1204~# dpkg -l | wc -l
2527
```

20.2.3. dpkg -l $package

Here is an example on how to get information on an individual package. The ii at the beginning means the package is installed.

```
root@debian6:~# dpkg -l rsync | tail -1 | tr -s ' '
ii rsync 3.0.7-2 fast remote file copy program (like rcp)
```

20.2.4. dpkg -S

You can find the package that installed a certain file on your computer with **dpkg -S**. This example shows how to find the package for three files on a typical Debian server.

```
root@debian6:~# dpkg -S /usr/share/doc/tmux/ /etc/ssh/ssh_config /sbin/ifconfig
tmux: /usr/share/doc/tmux/
openssh-client: /etc/ssh/ssh_config
net-tools: /sbin/ifconfig
```

20.2.5. dpkg -L

You can also get a list of all files that are installed by a certain program. Below is the list for the **tmux** package.

```
root@debian6:~# dpkg -L tmux
/.
/etc
/etc/init.d
/etc/init.d/tmux-cleanup
/usr
/usr/share
/usr/share/lintian
/usr/share/lintian/overrides
/usr/share/lintian/overrides/tmux
/usr/share/doc
```

```
/usr/share/doc/tmux
/usr/share/doc/tmux/TODO.gz
/usr/share/doc/tmux/FAQ.gz
/usr/share/doc/tmux/changelog.Debian.gz
/usr/share/doc/tmux/NEWS.Debian.gz
/usr/share/doc/tmux/changelog.gz
/usr/share/doc/tmux/copyright
/usr/share/doc/tmux/examples
/usr/share/doc/tmux/examples/tmux.vim.gz
/usr/share/doc/tmux/examples/h-boetes.conf
/usr/share/doc/tmux/examples/n-marriott.conf
/usr/share/doc/tmux/examples/screen-keys.conf
/usr/share/doc/tmux/examples/t-williams.conf
/usr/share/doc/tmux/examples/vim-keys.conf
/usr/share/doc/tmux/NOTES
/usr/share/man
/usr/share/man/man1
/usr/share/man/man1/tmux.1.gz
/usr/bin
/usr/bin/tmux
```

20.2.6. dpkg

You could use **dpkg -i** to install a package and **dpkg -r** to remove a package, but you'd have to manually keep track of dependencies. Using **apt-get** or **aptitude** is much easier.

20.3. apt-get

Debian has been using **apt-get** to manage packages since 1998. Today Debian and many Debian-based distributions still actively support **apt-get**, though some experts claim **aptitude** is better at handling dependencies than **apt-get**.

Both commands use the same configuration files and can be used alternately; whenever you see **apt-get** in documentation, feel free to type **aptitude**.

We will start with **apt-get** and discuss **aptitude** in the next section.

20.3.1. apt-get update

When typing **apt-get update** you are downloading the names, versions and short description of all packages available on all configured repositories for your system.

In the example below you can see some repositories at the url **be.archive.ubuntu.com** because this computer was installed in Belgium. This url can be different for you.

```
root@ubu1204~# apt-get update
Ign http://be.archive.ubuntu.com precise InRelease
Ign http://extras.ubuntu.com precise InRelease
Ign http://security.ubuntu.com precise-security InRelease
Ign http://archive.canonical.com precise InRelease
Ign http://be.archive.ubuntu.com precise-updates InRelease
...
Hit http://be.archive.ubuntu.com precise-backports/main Translation-en
Hit http://be.archive.ubuntu.com precise-backports/multiverse Translation-en
Hit http://be.archive.ubuntu.com precise-backports/restricted Translation-en
Hit http://be.archive.ubuntu.com precise-backports/universe Translation-en
Fetched 13.7 MB in 8s (1682 kB/s)
Reading package lists... Done
root@mac~#
```

Run **apt-get update** every time before performing other package operations.

20.3.2. apt-get upgrade

One of the nicest features of **apt-get** is that it allows for a secure update of **all software currently installed** on your computer with just **one** command.

```
root@debian6:~# apt-get upgrade
Reading package lists... Done
Building dependency tree
Reading state information... Done
0 upgraded, 0 newly installed, 0 to remove and 0 not upgraded.
root@debian6:~#
```

The above screenshot shows that all software is updated to the latest version available for my distribution.

20.3.3. apt-get clean

apt-get keeps a copy of downloaded packages in **/var/cache/apt/archives**, as can be seen in this screenshot.

```
root@ubu1204~# ls /var/cache/apt/archives/ | head
accountsservice_0.6.15-2ubuntu9.4_i386.deb
apport_2.0.1-0ubuntu14_all.deb
apport-gtk_2.0.1-0ubuntu14_all.deb
apt_0.8.16~exp12ubuntu10.3_i386.deb
apt-transport-https_0.8.16~exp12ubuntu10.3_i386.deb
apt-utils_0.8.16~exp12ubuntu10.3_i386.deb
bind9-host_1%3a9.8.1.dfsg.P1-4ubuntu0.4_i386.deb
chromium-browser_20.0.1132.47~r144678-0ubuntu0.12.04.1_i386.deb
chromium-browser-l10n_20.0.1132.47~r144678-0ubuntu0.12.04.1_all.deb
chromium-codecs-ffmpeg_20.0.1132.47~r144678-0ubuntu0.12.04.1_i386.deb
```

Running **apt-get clean** removes all .deb files from that directory.

```
root@ubu1204~# apt-get clean
root@ubu1204~# ls /var/cache/apt/archives/*.deb
ls: cannot access /var/cache/apt/archives/*.deb: No such file or directory
```

20.3.4. apt-cache search

Use **apt-cache search** to search for availability of a package. Here we look for **rsync**.

```
root@ubu1204~# apt-cache search rsync | grep ^rsync
rsync - fast, versatile, remote (and local) file-copying tool
rsyncrypto - rsync friendly encryption
```

20.3.5. apt-get install

You can install one or more applications by appending their name behind **apt-get install**. The screenshot shows how to install the **rsync** package.

```
root@ubu1204~# apt-get install rsync
Reading package lists... Done
Building dependency tree
Reading state information... Done
The following NEW packages will be installed:
  rsync
0 upgraded, 1 newly installed, 0 to remove and 8 not upgraded.
Need to get 299 kB of archives.
After this operation, 634 kB of additional disk space will be used.
Get:1 http://be.archive.ubuntu.com/ubuntu/ precise/main rsync i386 3.0.9-1ubuntu1 [299 kB]
Fetched 299 kB in 0s (740 kB/s)
Selecting previously unselected package rsync.
(Reading database ... 323649 files and directories currently installed.)
Unpacking rsync (from .../rsync_3.0.9-1ubuntu1_i386.deb) ...
Processing triggers for man-db ...
Processing triggers for ureadahead ...
Setting up rsync (3.0.9-1ubuntu1) ...
 Removing any system startup links for /etc/init.d/rsync ...
root@ubu1204~#
```

20.3.6. apt-get remove

You can remove one or more applications by appending their name behind **apt-get remove**. The screenshot shows how to remove the **rsync** package.

```
root@ubu1204~# apt-get remove rsync
Reading package lists... Done
Building dependency tree
Reading state information... Done
```

```
The following packages will be REMOVED:
  rsync ubuntu-standard
0 upgraded, 0 newly installed, 2 to remove and 8 not upgraded.
After this operation, 692 kB disk space will be freed.
Do you want to continue [Y/n]?
(Reading database ... 323681 files and directories currently installed.)
Removing ubuntu-standard ...
Removing rsync ...
 * Stopping rsync daemon rsync
Processing triggers for ureadahead ...
Processing triggers for man-db ...
root@ubu1204~#
```

Note however that some configuration information is not removed.

```
root@ubu1204~# dpkg -l rsync | tail -1 | tr -s ' '
rc rsync 3.0.9-1ubuntu1 fast, versatile, remote (and local) file-copying tool
```

20.3.7. apt-get purge

You can purge one or more applications by appending their name behind **apt-get purge**. Purging will also remove all existing configuration files related to that application. The screenshot shows how to purge the **rsync** package.

```
root@ubu1204~# apt-get purge rsync
Reading package lists... Done
Building dependency tree
Reading state information... Done
The following packages will be REMOVED:
  rsync*
0 upgraded, 0 newly installed, 1 to remove and 8 not upgraded.
After this operation, 0 B of additional disk space will be used.
Do you want to continue [Y/n]?
(Reading database ... 323651 files and directories currently installed.)
Removing rsync ...
Purging configuration files for rsync ...
Processing triggers for ureadahead ...
root@ubu1204~#
```

Note that **dpkg** has no information about a purged package, except that it is uninstalled and no configuration is left on the system.

```
root@ubu1204~# dpkg -l rsync | tail -1 | tr -s ' '
un rsync <none> (no description available)
```

20.4. aptitude

Most people use **aptitude** for package management on Debian, Mint and Ubuntu systems.

To synchronize with the repositories.

```
aptitude update
```

To patch and upgrade all software to the latest version on Debian.

```
aptitude upgrade
```

To patch and upgrade all software to the latest version on Ubuntu and Mint.

```
aptitude safe-upgrade
```

To install an application with all dependencies.

```
aptitude install $package
```

To search the repositories for applications that contain a certain string in their name or description.

```
aptitude search $string
```

To remove an application.

```
aptitude remove $package
```

To remove an application and all configuration files.

```
aptitude purge $package
```

20.5. apt

Both **apt-get** and **aptitude** use the same configuration information in **/etc/apt/**. Thus adding a repository for one of them, will automatically add it for both.

20.5.1. /etc/apt/sources.list

The resource list used by **apt-get** and **aptitude** is located in **/etc/apt/sources.list**. This file contains a list of http or ftp sources where packages for the distribution can be downloaded.

This is what that list looks like on my Debian server.

```
root@debian6:~# cat /etc/apt/sources.list
deb http://ftp.be.debian.org/debian/ squeeze main
deb-src http://ftp.be.debian.org/debian/ squeeze main

deb http://security.debian.org/ squeeze/updates main
deb-src http://security.debian.org/ squeeze/updates main

# squeeze-updates, previously known as 'volatile'
deb http://ftp.be.debian.org/debian/ squeeze-updates main
deb-src http://ftp.be.debian.org/debian/ squeeze-updates main
```

On my Ubuntu there are four times as many online repositories in use.

```
root@ubu1204~# wc -l /etc/apt/sources.list
63 /etc/apt/sources.list
```

There is much more to learn about **apt**, explore commands like **add-apt-repository**, **apt-key** and **apropos apt**.

20.6. rpm

20.6.1. about rpm

The **Red Hat package manager** can be used on the command line with **rpm** or in a graphical way going to Applications--System Settings--Add/Remove Applications. Type **rpm --help** to see some of the options.

Software distributed in the **rpm** format will be named **foo-version.platform.rpm** .

20.6.2. rpm -qa

To obtain a list of all installed software, use the **rpm -qa** command.

```
[root@RHEL52 ~]# rpm -qa | grep samba
system-config-samba-1.2.39-1.el5
samba-3.0.28-1.el5_2.1
samba-client-3.0.28-1.el5_2.1
samba-common-3.0.28-1.el5_2.1
```

20.6.3. rpm -q

To verify whether one package is installed, use **rpm -q**.

```
root@RHELv4u4:~# rpm -q gcc
gcc-3.4.6-3
root@RHELv4u4:~# rpm -q laika
package laika is not installed
```

20.6.4. rpm -Uvh

To install or upgrade a package, use the -Uvh switches. The -U switch is the same as -i for install, except that older versions of the software are removed. The -vh switches are for nicer output.

```
root@RHELv4u4:~# rpm -Uvh gcc-3.4.6-3
```

20.6.5. rpm -e

To remove a package, use the -e switch.

```
root@RHELv4u4:~# rpm -e gcc-3.4.6-3
```

rpm -e verifies dependencies, and thus will prevent you from accidentailly erasing packages that are needed by other packages.

```
[root@RHEL52 ~]# rpm -e gcc-4.1.2-42.el5
error: Failed dependencies:
gcc = 4.1.2-42.el5 is needed by (installed) gcc-c++-4.1.2-42.el5.i386
gcc = 4.1.2-42.el5 is needed by (installed) gcc-gfortran-4.1.2-42.el5.i386
gcc is needed by (installed) systemtap-0.6.2-1.el5_2.2.i386
```

20.6.6. /var/lib/rpm

The **rpm** database is located at **/var/lib/rpm**. This database contains all meta information about packages that are installed (via rpm). It keeps track of all files, which enables complete removes of software.

20.6.7. rpm2cpio

We can use **rpm2cpio** to convert an **rpm** to a **cpio** archive.

```
[root@RHEL53 ~]# file kernel.src.rpm
kernel.src.rpm: RPM v3 src PowerPC kernel-2.6.18-92.1.13.el5
[root@RHEL53 ~]# rpm2cpio kernel.src.rpm > kernel.cpio
[root@RHEL53 ~]# file kernel.cpio
kernel.cpio: ASCII cpio archive (SVR4 with no CRC)
```

But why would you want to do this ?

Perhaps just to see of list of files in the **rpm** file.

```
[root@RHEL53 ~]# rpm2cpio kernel.src.rpm | cpio -t | head -5
COPYING.modules
Config.mk
Module.kabi_i686
Module.kabi_i686PAE
Module.kabi_i686xen
```

Or to extract one file from an **rpm** package.

```
[root@RHEL53 ~]# rpm2cpio kernel.src.rpm | cpio -iv Config.mk
Config.mk
246098 blocks
```

20.7. yum

20.7.1. about yum

The **Yellowdog Updater, Modified (yum)** is an easier command to work with **rpm** packages. It is installed by default on Fedora and Red Hat Enterprise Linux since version 5.2.

20.7.2. yum list

Issue **yum list available** to see a list of available packages. The **available** parameter is optional.

```
root@rhel65:/etc# yum list | wc -l
This system is receiving updates from Red Hat Subscription Management.
3935
root@rhel65:/etc#
```

Issue **yum list $package** to get all versions (in different repositories) of one package.

```
[root@rhel55 ~]# yum list samba
Loaded plugins: rhnplugin, security
Installed Packages
samba.i386                    3.0.33-3.28.el5         installed
Available Packages
samba.i386                    3.0.33-3.29.el5_5       rhel-i386-server-5
```

20.7.3. yum search

To search for a package containing a certain string in the description or name use **yum search $string**.

```
[root@rhel55 ~]# yum search gcc44
Loaded plugins: rhnplugin, security
========================== Matched: gcc44 ===========================
gcc44.i386 : Preview of GCC version 4.4
gcc44-c++.i386 : C++ support for GCC version 4.4
gcc44-gfortran.i386 : Fortran support for GCC 4.4 previe
```

20.7.4. yum provides

To search for a package containing a certain file (you might need for compiling things) use **yum provides $filename**.

```
root@rhel65:/etc# yum provides /usr/share/man/man5/passwd.5.gz
Loaded plugins: product-id, subscription-manager
This system is receiving updates from Red Hat Subscription Management.
rhel-6-server-cf-tools-1-rpms                                    | 2.8 kB     00:00
rhel-6-server-rpms                                               | 3.7 kB     00:00
man-pages-3.22-12.el6.noarch : Man (manual) pages from the Linux Documenta...
Repo        : rhel-6-server-rpms
Matched from:
Filename    : /usr/share/man/man5/passwd.5.gz



man-pages-3.22-20.el6.noarch : Man (manual) pages from the Linux Documenta...
Repo        : rhel-6-server-rpms
Matched from:
Filename    : /usr/share/man/man5/passwd.5.gz



man-pages-3.22-17.el6.noarch : Man (manual) pages from the Linux Documenta...
Repo        : rhel-6-server-rpms
Matched from:
Filename    : /usr/share/man/man5/passwd.5.gz



man-pages-3.22-20.el6.noarch : Man (manual) pages from the Linux Documenta...
Repo        : installed
Matched from:
Other       : Provides-match: /usr/share/man/man5/passwd.5.gz



root@rhel65:/etc#
```

20.7.5. yum install

To install an application, use **yum install $package**. Naturally **yum** will install all the necessary dependencies.

```
[root@rhel55 ~]# yum install sudo
Loaded plugins: rhnplugin, security
Setting up Install Process
Resolving Dependencies
--> Running transaction check
---> Package sudo.i386 0:1.7.2p1-7.el5_5 set to be updated
--> Finished Dependency Resolution

Dependencies Resolved

======================================================================
 Package     Arch      Version              Repository              Size
======================================================================
Installing:
 sudo        i386      1.7.2p1-7.el5_5      rhel-i386-server-5      230 k

Transaction Summary
======================================================================
Install       1 Package(s)
Upgrade       0 Package(s)

Total download size: 230 k
Is this ok [y/N]: y
Downloading Packages:
sudo-1.7.2p1-7.el5_5.i386.rpm                         | 230 kB     00:00
Running rpm_check_debug
Running Transaction Test
Finished Transaction Test
Transaction Test Succeeded
Running Transaction
  Installing     : sudo                                          1/1

Installed:
  sudo.i386 0:1.7.2p1-7.el5_5

Complete!
```

You can add more than one parameter here.

```
yum install $package1 $package2 $package3
```

20.7.6. yum update

To bring all applications up to date, by downloading and installing them, issue **yum update**. All software that was installed via **yum** will be updated to the latest version that is available in the repository.

```
yum update
```

If you only want to update one package, use **yum update $package**.

```
[root@rhel55 ~]# yum update sudo
Loaded plugins: rhnplugin, security
Skipping security plugin, no data
Setting up Update Process
Resolving Dependencies
Skipping security plugin, no data
--> Running transaction check
---> Package sudo.i386 0:1.7.2p1-7.el5_5 set to be updated
--> Finished Dependency Resolution

Dependencies Resolved

======================================================================
 Package     Arch     Version            Repository               Size
======================================================================
Updating:
 sudo        i386     1.7.2p1-7.el5_5    rhel-i386-server-5       230 k

Transaction Summary
======================================================================
Install       0 Package(s)
Upgrade       1 Package(s)

Total download size: 230 k
Is this ok [y/N]: y
Downloading Packages:
sudo-1.7.2p1-7.el5_5.i386.rpm                       | 230 kB     00:00
Running rpm_check_debug
Running Transaction Test
Finished Transaction Test
Transaction Test Succeeded
Running Transaction
  Updating       : sudo                                              1/2
  Cleanup        : sudo                                              2/2

Updated:
  sudo.i386 0:1.7.2p1-7.el5_5

Complete!
```

20.7.7. yum software groups

Issue **yum grouplist** to see a list of all available software groups.

```
[root@rhel55 ~]# yum grouplist
Loaded plugins: rhnplugin, security
Setting up Group Process
Installed Groups:
   Administration Tools
   Authoring and Publishing
   DNS Name Server
   Development Libraries
   Development Tools
   Editors
   GNOME Desktop Environment
   GNOME Software Development
   Graphical Internet
   Graphics
   Legacy Network Server
   Legacy Software Development
   Legacy Software Support
   Mail Server
   Network Servers
   Office/Productivity
   Printing Support
   Server Configuration Tools
   System Tools
   Text-based Internet
   Web Server
   Windows File Server
   X Software Development
   X Window System
Available Groups:
   Engineering and Scientific
   FTP Server
   Games and Entertainment
   Java Development
   KDE (K Desktop Environment)
   KDE Software Development
   MySQL Database
   News Server
   OpenFabrics Enterprise Distribution
   PostgreSQL Database
   Sound and Video
Done
```

To install a set of applications, brought together via a group, use **yum groupinstall $groupname**.

```
[root@rhel55 ~]# yum groupinstall 'Sound and video'
Loaded plugins: rhnplugin, security
Setting up Group Process
Package alsa-utils-1.0.17-1.el5.i386 already installed and latest version
Package sox-12.18.1-1.i386 already installed and latest version
Package 9:mkisofs-2.01-10.7.el5.i386 already installed and latest version
Package 9:cdrecord-2.01-10.7.el5.i386 already installed and latest version
Package cdrdao-1.2.1-2.i386 already installed and latest version
Resolving Dependencies
--> Running transaction check
---> Package cdda2wav.i386 9:2.01-10.7.el5 set to be updated
---> Package cdparanoia.i386 0:alpha9.8-27.2 set to be updated
---> Package sound-juicer.i386 0:2.16.0-3.el5 set to be updated
--> Processing Dependency: libmusicbrainz >= 2.1.0 for package: sound-juicer
--> Processing Dependency: libmusicbrainz.so.4 for package: sound-juicer
---> Package vorbis-tools.i386 1:1.1.1-3.el5 set to be updated
--> Processing Dependency: libao >= 0.8.4 for package: vorbis-tools
--> Processing Dependency: libao.so.2 for package: vorbis-tools
--> Running transaction check
---> Package libao.i386 0:0.8.6-7 set to be updated
---> Package libmusicbrainz.i386 0:2.1.1-4.1 set to be updated
--> Finished Dependency Resolution
...
```

Read the manual page of **yum** for more information about managing groups in **yum**.

20.7.8. /etc/yum.conf and repositories

The configuration of **yum** repositories is done in **/etc/yum/yum.conf** and **/etc/yum/repos.d/**
.

Configurating **yum** itself is done in **/etc/yum.conf**. This file will contain the location of a log file and a cache directory for **yum** and can also contain a list of repositories.

Recently **yum** started accepting several **repo** files with each file containing a list of **repositories**. These **repo** files are located in the **/etc/yum.repos.d/** directory.

One important flag for yum is **enablerepo**. Use this command if you want to use a repository that is not enabled by default.

```
yum $command $foo --enablerepo=$repo
```

An example of the contents of the repo file: MyRepo.repo

```
[$repo]
name=My Repository
baseurl=http://path/to/MyRepo
gpgcheck=1
gpgkey=file:///etc/pki/rpm-gpg/RPM-GPG-KEY-MyRep
```

20.8. alien

alien is experimental software that converts between **rpm** and **deb** package formats (and others).

Below an example of how to use **alien** to convert an **rpm** package to a **deb** package.

```
paul@barry:~$ ls -l netcat*
-rw-r--r-- 1 paul paul 123912 2009-06-04 14:58 netcat-0.7.1-1.i386.rpm
paul@barry:~$ alien --to-deb netcat-0.7.1-1.i386.rpm
netcat_0.7.1-2_i386.deb generated
paul@barry:~$ ls -l netcat*
-rw-r--r-- 1 paul paul 123912 2009-06-04 14:58 netcat-0.7.1-1.i386.rpm
-rw-r--r-- 1 root root 125236 2009-06-04 14:59 netcat_0.7.1-2_i386.deb
```

*In real life, use the **netcat** tool provided by your distribution, or use the .deb file from their website.*

20.9. downloading software outside the repository

First and most important, whenever you download software, start by reading the README file!

Normally the readme will explain what to do after download. You will probably receive a .tar.gz or a .tgz file. Read the documentation, then put the compressed file in a directory. You can use the following to find out where the package wants to install.

```
tar tvzpf $downloadedFile.tgz
```

You unpack them like with **tar xzf**, it will create a directory called applicationName-1.2.3

```
tar xzf $applicationName.tgz
```

Replace the z with a j when the file ends in .tar.bz2. The **tar**, **gzip** and **bzip2** commands are explained in detail in the Linux Fundamentals course.

If you download a **.deb** file, then you'll have to use **dpkg** to install it, **.rpm**'s can be installed with the **rpm** command.

20.10. compiling software

First and most important, whenever you download source code for installation, start by reading the README file!

Usually the steps are always the same three : running **./configure** followed by **make** (which is the actual compiling) and then by **make install** to copy the files to their proper location.

```
./configure
make
make install
```

20.11. practice: package management

1. Verify whether gcc, sudo and wesnoth are installed.

2. Use yum or aptitude to search for and install the scp, tmux, and man-pages packages. Did you find them all ?

3. Search the internet for 'webmin' and figure out how to install it.

4. If time permits, search for and install samba including the samba docs pdf files (thousands of pages in two pdf's).

20.12. solution: package management

1. Verify whether gcc, sudo and wesnoth are installed.

```
On Red Hat/CentOS:
rpm -qa | grep gcc
rpm -qa | grep sudo
rpm -qa | grep wesnoth

On Debian/Ubuntu:
dpkg -l | grep gcc
dpkg -l | grep sudo
dpkg -l | grep wesnoth
```

2. Use yum or aptitude to search for and install the scp, tmux, and man-pages packages. Did you find them all ?

```
On Red Hat/CentOS:
yum search scp
yum search tmux
yum search man-pages

On Debian/Ubuntu:
aptitude search scp
aptitude search tmux
aptitude search man-pages
```

3. Search the internet for 'webmin' and figure out how to install it.

```
Google should point you to webmin.com.

There are several formats available there choose .rpm, .deb or .tgz .
```

4. If time permits, search for and install samba including the samba docs pdf files (thousands of pages in two pdf's).

Part V. network management

Table of Contents

Chapter 21. general networking

While this chapter is not directly about **Linux**, it does contain general networking concepts that will help you in troubleshooting networks on **Linux**.

21.1. network layers

21.1.1. seven OSI layers

When talking about protocol layers, people usually mention the seven layers of the **osi** protocol (Application, Presentation, Session, Transport, Network, Data Link and Physical). We will discuss layers 2 and 3 in depth, and focus less on the other layers. The reason is that these layers are important for understanding networks. You will hear administrators use words like "this is a layer 2 device" or "this is a layer 3 broadcast", and you should be able to understand what they are talking about.

21.1.2. four DoD layers

The **DoD** (or tcp/ip) model has only four layers, roughly mapping its **network access layer** to OSI layers 1 and 2 (Physical and Datalink), its **internet** (IP) layer to the OSI **network layer**, its **host-to-host** (tcp, udp) layer to OSI layer 4 (transport) and its **application layer** to OSI layers 5, 6 and 7.

Below an attempt to put OSI and DoD layers next to some protocols and devices.

OSI Model	DoD Model	protocols	devices/apps
layer 5, 6, 7	application	dns, dhcp, ntp, snmp, https, ftp, ssh, telnet, http, pop3... others	web server, mail server, browser, mail client...
layer 4	host-to-host	tcp udp	gateway
layer 3	internet	ip, icmp, igmp	router, firewall layer 3 switch
layer 2	network access	arp (mac), rarp	bridge layer 2 switch
layer 1		ethernet, token ring	hub

21.1.3. short introduction to the physical layer

The physical layer, or **layer 1**, is all about voltage, electrical signals and mechanical connections. Some networks might still use **coax** cables, but most will have migrated to **utp** (cat 5 or better) with **rj45** connectors.

Devices like **repeaters** and **hubs** are part of this layer. You cannot use software to 'see' a **repeater** or **hub** on the network. The only thing these devices are doing is amplifying electrical signals on cables. **Passive hubs** are multiport amplifiers that amplify an incoming electrical signal on all other connections. **Active hubs** do this by reading and retransmitting bits, without interpreting any meaning in those bits.

Network technologies like **csma/cd** and **token ring** are defined on this layer.

This is all we have to say about **layer 1** in this book.

21.1.4. short introduction to the data link layer

The data link layer, or **layer 2** is about frames. A frame has a **crc** (cyclic redundancy check). In the case of ethernet (802.3), each network card is identifiable by a unique 48-bit **mac** address (media access control address).

On this layer we find devices like bridges and switches. A bridge is more intelligent than a hub because a **bridge** can make decisions based on the mac address of computers. A **switch** also understands mac addresses.

In this book we will discuss commands like **arp** and **ifconfig** to explore this layer.

21.1.5. short introduction to the network layer

Layer 3 is about ip packets. This layer gives every host a unique 32-bit ip address. But **ip** is not the only protocol on this layer, there is also icmp, igmp, ipv6 and more. A complete list can be found in the **/etc/protocols** file.

On this layer we find devices like **routers** and layer 3 switches, devices that know (and have) an ip address.

In tcp/ip this layer is commonly referred to as the **internet layer**.

21.1.6. short introduction to the transport layer

We will discuss the **tcp** and **udp** protocols in the context of layer 4. The DoD model calls this the host-to-host layer.

21.1.7. layers 5, 6 and 7

The tcp/ip application layer includes layers 5, 6 and 7. Details on the difference between these layers are out of scope of this course.

21.1.8. network layers in this book

Stacking of layers in this book is based on the **Protocols in Frame** explanation in the **wireshark** sniffer. When sniffing a dhcp packet, we notice the following in the sniffer.

```
[Protocols in Frame: eth:ip:udp:bootp]
```

Sniffing for ntp (Network Time Protocol) packets gives us this line, which makes us conclude to put **ntp** next to **bootp** in the protocol chart below.

```
[Protocols in Frame: eth:ip:udp:ntp]
```

Sniffing an **arp** broadcast makes us put arp next to **ip**. All these protocols are explained later in this chapter.

```
[Protocols in Frame: eth:arp]
```

Below is a protocol chart based on wireshark's knowledge. It contains some very common protocols that are discussed in this book. The chart does not contain all protocols.

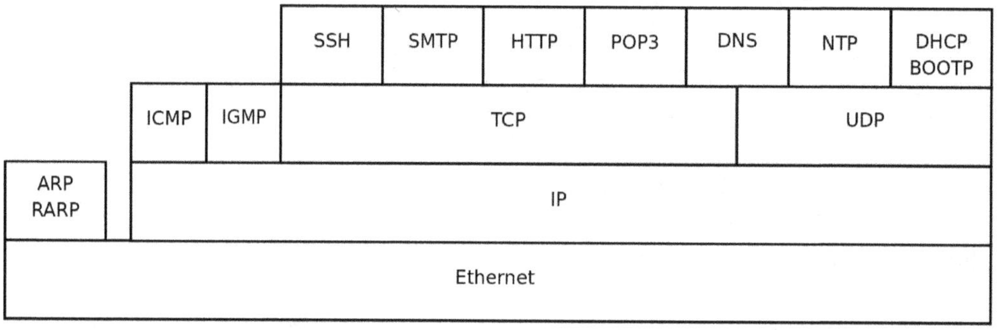

21.2. unicast, multicast, broadcast, anycast

21.2.1. unicast

A **unicast** communication originates from one computer and is destined for exactly one other computer (or host). It is common for computers to have many **unicast** communications.

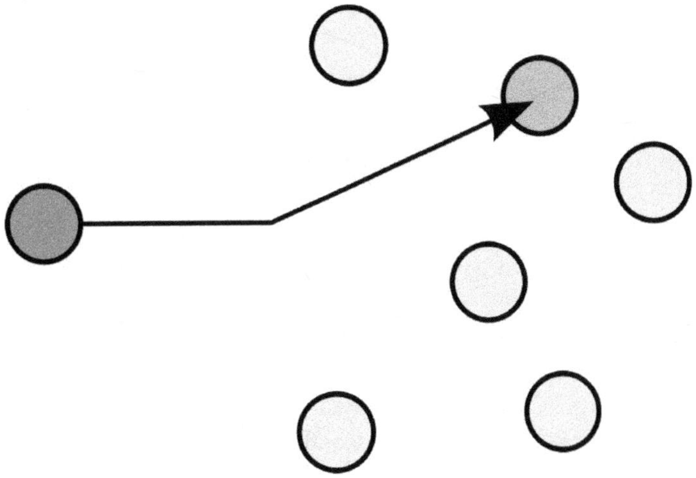

21.2.2. multicast

A **multicast** is destined for a group (of computers).

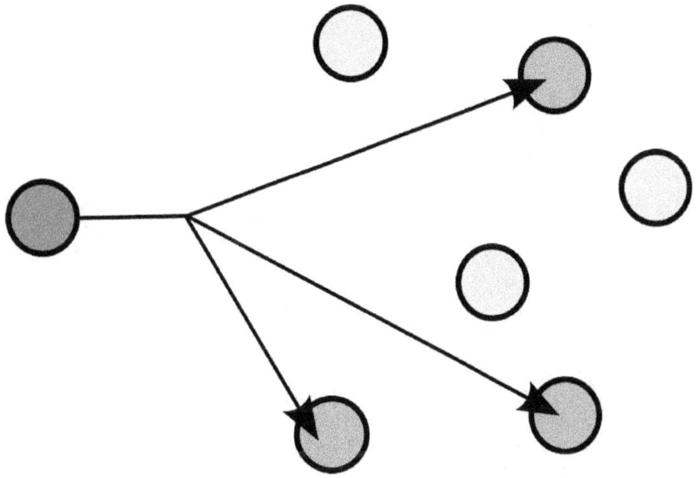

Some examples of **multicast** are Realplayer (.sdp files) and **ripv2** (a routing protocol).

21.2.3. broadcast

A **broadcast** is meant for everyone.

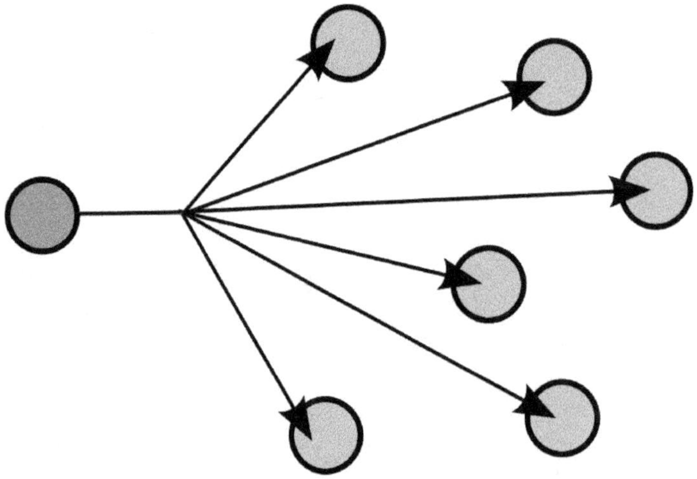

Typical example here is the BBC (British Broadcasting Corporation) broadcasting to everyone. In datacommunications a broadcast is most common confined to the **lan**.

Careful, a **layer 2 broadcast** is very different from a **layer 3 broadcast**. A layer two broadcast is received by all network cards on the same segment (it does not pass any router), whereas a layer 3 broadcast is received by all hosts in the same ip subnet.

21.2.4. anycast

The **root name servers** of the internet use **anycast**. An **anycast** signal goes the the (geographically) nearest of a well defined group.

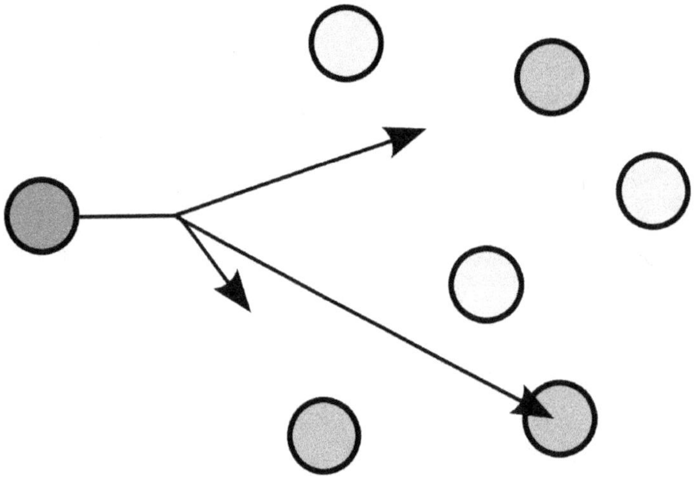

With thanks to the nice anonymous wikipedia contributor to put these pictures in the public domain.

21.3. lan-wan-man

The term **lan** is used for local area networks, as opposed to a **wan** for wide area networks. The difference between the two is determined by the **distance** between the computers, and not by the number of computers in a network. Some protocols like **atm** are designed for use in a **wan**, others like **ethernet** are designed for use in a **lan**.

21.3.1. lan

A **lan** (Local Area Network) is a local network. This can be one room, or one floor, or even one big building. We say **lan** as long as computers are **close** to each other. You can also define a **lan** when all computers are **ethernet** connected.

A **lan** can contain multiple smaller **lan**'s. The picture below shows three **lan**'s that together make up one **lan**.

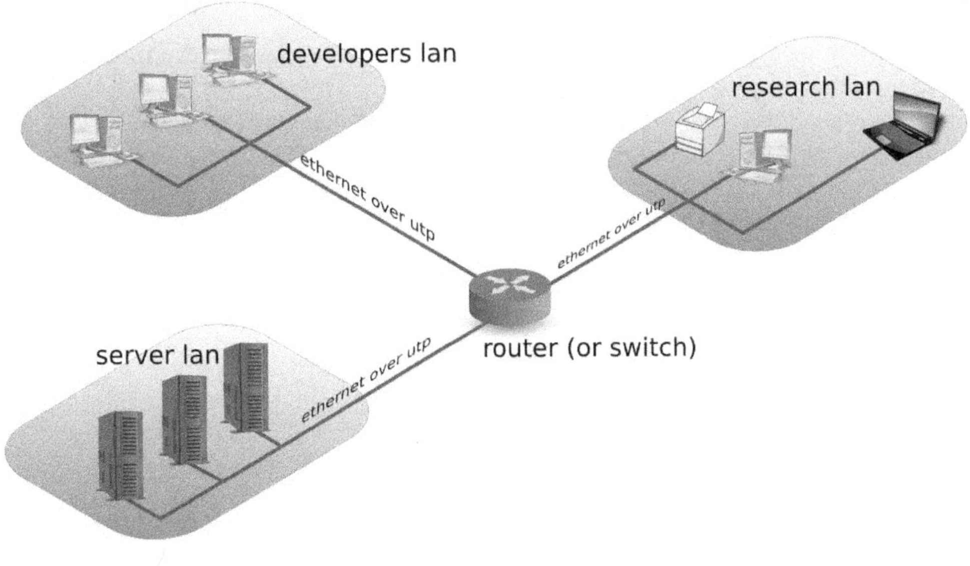

21.3.2. man

A **man** (Metropolitan Area Network) is something inbetween a **lan** and a **wan**, often comprising several buildings on the same campus or in the same city. A **man** can use **fddi** or **ethernet** or other protocols for connectivity.

21.3.3. wan

A **wan** (Wide Area Network) is a network with a lot of distance between the computers (or hosts). These hosts are often connected by **leased lines**. A **wan** does not use **ethernet**, but protocols like **fddi**, **frame relay**, **ATM** or **X.25** to connect computers (and networks).

The picture below shows a branch office that is connected through **Frame Relay** with headquarters.

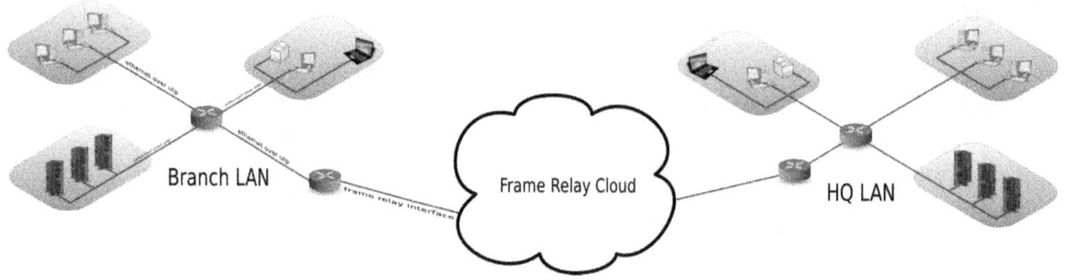

The acronym **wan** is also used for large surface area networks like the **internet**.

Cisco is known for their **wan** technology. They make **routers** that connect many **lan** networks using **wan** protocols.

21.3.4. pan-wpan

Your home network is called a **pan** (Personal Area Network). A wireless **pan** is a **wpan**.

21.4. internet - intranet - extranet

The **internet** is a global network. It connects many networks using the **tcp/ip** protocol stack.

The origin of the **internet** is the **arpanet**. The **arpanet** was created in 1969, that year only four computers were connected in the network. In 1971 the first **e-mail** was sent over the **arpanet**. **E-mail** took 75 percent of all **arpanet** traffic in 1973. 1973 was also the year **ftp** was introduced, and saw the connection of the first European countries (Norway and UK). In 2009 the internet was available to 25 percent of the world population. In 2011 it is estimated that only a quarter of internet webpages are in English.

An **intranet** is a private **tcp/ip** network. An **intranet** uses the same protocols as the **internet**, but is only accessible to people from within one organization.

An **extranet** is similar to an **intranet**, but some trusted organizations (partners/clients/suppliers/...) also get access.

21.5. tcp/ip

21.5.1. history of tcp/ip

In the Sixties development of the **tcp/ip** protocol stack was started by the US Department of Defense. In the Eighties a lot of commercial enterprises developed their own protocol stack: IBM created **sna**, Novell had **ipx/spx**, Microsoft completed **netbeui** and Apple worked with **appletalk**. All the efforts from the Eighties failed to survive the Nineties. By the end of the Nineties, almost all computers in the world were able to speak tcp/ip.

In my humble opinion, the main reason for the survival of **tcp/ip** over all the other protocols is its openness. Everyone is free to develop and use the tcp/ip protocol suite.

21.5.2. rfc (request for comment)

The protocols that are used on the internet are defined in **rfc's**. An rfc or **request for comment** describes the inner working of all internet protocols. The **IETF** (Internet Engineering Task Force) is the sole publisher of these protocols since 1986.

The official website for the rfc's is **http://www.rfc-editor.org**. This website contains all rfc's in plain text, for example rfc2132 (which defines dhcp and bootp) is accessible at http://www.rfc-editor.org/rfc/rfc2132.txt.

21.5.3. many protocols

For reliable connections, you use **tcp**, whereas **udp** is connectionless but faster. The **icmp** error messages are used by **ping**, multicast groups are managed by **igmp**.

These protocols are visible in the protocol field of the ip header, and are listed in the **/etc/protocols** file.

```
paul@debian5:~$ grep tcp /etc/protocols
tcp     6       TCP             # transmission control protocol
```

21.5.4. many services

Network cards are uniquely identified by their **mac address**, hosts by their **ip address** and applications by their **port number**.

Common application level protocols like smtp, http, ssh, telnet and ftp have fixed **port numbers**. There is a list of **port numbers** in **/etc/services**.

```
paul@ubu1010:~$ grep ssh /etc/services
ssh             22/tcp                  # SSH Remote Login Protocol
ssh             22/udp
```

Chapter 22. interface configuration

This chapter explains how to configure **network interface cards** to work with **tcp/ip**.

22.1. to gui or not to gui

Recent Linux distributions often include a graphical application to configure the network. Some people complain that these applications mess networking configurations up when used simultaneously with command line configurations. Notably **Network Manager** (often replaced by **wicd**) and **yast** are known to not care about configuration changes via the command line.

Since the goal of this course is **server** administration, we will assume our Linux servers are always administered through the command line.

This chapter only focuses on using the command line for network interface configuration!

Unfortunately there is no single combination of Linux commands and **/etc** files that works on all Linux distributions. We discuss networking on two (large but distinct) Linux distribution families.

We start with **Debian** (this should also work on Ubuntu and Mint), then continue with **RHEL** (which is identical to CentOS and Fedora).

22.2. Debian nic configuration

22.2.1. /etc/network/interfaces

The **/etc/network/interfaces** file is a core network interface card configuration file on **debian**.

dhcp client

The screenshot below shows that our computer is configured for **dhcp** on **eth0** (the first network interface card or nic).

```
paul@debian8:~$ cat /etc/network/interfaces
# This file describes the network interfaces available on your system
# and how to activate them. For more information, see interfaces(5).

# The loopback network interface
auto lo
iface lo inet loopback

auto eth0
iface eth0 inet dhcp
```

Configuring network cards for **dhcp** is good practice for clients, but servers usually require a **fixed ip address**.

fixed ip

The screenshot below shows **/etc/network/interfaces** configured with a **fixed ip address**.

```
root@debian7~# cat /etc/network/interfaces
auto lo
iface lo inet loopback

auto  eth0
iface eth0 inet static
address   10.42.189.198
broadcast 10.42.189.207
netmask   255.255.255.240
gateway   10.42.189.193
```

The screenshot above also shows that you can provide more configuration than just the ip address. See **interfaces(5)** for help on setting a **gateway**, **netmask** or any of the other options.

22.2.2. /sbin/ifdown

It is adviced (but not mandatory) to down an interface before changing its configuration. This can be done with the **ifdown** command.

The command will not give any output when downing an interface with a fixed ip address. However **ifconfig** will no longer show the interface.

```
root@ubu1104srv:~# ifdown eth0
root@ubu1104srv:~# ifconfig
lo    Link encap:Local Loopback
      inet addr:127.0.0.1  Mask:255.0.0.0
      inet6 addr: ::1/128 Scope:Host
      UP LOOPBACK RUNNING  MTU:16436  Metric:1
      RX packets:106 errors:0 dropped:0 overruns:0 frame:0
      TX packets:106 errors:0 dropped:0 overruns:0 carrier:0
      collisions:0 txqueuelen:0
      RX bytes:11162 (11.1 KB)  TX bytes:11162 (11.1 KB)
```

An interface that is down cannot be used to connect to the network.

22.2.3. /sbin/ifup

Below a screenshot of **ifup** bringing the **eth0** ethernet interface up using dhcp. (Note that this is a Ubuntu 10.10 screenshot, Ubuntu 11.04 omits **ifup** output by default.)

```
root@ubu1010srv:/etc/network# ifup eth0
Internet Systems Consortium DHCP Client V3.1.3
Copyright 2004-2009 Internet Systems Consortium.
All rights reserved.
For info, please visit https://www.isc.org/software/dhcp/

Listening on LPF/eth0/08:00:27:cd:7f:fc
Sending on   LPF/eth0/08:00:27:cd:7f:fc
Sending on   Socket/fallback
DHCPREQUEST of 192.168.1.34 on eth0 to 255.255.255.255 port 67
DHCPNAK from 192.168.33.100
DHCPDISCOVER on eth0 to 255.255.255.255 port 67 interval 3
DHCPOFFER of 192.168.33.77 from 192.168.33.100
DHCPREQUEST of 192.168.33.77 on eth0 to 255.255.255.255 port 67
DHCPACK of 192.168.33.77 from 192.168.33.100
bound to 192.168.33.77 -- renewal in 95 seconds.
ssh stop/waiting
ssh start/running, process 1301
root@ubu1010srv:/etc/network#
```

The details of **dhcp** are covered in a separate chapter in the **Linux Servers** course.

22.3. RHEL nic configuration

22.3.1. /etc/sysconfig/network

The **/etc/sysconfig/network** file is a global (across all network cards) configuration file. It allows us to define whether we want networking (NETWORKING=yes|no), what the hostname should be (HOSTNAME=) and which gateway to use (GATEWAY=).

```
[root@rhel6 ~]# cat /etc/sysconfig/network
NETWORKING=yes
HOSTNAME=rhel6
GATEWAY=192.168.1.1
```

There are a dozen more options settable in this file, details can be found in **/usr/share/doc/initscripts-*/sysconfig.txt**.

Note that this file contains no settings at all in a default RHEL7 install (with networking enabled).

```
[root@rhel71 ~]# cat /etc/sysconfig/network
# Created by anaconda
```

22.3.2. /etc/sysconfig/network-scripts/ifcfg-

Each network card can be configured individually using the **/etc/sysconfig/network-scripts/ifcfg-*** files. When you have only one network card, then this will probably be **/etc/sysconfig/network-scripts/ifcfg-eth0**.

dhcp client

Below a screenshot of **/etc/sysconfig/network-scripts/ifcfg-eth0** configured for dhcp (BOOTPROTO="dhcp"). Note also the NM_CONTROLLED paramater to disable control of this nic by **Network Manager**. This parameter is not explained (not even mentioned) in **/usr/share/doc/initscripts-*/sysconfig.txt**, but many others are.

```
[root@rhel6 ~]# cat /etc/sysconfig/network-scripts/ifcfg-eth0
DEVICE="eth0"
HWADDR="08:00:27:DD:0D:5C"
NM_CONTROLLED="no"
BOOTPROTO="dhcp"
ONBOOT="yes"
```

The BOOTPROTO variable can be set to either **dhcp** or **bootp**, anything else will be considered **static** meaning there should be no protocol used at boot time to set the interface values.

RHEL7 adds **ipv6** variables to this file.

```
[root@rhel71 network-scripts]# cat ifcfg-enp0s3
TYPE="Ethernet"
BOOTPROTO="dhcp"
DEFROUTE="yes"
PEERDNS="yes"
PEERROUTES="yes"
IPV4_FAILURE_FATAL="no"
```

```
IPV6INIT="yes"
IPV6_AUTOCONF="yes"
IPV6_DEFROUTE="yes"
IPV6_PEERDNS="yes"
IPV6_PEERROUTES="yes"
IPV6_FAILURE_FATAL="no"
NAME="enp0s3"
UUID="9fa6a83a-2f8e-4ecc-962c-5f614605f4ee"
DEVICE="enp0s3"
ONBOOT="yes"
[root@rhel71 network-scripts]#
```

fixed ip

Below a screenshot of a **fixed ip** configuration in **/etc/sysconfig/network-scripts/ifcfg-eth0**.

```
[root@rhel6 ~]# cat /etc/sysconfig/network-scripts/ifcfg-eth0
DEVICE="eth0"
HWADDR="08:00:27:DD:0D:5C"
NM_CONTROLLED="no"
BOOTPROTO="none"
IPADDR="192.168.1.99"
NETMASK="255.255.255.0"
GATEWAY="192.168.1.1"
ONBOOT="yes"
```

The HWADDR can be used to make sure that each network card gets the correct name when multiple network cards are present in the computer. It can not be used to assign a **mac address** to a network card. For this, you need to specify the MACADDR variable. Do not use HWADDR and MACADDR in the same **ifcfg-ethx** file.

The BROADCAST= and NETWORK= parameters from previous RHEL/Fedora versions are obsoleted.

22.3.3. nmcli

On RHEL7 you should run **nmcli connection reload** if you changed configuration files in **/etc/sysconfig/** to enable your changes.

The **nmcli** tool has many options to configure networking on the command line in RHEL7/CentOS7

```
man nmcli
```

22.3.4. nmtui

Another recommendation for RHEL7/CentOS7 is to use **nmtui**. This tool will use a 'windowed' interface in command line to manage network interfaces.

```
nmtui
```

22.3.5. /sbin/ifup and /sbin/ifdown

The **ifup** and **ifdown** commands will set an interface up or down, using the configuration discussed above. This is identical to their behaviour in Debian and Ubuntu.

```
[root@rhel6 ~]# ifdown eth0 && ifup eth0
[root@rhel6 ~]# ifconfig eth0
eth0 Link encap:Ethernet  HWaddr 08:00:27:DD:0D:5C
     inet addr:192.168.1.99  Bcast:192.168.1.255  Mask:255.255.255.0
     inet6 addr: fe80::a00:27ff:fedd:d5c/64 Scope:Link
     UP BROADCAST RUNNING MULTICAST  MTU:1500  Metric:1
     RX packets:2452 errors:0 dropped:0 overruns:0 frame:0
     TX packets:1881 errors:0 dropped:0 overruns:0 carrier:0
     collisions:0 txqueuelen:1000
     RX bytes:257036 (251.0 KiB)  TX bytes:184767 (180.4 KiB)
```

22.4. ifconfig

The use of **/sbin/ifconfig** without any arguments will present you with a list of all active network interface cards, including wireless and the loopback interface. In the screenshot below **eth0** has no ip address.

```
root@ubu1010:~# ifconfig
eth0 Link encap:Ethernet  HWaddr 00:26:bb:5d:2e:52
     UP BROADCAST MULTICAST  MTU:1500  Metric:1
     RX packets:0 errors:0 dropped:0 overruns:0 frame:0
     TX packets:0 errors:0 dropped:0 overruns:0 carrier:0
     collisions:0 txqueuelen:1000
     RX bytes:0 (0.0 B)  TX bytes:0 (0.0 B)
     Interrupt:43 Base address:0xe000

eth1 Link encap:Ethernet  HWaddr 00:26:bb:12:7a:5e
     inet addr:192.168.1.30  Bcast:192.168.1.255  Mask:255.255.255.0
     inet6 addr: fe80::226:bbff:fe12:7a5e/64 Scope:Link
     UP BROADCAST RUNNING MULTICAST  MTU:1500  Metric:1
     RX packets:11141791 errors:202 dropped:0 overruns:0 frame:11580126
     TX packets:6473056 errors:3860 dropped:0 overruns:0 carrier:0
     collisions:0 txqueuelen:1000
     RX bytes:3476531617 (3.4 GB)  TX bytes:2114919475 (2.1 GB)
     Interrupt:23

lo   Link encap:Local Loopback
     inet addr:127.0.0.1  Mask:255.0.0.0
     inet6 addr: ::1/128 Scope:Host
     UP LOOPBACK RUNNING  MTU:16436  Metric:1
     RX packets:2879 errors:0 dropped:0 overruns:0 frame:0
     TX packets:2879 errors:0 dropped:0 overruns:0 carrier:0
     collisions:0 txqueuelen:0
     RX bytes:486510 (486.5 KB)  TX bytes:486510 (486.5 KB)
```

You can also use **ifconfig** to obtain information about just one network card.

```
[root@rhel6 ~]# ifconfig eth0
eth0 Link encap:Ethernet  HWaddr 08:00:27:DD:0D:5C
     inet addr:192.168.1.99  Bcast:192.168.1.255  Mask:255.255.255.0
     inet6 addr: fe80::a00:27ff:fedd:d5c/64 Scope:Link
     UP BROADCAST RUNNING MULTICAST  MTU:1500  Metric:1
     RX packets:2969 errors:0 dropped:0 overruns:0 frame:0
     TX packets:1918 errors:0 dropped:0 overruns:0 carrier:0
     collisions:0 txqueuelen:1000
```

```
          RX bytes:335942 (328.0 KiB)  TX bytes:190157 (185.7 KiB)
```

When **/sbin** is not in the **$PATH** of a normal user you will have to type the full path, as seen here on Debian.

```
paul@debian5:~$ /sbin/ifconfig eth3
eth3 Link encap:Ethernet  HWaddr 08:00:27:ab:67:30
     inet addr:192.168.1.29  Bcast:192.168.1.255  Mask:255.255.255.0
     inet6 addr: fe80::a00:27ff:feab:6730/64 Scope:Link
     UP BROADCAST RUNNING MULTICAST  MTU:1500  Metric:1
     RX packets:27155 errors:0 dropped:0 overruns:0 frame:0
     TX packets:30527 errors:0 dropped:0 overruns:0 carrier:0
     collisions:0 txqueuelen:1000
     RX bytes:13095386 (12.4 MiB)  TX bytes:25767221 (24.5 MiB)
```

22.4.1. up and down

You can also use **ifconfig** to bring an interface up or down. The difference with **ifup** is that **ifconfig eth0 up** will re-activate the nic keeping its existing (current) configuration, whereas **ifup** will read the correct file that contains a (possibly new) configuration and use this config file to bring the interface up.

```
[root@rhel6 ~]# ifconfig eth0 down
[root@rhel6 ~]# ifconfig eth0 up
[root@rhel6 ~]# ifconfig eth0
eth0 Link encap:Ethernet  HWaddr 08:00:27:DD:0D:5C
     inet addr:192.168.1.99  Bcast:192.168.1.255  Mask:255.255.255.0
     inet6 addr: fe80::a00:27ff:fedd:d5c/64 Scope:Link
     UP BROADCAST RUNNING MULTICAST  MTU:1500  Metric:1
     RX packets:2995 errors:0 dropped:0 overruns:0 frame:0
     TX packets:1927 errors:0 dropped:0 overruns:0 carrier:0
     collisions:0 txqueuelen:1000
     RX bytes:339030 (331.0 KiB)  TX bytes:191583 (187.0 KiB)
```

22.4.2. setting ip address

You can **temporary** set an ip address with **ifconfig**. This ip address is only valid until the next **ifup/ifdown** cycle or until the next **reboot**.

```
[root@rhel6 ~]# ifconfig eth0 | grep 192
     inet addr:192.168.1.99  Bcast:192.168.1.255  Mask:255.255.255.0
[root@rhel6 ~]# ifconfig eth0 192.168.33.42 netmask 255.255.0.0
[root@rhel6 ~]# ifconfig eth0 | grep 192
     inet addr:192.168.33.42  Bcast:192.168.255.255  Mask:255.255.0.0
[root@rhel6 ~]# ifdown eth0 && ifup eth0
[root@rhel6 ~]# ifconfig eth0 | grep 192
     inet addr:192.168.1.99  Bcast:192.168.1.255  Mask:255.255.255.0
```

22.4.3. setting mac address

You can also use **ifconfig** to set another **mac address** than the one hard coded in the network card. This screenshot shows you how.

```
[root@rhel6 ~]# ifconfig eth0 | grep HWaddr
eth0 Link encap:Ethernet  HWaddr 08:00:27:DD:0D:5C
[root@rhel6 ~]# ifconfig eth0 hw ether 00:42:42:42:42:42
[root@rhel6 ~]# ifconfig eth0 | grep HWaddr
eth0 Link encap:Ethernet  HWaddr 00:42:42:42:42:42
```

22.5. ip

The **ifconfig** tool is deprecated on some systems. Use the **ip** tool instead.

To see ip addresses on RHEL7 for example, use this command:

```
[root@rhel71 ~]# ip a
1: lo: <LOOPBACK,UP,LOWER_UP> mtu 65536 qdisc noqueue state UNKNOWN
    link/loopback 00:00:00:00:00:00 brd 00:00:00:00:00:00
    inet 127.0.0.1/8 scope host lo
       valid_lft forever preferred_lft forever
    inet6 ::1/128 scope host
       valid_lft forever preferred_lft forever
2: enp0s3: <BROADCAST,MULTICAST,UP,LOWER_UP> mtu 1500 qdisc pfifo_fast state UP qlen 1000
    link/ether 08:00:27:89:22:33 brd ff:ff:ff:ff:ff:ff
    inet 192.168.1.135/24 brd 192.168.1.255 scope global dynamic enp0s3
       valid_lft 6173sec preferred_lft 6173sec
    inet6 fe80::a00:27ff:fe89:2233/64 scope link
       valid_lft forever preferred_lft forever
[root@rhel71 ~]#
```

22.6. dhclient

Home and client Linux desktops often have **/sbin/dhclient** running. This is a daemon that enables a network interface to lease an ip configuration from a **dhcp server**. When your adapter is configured for **dhcp** or **bootp**, then **/sbin/ifup** will start the **dhclient** daemon.

When a lease is renewed, **dhclient** will override your **ifconfig** set ip address!

22.7. hostname

Every host receives a **hostname**, often placed in a **DNS name space** forming the **fqdn** or Fully Qualified Domain Name.

This screenshot shows the **hostname** command and the configuration of the hostname on Red Hat/Fedora.

```
[root@rhel6 ~]# grep HOSTNAME /etc/sysconfig/network
HOSTNAME=rhel6
[root@rhel6 ~]# hostname
rhel6
```

Starting with RHEL7/CentOS7 this file is empty. The hostname is configured in the standard **/etc/hostname** file.

```
[root@rhel71 ~]# cat /etc/hostname
rhel71.linux-training.be
[root@rhel71 ~]#
```

Ubuntu/Debian uses the **/etc/hostname** file to configure the **hostname**.

```
paul@debian8:~$ cat /etc/hostname
server42
paul@debian8:~$ hostname
server42
```

On all Linux distributions you can change the **hostname** using the **hostname $newname** command. This is not a permanent change.

```
[root@rhel6 ~]# hostname server42
[root@rhel6 ~]# hostname
server42
```

On any Linux you can use **sysctl** to display and set the hostname.

```
[root@rhel6 ~]# sysctl kernel.hostname
kernel.hostname = server42
[root@rhel6 ~]# sysctl kernel.hostname=rhel6
kernel.hostname = rhel6
[root@rhel6 ~]# sysctl kernel.hostname
kernel.hostname = rhel6
[root@rhel6 ~]# hostname
rhel6
```

22.8. arp

The **ip to mac** resolution is handled by the **layer two broadcast** protocol **arp**. The **arp table** can be displayed with the **arp tool**. The screenshot below shows the list of computers that this computer recently communicated with.

```
root@barry:~# arp -a
? (192.168.1.191) at 00:0C:29:3B:15:80 [ether] on eth1
agapi (192.168.1.73) at 00:03:BA:09:7F:D2 [ether] on eth1
anya (192.168.1.1) at 00:12:01:E2:87:FB [ether] on eth1
faith (192.168.1.41) at 00:0E:7F:41:0D:EB [ether] on eth1
kiss (192.168.1.49) at 00:D0:E0:91:79:95 [ether] on eth1
laika (192.168.1.40) at 00:90:F5:4E:AE:17 [ether] on eth1
pasha (192.168.1.71) at 00:03:BA:02:C3:82 [ether] on eth1
shaka (192.168.1.72) at 00:03:BA:09:7C:F9 [ether] on eth1
root@barry:~#
```

Anya is a Cisco Firewall, faith is a laser printer, kiss is a Kiss DP600, laika is a laptop and Agapi, Shaka and Pasha are SPARC servers. The question mark is a Red Hat Enterprise Linux server running on a virtual machine.

You can use **arp -d** to remove an entry from the **arp table**.

```
[root@rhel6 ~]# arp
Address                  HWtype  HWaddress           Flags Mask            Iface
ubu1010                  ether   00:26:bb:12:7a:5e   C                     eth0
anya                     ether   00:02:cf:aa:68:f0   C                     eth0
[root@rhel6 ~]# arp -d anya
[root@rhel6 ~]# arp
Address                  HWtype  HWaddress           Flags Mask            Iface
ubu1010                  ether   00:26:bb:12:7a:5e   C                     eth0
anya                             (incomplete)                              eth0
[root@rhel6 ~]# ping anya
PING anya (192.168.1.1) 56(84) bytes of data.
64 bytes from anya (192.168.1.1): icmp_seq=1 ttl=254 time=10.2 ms
...
[root@rhel6 ~]# arp
Address                  HWtype  HWaddress           Flags Mask            Iface
ubu1010                  ether   00:26:bb:12:7a:5e   C                     eth0
anya                     ether   00:02:cf:aa:68:f0   C                     eth0
```

22.9. route

You can see the computer's local routing table with the **/sbin/route** command (and also with **netstat -r**).

```
root@RHEL4b ~]# netstat -r
Kernel IP routing table
Destination     Gateway    Genmask          Flags   MSS Window  irtt Iface
192.168.1.0     *          255.255.255.0    U         0 0          0 eth0
[root@RHEL4b ~]# route
Kernel IP routing table
Destination     Gateway    Genmask          Flags Metric Ref    Use Iface
192.168.1.0     *          255.255.255.0    U     0      0        0 eth0
[root@RHEL4b ~]#
```

It appears this computer does not have a **gateway** configured, so we use **route add default gw** to add a **default gateway** on the fly.

```
[root@RHEL4b ~]# route add default gw 192.168.1.1
[root@RHEL4b ~]# route
Kernel IP routing table
Destination     Gateway      Genmask         Flags Metric Ref    Use Iface
192.168.1.0     *            255.255.255.0   U     0      0        0 eth0
default         192.168.1.1  0.0.0.0         UG    0      0        0 eth0
[root@RHEL4b ~]#
```

Unless you configure the gateway in one of the **/etc/** file from the start of this chapter, your computer will forget this **gateway** after a reboot.

22.10. ping

If you can **ping** to another host, then **tcp/ip** is configured.

```
[root@RHEL4b ~]# ping 192.168.1.5
PING 192.168.1.5 (192.168.1.5) 56(84) bytes of data.
64 bytes from 192.168.1.5: icmp_seq=0 ttl=64 time=1004 ms
64 bytes from 192.168.1.5: icmp_seq=1 ttl=64 time=1.19 ms
64 bytes from 192.168.1.5: icmp_seq=2 ttl=64 time=0.494 ms
64 bytes from 192.168.1.5: icmp_seq=3 ttl=64 time=0.419 ms

--- 192.168.1.5 ping statistics ---
4 packets transmitted, 4 received, 0% packet loss, time 3009ms
rtt min/avg/max/mdev = 0.419/251.574/1004.186/434.520 ms, pipe 2
[root@RHEL4b ~]#
```

22.11. optional: ethtool

To display or change network card settings, use **ethtool**. The results depend on the capabilities of your network card. The example shows a network that auto-negotiates it's bandwidth.

```
root@laika:~# ethtool eth0
Settings for eth0:
 Supported ports: [ TP ]
 Supported link modes:   10baseT/Half 10baseT/Full
                         100baseT/Half 100baseT/Full
                         1000baseT/Full
 Supports auto-negotiation: Yes
 Advertised link modes:  10baseT/Half 10baseT/Full
                         100baseT/Half 100baseT/Full
                         1000baseT/Full
 Advertised auto-negotiation: Yes
 Speed: 1000Mb/s
 Duplex: Full
 Port: Twisted Pair
 PHYAD: 0
 Transceiver: internal
 Auto-negotiation: on
 Supports Wake-on: pumbg
 Wake-on: g
 Current message level: 0x00000033 (51)
 Link detected: yes
```

This example shows how to use ethtool to switch the bandwidth from 1000Mbit to 100Mbit and back. Note that some time passes before the nic is back to 1000Mbit.

```
root@laika:~# ethtool eth0 | grep Speed
 Speed: 1000Mb/s
root@laika:~# ethtool -s eth0 speed 100
root@laika:~# ethtool eth0 | grep Speed
 Speed: 100Mb/s
root@laika:~# ethtool -s eth0 speed 1000
root@laika:~# ethtool eth0 | grep Speed
 Speed: 1000Mb/s
```

22.12. practice: interface configuration

1. Verify whether **dhclient** is running.

2. Display your current ip address(es).

3. Display the configuration file where this **ip address** is defined.

4. Follow the **nic configuration** in the book to change your ip address from **dhcp client** to **fixed**. Keep the same **ip address** to avoid conflicts!

5. Did you also configure the correct **gateway** in the previous question ? If not, then do this now.

6. Verify that you have a gateway.

7. Verify that you can connect to the gateway, that it is alive.

8. Change the last two digits of your **mac address**.

9. Which ports are used by http, pop3, ssh, telnet, nntp and ftp ?

10. Explain why e-mail and websites are sent over **tcp** and not **udp**.

11. Display the **hostname** of your computer.

12. Which ip-addresses did your computer recently have contact with ?

22.13. solution: interface configuration

1. Verify whether **dhclient** is running.

```
paul@debian5:~$ ps fax | grep dhclient
```

2. Display your current ip address(es).

```
paul@debian5:~$ /sbin/ifconfig | grep 'inet '
          inet addr:192.168.1.31  Bcast:192.168.1.255  Mask:255.255.255.0
          inet addr:127.0.0.1  Mask:255.0.0.0
```

3. Display the configuration file where this **ip address** is defined.

```
Ubuntu/Debian: cat /etc/network/interfaces
Redhat/Fedora: cat /etc/sysconfig/network-scripts/ifcfg-eth*
```

4. Follow the **nic configuration** in the book to change your ip address from **dhcp client** to **fixed**. Keep the same **ip address** to avoid conflicts!

```
Ubuntu/Debian:
ifdown eth0
vi /etc/network/interfaces
ifup eth0
```

```
Redhat/Fedora:
ifdown eth0
vi /etc/sysconfig/network-scripts/ifcfg-eth0
ifup eth0
```

5. Did you also configure the correct **gateway** in the previous question ? If not, then do this now.

6. Verify that you have a gateway.

```
paul@debian5:~$ /sbin/route
Kernel IP routing table
Destination     Gateway         Genmask         Flags Metric Ref    Use Iface
192.168.1.0     *               255.255.255.0   U     0      0        0 eth0
default         192.168.1.1     0.0.0.0         UG    0      0        0 eth0
```

7. Verify that you can connect to the gateway, that it is alive.

```
paul@debian5:~$ ping -c3 192.168.1.1
PING 192.168.1.1 (192.168.1.1) 56(84) bytes of data.
64 bytes from 192.168.1.1: icmp_seq=1 ttl=254 time=2.28 ms
64 bytes from 192.168.1.1: icmp_seq=2 ttl=254 time=2.94 ms
64 bytes from 192.168.1.1: icmp_seq=3 ttl=254 time=2.34 ms

--- 192.168.1.1 ping statistics ---
3 packets transmitted, 3 received, 0% packet loss, time 2008ms
rtt min/avg/max/mdev = 2.283/2.524/2.941/0.296 ms
```

8. Change the last two digits of your **mac address**.

```
[root@rhel6 ~]# ifconfig eth0 hw ether 08:00:27:ab:67:XX
```

9. Which ports are used by http, pop3, ssh, telnet, nntp and ftp ?

```
root@rhel6 ~# grep ^'http ' /etc/services
```

```
http        80/tcp          www www-http    # WorldWideWeb HTTP
http        80/udp          www www-http    # HyperText Transfer Protocol
root@rhel6 ~# grep ^'smtp ' /etc/services
smtp        25/tcp          mail
smtp        25/udp          mail
root@rhel6 ~# grep ^'ssh ' /etc/services
ssh         22/tcp                          # The Secure Shell (SSH) Protocol
ssh         22/udp                          # The Secure Shell (SSH) Protocol
root@rhel6 ~# grep ^'telnet ' /etc/services
telnet      23/tcp
telnet      23/udp
root@rhel6 ~# grep ^'nntp ' /etc/services
nntp        119/tcp         readnews untp   # USENET News Transfer Protocol
nntp        119/udp         readnews untp   # USENET News Transfer Protocol
root@rhel6 ~# grep ^'ftp ' /etc/services
ftp         21/tcp
ftp         21/udp          fsp fspd
```

10. Explain why e-mail and websites are sent over **tcp** and not **udp**.

```
Because tcp is reliable and udp is not.
```

11. Display the **hostname** of your computer.

```
paul@debian5:~$ hostname
debian5
```

12. Which ip-addresses did your computer recently have contact with ?

```
root@rhel6 ~# arp -a
? (192.168.1.1) at 00:02:cf:aa:68:f0 [ether] on eth2
? (192.168.1.30) at 00:26:bb:12:7a:5e [ether] on eth2
? (192.168.1.31) at 08:00:27:8e:8a:a8 [ether] on eth2
```

Chapter 23. network sniffing

A network administrator should be able to use a sniffer like **wireshark** or **tcpdump** to troubleshoot network problems.

A student should often use a sniffer to learn about networking. This chapter introduces you to **network sniffing**.

23.1. wireshark

23.1.1. installing wireshark

This example shows how to install **wireshark** on **.deb** based distributions (including Debian, Mint, Xubuntu, and others).

```
root@debian8:~# apt-get install wireshark
Reading package lists... Done
Building dependency tree
Reading state information... Done
... (output truncated)
```

On **.rpm** based distributions like CentOS, RHEL and Fedora you can use **yum** to install **wireshark**.

```
[root@centos7 ~]# yum install wireshark
Loaded plugins: fastestmirror
Loading mirror speeds from cached hostfile
... (output truncated)
```

23.1.2. selecting interface

When you start **wireshark** for the first time, you will need to select an interface. You will see a dialog box that looks similar to this one.

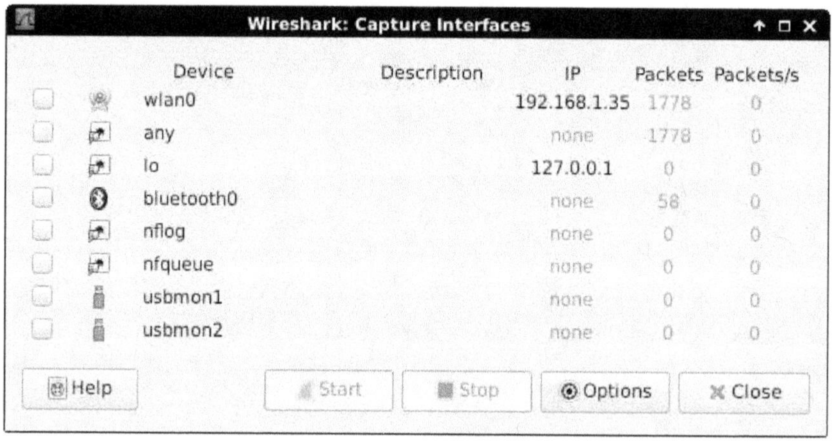

It is possible that there are no interfaces available because some distributions only allow root to sniff the network. You may need to use **sudo wireshark**.

Or you can follow the general advice to sniff using **tcpdump** or any other tool, and save the capture to a file. Any saved capture can be analyzed using **wireshark** at a later time.

23.1.3. minimize traffic

Sniffing a network can generate many thousands of packets in a very short time. This can be overwhelming. Try to mitigate by isolating your sniffer on the network. Preferably sniff an isolated virtual network interface over which you control all traffic.

If you are at home to learn sniffing, then it could help to close all network programs on your computer, and disconnect other computers and devices like smartphones and tablets to minimize the traffic.

Even more important than this is the use of **filters** which will be discussed in this chapter.

23.1.4. sniffing ping

I started the sniffer and captured all packets while doing these three **ping** commands (there is no need for root to do this):

```
root@debian7:~# ping -c2 ns1.paul.local
PING ns1.paul.local (10.104.33.30) 56(84) bytes of data.
64 bytes from 10.104.33.30: icmp_req=1 ttl=64 time=0.010 ms
64 bytes from 10.104.33.30: icmp_req=2 ttl=64 time=0.023 ms

--- ns1.paul.local ping statistics ---
2 packets transmitted, 2 received, 0% packet loss, time 1001ms
rtt min/avg/max/mdev = 0.010/0.016/0.023/0.007 ms
root@debian7:~# ping -c3 linux-training.be
PING linux-training.be (188.93.155.87) 56(84) bytes of data.
64 bytes from antares.ginsys.net (188.93.155.87): icmp_req=1 ttl=56 time=15.6 ms
64 bytes from antares.ginsys.net (188.93.155.87): icmp_req=2 ttl=56 time=17.8 ms
64 bytes from antares.ginsys.net (188.93.155.87): icmp_req=3 ttl=56 time=14.7 ms

--- linux-training.be ping statistics ---
3 packets transmitted, 3 received, 0% packet loss, time 2003ms
rtt min/avg/max/mdev = 14.756/16.110/17.881/1.309 ms
root@debian7:~# ping -c1 centos7.paul.local
PING centos7.paul.local (10.104.33.31) 56(84) bytes of data.
64 bytes from 10.104.33.31: icmp_req=1 ttl=64 time=0.590 ms

--- centos7.paul.local ping statistics ---
1 packets transmitted, 1 received, 0% packet loss, time 0ms
rtt min/avg/max/mdev = 0.590/0.590/0.590/0.000 ms
```

In total more than 200 packets were sniffed from the network. Things become clearer when you enter **icmp** in the filter field and press the **apply** button.

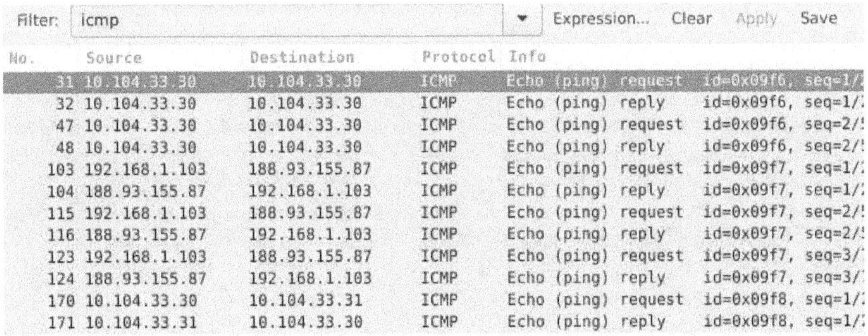

23.1.5. sniffing ping and dns

Using the same capture as before, but now with a different **filter**. We want to see both **dns** and **icmp** traffic, so we enter both in the filter field.

We put **dns or icmp** in the filter to achieve this. Putting **dns and icmp** would render nothing because there is no packet that matches both protocols.

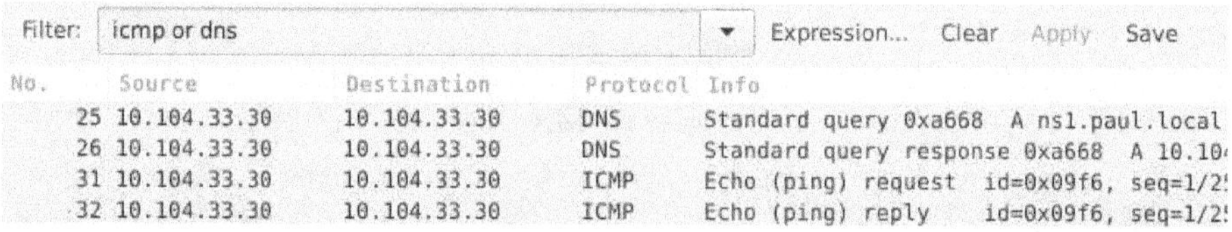

In the screenshot above you can see that packets 25 and 26 both have 10.104.33.30 as **source** and **destination** ip address. That is because the dns client is the same computer as the dns server.

The same is true for packets 31 and 32, since the machine is actually pinging itself.

23.1.6. specific ip address

This is a screenshot that filters for **dns** packets that contain a certain **ip address**. The filter in use is **ip.addr==10.104.33.30 and dns**. The **and** directive forces each displayed packet to match both conditions.

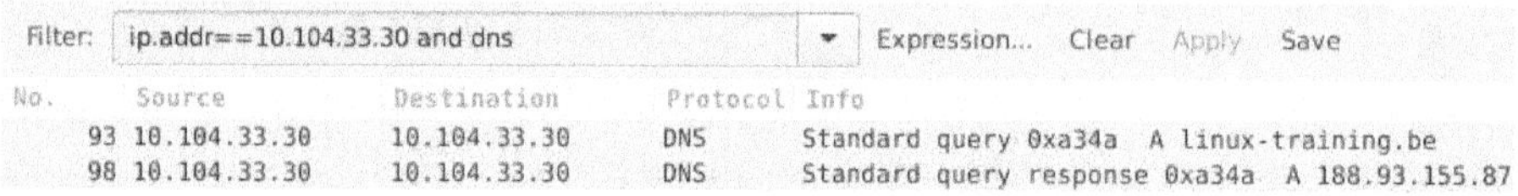

Packet 93 is the **dns query** for the A record of linux-training.be. Packet 98 is the response from the **dns server**. What do you think happened in the packets between 93 and 98 ? Try to answer this before reading on (it always helps to try to predict what you will see, and then checking your prediction).

23.1.7. filtering by frame

The correct technical term for a **packet** as sniffed is a **frame** (because we sniff on layer two). So to display packets with certain numbers, we use **frame.number** in the filter.

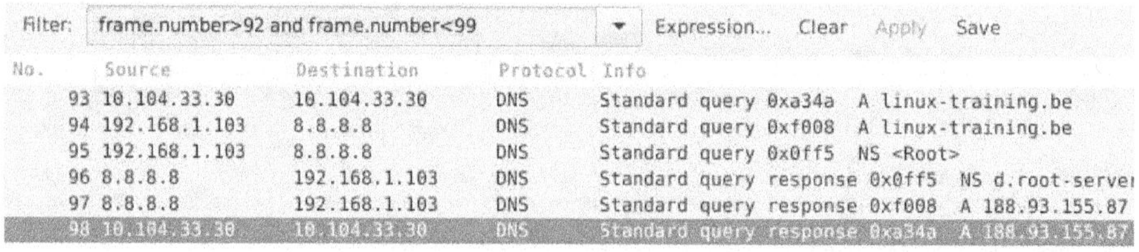

23.1.8. looking inside packets

The middle pane can be expanded. When selecting a line in this pane, you can see the corresponding bytes in the frame in the bottom panel.

This screenshot shows the middle pane with the source address of my laptop selected.

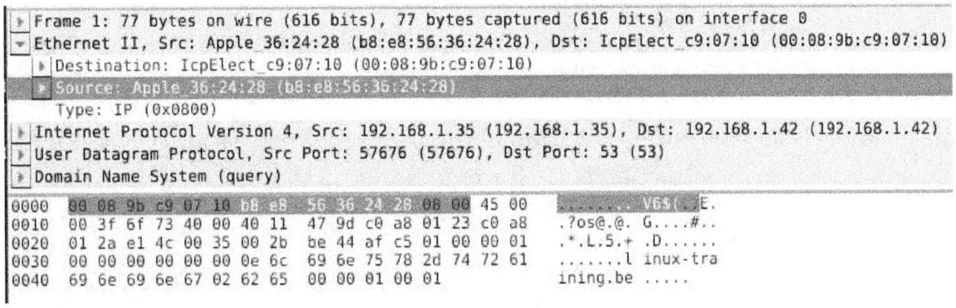

Note that the above works fine when sniffing one interface. When sniffing with for example **tcpdump -i any** you will end up with **Linux cooked** at this level.

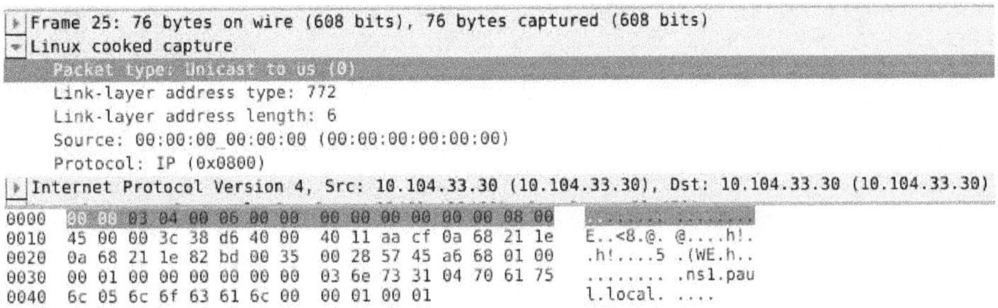

23.1.9. other filter examples

You can combine two protocols with a logical **or** between them. The example below shows how to filter only **arp** and **bootp** (or **dhcp**) packets.

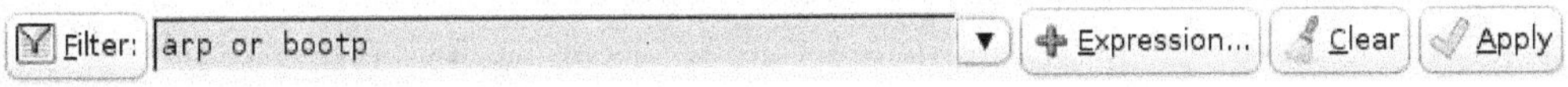

This example shows how to filter for **dns** traffic containing a certain **ip address**.

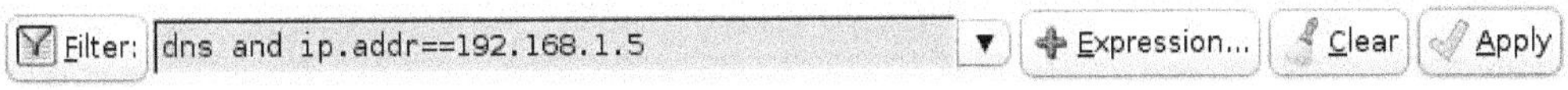

23.2. tcpdump

Sniffing on the command line can be done with **tcpdump**. Here are some examples.

Using the **tcpdump host $ip** command displays all traffic with one host (192.168.1.38 in this example).

```
root@ubuntu910:~# tcpdump host 192.168.1.38
tcpdump: verbose output suppressed, use -v or -vv for full protocol decode
listening on eth0, link-type EN10MB (Ethernet), capture size 96 bytes
```

Capturing only ssh (tcp port 22) traffic can be done with **tcpdump tcp port $port**. This screenshot is cropped to 76 characters for readability in the pdf.

```
root@deb503:~# tcpdump tcp port 22
tcpdump: verbose output suppressed, use -v or -vv for full protocol decode
listening on eth1, link-type EN10MB (Ethernet), capture size 96 bytes
14:22:20.716313 IP deb503.local.37973 > rhel53.local.ssh: P 666050963:66605
14:22:20.719936 IP rhel53.local.ssh > deb503.local.37973: P 1:49(48) ack 48
14:22:20.720922 IP rhel53.local.ssh > deb503.local.37973: P 49:113(64) ack
14:22:20.721321 IP rhel53.local.ssh > deb503.local.37973: P 113:161(48) ack
14:22:20.721820 IP deb503.local.37973 > rhel53.local.ssh: . ack 161 win 200
14:22:20.722492 IP rhel53.local.ssh > deb503.local.37973: P 161:225(64) ack
14:22:20.760602 IP deb503.local.37973 > rhel53.local.ssh: . ack 225 win 200
14:22:23.108106 IP deb503.local.54424 > ubuntu910.local.ssh: P 467252637:46
14:22:23.116804 IP ubuntu910.local.ssh > deb503.local.54424: P 1:81(80) ack
14:22:23.116844 IP deb503.local.54424 > ubuntu910.local.ssh: . ack 81 win 2
^C
10 packets captured
10 packets received by filter
0 packets dropped by kernel
```

Same as above, but write the output to a file with the **tcpdump -w $filename** command.

```
root@ubuntu910:~# tcpdump -w sshdump.tcpdump tcp port 22
tcpdump: listening on eth0, link-type EN10MB (Ethernet), capture size 96 bytes
^C
17 packets captured
17 packets received by filter
0 packets dropped by kernel
```

With **tcpdump -r $filename** the file created above can be displayed.

```
root@ubuntu910:~# tcpdump -r sshdump.tcpdump
```

Many more examples can be found in the manual page of **tcpdump**.

23.3. practice: network sniffing

1. Install wireshark on your computer (not inside a virtual machine).

2. Start a ping between your computer and another computer.

3. Start sniffing the network.

4. Display only the ping echo's in the top pane using a filter.

5. Now ping to a name (like www.linux-training.be) and try to sniff the DNS query and response. Which DNS server was used ? Was it a tcp or udp query and response ?

6. Find an amateur/hobby/club website that features a login prompt. Attempt to login with user 'paul' and password 'hunter2' while your sniffer is running. Now find this information in the sniffer.

23.4. solution: network sniffing

1. Install wireshark on your computer (not inside a virtual machine).

```
Debian/Ubuntu: aptitude install wireshark
```

```
Red Hat/Mandriva/Fedora: yum install wireshark
```

2. Start a ping between your computer and another computer.

```
ping $ip_address
```

3. Start sniffing the network.

```
(sudo) wireshark
```

```
select an interface (probably eth0)
```

4. Display only the ping echo's in the top pane using a filter.

```
type 'icmp' (without quotes) in the filter box, and then click 'apply'
```

5. Now ping to a name (like www.linux-training.be) and try to sniff the DNS query and response. Which DNS server was used ? Was it a tcp or udp query and response ?

```
First start the sniffer.
```

```
Enter 'dns' in the filter box and click apply.
```

```
root@ubuntu910:~# ping www.linux-training.be
PING www.linux-training.be (88.151.243.8) 56(84) bytes of data.
64 bytes from fosfor.openminds.be (88.151.243.8): icmp_seq=1 ttl=58 time=14.9 ms
64 bytes from fosfor.openminds.be (88.151.243.8): icmp_seq=2 ttl=58 time=16.0 ms
^C
--- www.linux-training.be ping statistics ---
2 packets transmitted, 2 received, 0% packet loss, time 1002ms
rtt min/avg/max/mdev = 14.984/15.539/16.095/0.569 ms
```

The wireshark screen should look something like this.

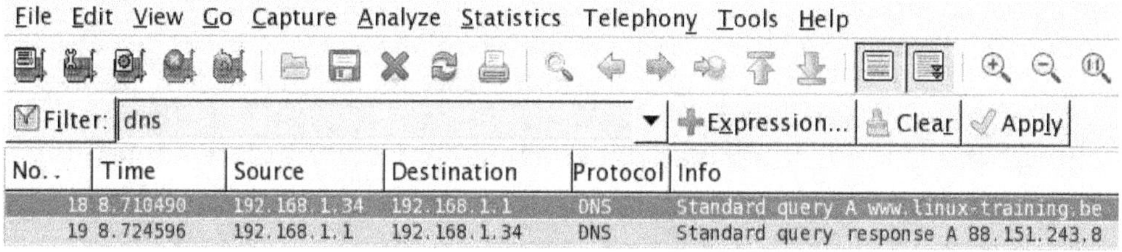

The details in wireshark will say the DNS query was inside a udp packet.

6. Find an amateur/hobby/club website that features a login prompt. Attempt to login with user 'paul' and password 'hunter2' while your sniffer is running. Now find this information in the sniffer.

Chapter 24. binding and bonding

Sometimes a server needs more than one **ip address** on the same network card, we call this **binding** ip addresses.

Linux can also activate multiple network cards behind the same **ip address**, this is called **bonding**.

This chapter will teach you how to configure **binding** and **bonding** on the most common Linux distributions.

24.1. binding on Redhat/Fedora

24.1.1. binding extra ip addresses

To bind more than one **ip address** to the same interface, use **ifcfg-eth0:0**, where the last zero can be anything else. Only two directives are required in the files.

```
[root@rhel6 ~]# cat /etc/sysconfig/network-scripts/ifcfg-eth0:0
DEVICE="eth0:0"
IPADDR="192.168.1.133"
[root@rhel6 ~]# cat /etc/sysconfig/network-scripts/ifcfg-eth0:1
DEVICE="eth0:0"
IPADDR="192.168.1.142"
```

24.1.2. enabling extra ip-addresses

To activate a virtual network interface, use **ifup**, to deactivate it, use **ifdown**.

```
[root@rhel6 ~]# ifup eth0:0
[root@rhel6 ~]# ifconfig | grep 'inet '
          inet addr:192.168.1.99  Bcast:192.168.1.255  Mask:255.255.255.0
          inet addr:192.168.1.133  Bcast:192.168.1.255  Mask:255.255.255.0
          inet addr:127.0.0.1  Mask:255.0.0.0
[root@rhel6 ~]# ifup eth0:1
[root@rhel6 ~]# ifconfig | grep 'inet '
          inet addr:192.168.1.99  Bcast:192.168.1.255  Mask:255.255.255.0
          inet addr:192.168.1.133  Bcast:192.168.1.255  Mask:255.255.255.0
          inet addr:192.168.1.142  Bcast:192.168.1.255  Mask:255.255.255.0
          inet addr:127.0.0.1  Mask:255.0.0.0
```

24.1.3. verifying extra ip-addresses

Use **ping** from another computer to check the activation, or use **ifconfig** like in this screenshot.

```
[root@rhel6 ~]# ifconfig
eth0      Link encap:Ethernet  HWaddr 08:00:27:DD:0D:5C
          inet addr:192.168.1.99  Bcast:192.168.1.255  Mask:255.255.255.0
          inet6 addr: fe80::a00:27ff:fedd:d5c/64 Scope:Link
          UP BROADCAST RUNNING MULTICAST  MTU:1500  Metric:1
          RX packets:1259 errors:0 dropped:0 overruns:0 frame:0
          TX packets:545 errors:0 dropped:0 overruns:0 carrier:0
          collisions:0 txqueuelen:1000
          RX bytes:115260 (112.5 KiB)  TX bytes:84293 (82.3 KiB)

eth0:0    Link encap:Ethernet  HWaddr 08:00:27:DD:0D:5C
          inet addr:192.168.1.133  Bcast:192.168.1.255  Mask:255.255.255.0
          UP BROADCAST RUNNING MULTICAST  MTU:1500  Metric:1

eth0:1    Link encap:Ethernet  HWaddr 08:00:27:DD:0D:5C
          inet addr:192.168.1.142  Bcast:192.168.1.255  Mask:255.255.255.0
          UP BROADCAST RUNNING MULTICAST  MTU:1500  Metric:1
```

24.2. binding on Debian/Ubuntu

24.2.1. binding extra ip addresses

The configuration of multiple ip addresses on the same network card is done in **/etc/network/interfaces** by adding **eth0:x** devices. Adding the **netmask** is mandatory.

```
debian5:~# cat /etc/network/interfaces
# This file describes the network interfaces available on your system
# and how to activate them. For more information, see interfaces(5).

# The loopback network interface
auto lo
iface lo inet loopback

# The primary network interface
iface eth0 inet static
address 192.168.1.34
network 192.168.1.0
netmask 255.255.255.0
gateway 192.168.1.1
auto eth0

auto eth0:0
iface eth0:0 inet static
address 192.168.1.233
netmask 255.255.255.0

auto eth0:1
iface eth0:1 inet static
address 192.168.1.242
netmask 255.255.255.0
```

24.2.2. enabling extra ip-addresses

Use **ifup** to enable the extra addresses.

```
debian5:~# ifup eth0:0
debian5:~# ifup eth0:1
```

24.2.3. verifying extra ip-addresses

Use **ping** from another computer to check the activation, or use **ifconfig** like in this screenshot.

```
debian5:~# ifconfig | grep 'inet '
      inet addr:192.168.1.34  Bcast:192.168.1.255  Mask:255.255.255.0
      inet addr:192.168.1.233  Bcast:192.168.1.255  Mask:255.255.255.0
      inet addr:192.168.1.242  Bcast:192.168.1.255  Mask:255.255.255.0
      inet addr:127.0.0.1  Mask:255.0.0.0
```

24.3. bonding on Redhat/Fedora

We start with **ifconfig -a** to get a list of all the network cards on our system.

```
[root@rhel6 network-scripts]# ifconfig -a | grep Ethernet
eth0      Link encap:Ethernet  HWaddr 08:00:27:DD:0D:5C
eth1      Link encap:Ethernet  HWaddr 08:00:27:DA:C1:49
eth2      Link encap:Ethernet  HWaddr 08:00:27:40:03:3B
```

In this demo we decide to bond **eth1** and **eth2**.

We will name our bond **bond0** and add this entry to **modprobe** so the kernel can load the **bonding module** when we bring the interface up.

```
[root@rhel6 network-scripts]# cat /etc/modprobe.d/bonding.conf
alias bond0 bonding
```

Then we create **/etc/sysconfig/network-scripts/ifcfg-bond0** to configure our **bond0** interface.

```
[root@rhel6 network-scripts]# pwd
/etc/sysconfig/network-scripts
[root@rhel6 network-scripts]# cat ifcfg-bond0
DEVICE=bond0
IPADDR=192.168.1.199
NETMASK=255.255.255.0
ONBOOT=yes
BOOTPROTO=none
USERCTL=no
```

Next we create two files, one for each network card that we will use as slave in **bond0**.

```
[root@rhel6 network-scripts]# cat ifcfg-eth1
DEVICE=eth1
BOOTPROTO=none
ONBOOT=yes
MASTER=bond0
SLAVE=yes
USERCTL=no
[root@rhel6 network-scripts]# cat ifcfg-eth2
DEVICE=eth2
BOOTPROTO=none
ONBOOT=yes
MASTER=bond0
SLAVE=yes
USERCTL=no
```

Finally we bring the interface up with **ifup bond0**.

```
[root@rhel6 network-scripts]# ifup bond0
[root@rhel6 network-scripts]# ifconfig bond0
bond0     Link encap:Ethernet  HWaddr 08:00:27:DA:C1:49
          inet addr:192.168.1.199  Bcast:192.168.1.255  Mask:255.255.255.0
          inet6 addr: fe80::a00:27ff:feda:c149/64 Scope:Link
          UP BROADCAST RUNNING MASTER MULTICAST  MTU:1500  Metric:1
          RX packets:251 errors:0 dropped:0 overruns:0 frame:0
          TX packets:21 errors:0 dropped:0 overruns:0 carrier:0
          collisions:0 txqueuelen:0
          RX bytes:39852 (38.9 KiB)  TX bytes:1070 (1.0 KiB)
```

The **bond** should also be visible in **/proc/net/bonding**.

```
[root@rhel6 network-scripts]# cat /proc/net/bonding/bond0
Ethernet Channel Bonding Driver: v3.5.0 (November 4, 2008)

Bonding Mode: load balancing (round-robin)
MII Status: up
MII Polling Interval (ms): 0
Up Delay (ms): 0
Down Delay (ms): 0

Slave Interface: eth1
MII Status: up
Link Failure Count: 0
Permanent HW addr: 08:00:27:da:c1:49

Slave Interface: eth2
MII Status: up
Link Failure Count: 0
Permanent HW addr: 08:00:27:40:03:3b
```

24.4. bonding on Debian/Ubuntu

We start with **ifconfig -a** to get a list of all the network cards on our system.

```
debian5:~# ifconfig -a | grep Ethernet
eth0      Link encap:Ethernet  HWaddr 08:00:27:bb:18:a4
eth1      Link encap:Ethernet  HWaddr 08:00:27:63:9a:95
eth2      Link encap:Ethernet  HWaddr 08:00:27:27:a4:92
```

In this demo we decide to bond **eth1** and **eth2**.

We also need to install the **ifenslave** package.

```
debian5:~# aptitude search ifenslave
p ifenslave     - Attach and detach slave interfaces to a bonding device
p ifenslave-2.6 - Attach and detach slave interfaces to a bonding device
debian5:~# aptitude install ifenslave
Reading package lists... Done
...
```

Next we update the **/etc/network/interfaces** file with information about the **bond0** interface.

```
debian5:~# tail -7 /etc/network/interfaces
iface bond0 inet static
 address 192.168.1.42
 netmask 255.255.255.0
 gateway 192.168.1.1
 slaves eth1 eth2
 bond-mode active-backup
 bond_primary eth1
```

On older version of Debian/Ubuntu you needed to **modprobe bonding**, but this is no longer required. Use **ifup** to bring the interface up, then test that it works.

```
debian5:~# ifup bond0
debian5:~# ifconfig bond0
bond0     Link encap:Ethernet  HWaddr 08:00:27:63:9a:95
          inet addr:192.168.1.42  Bcast:192.168.1.255  Mask:255.255.255.0
          inet6 addr: fe80::a00:27ff:fe63:9a95/64 Scope:Link
          UP BROADCAST RUNNING MASTER MULTICAST  MTU:1500  Metric:1
          RX packets:212 errors:0 dropped:0 overruns:0 frame:0
          TX packets:39 errors:0 dropped:0 overruns:0 carrier:0
          collisions:0 txqueuelen:0
          RX bytes:31978 (31.2 KiB)  TX bytes:6709 (6.5 KiB)
```

The **bond** should also be visible in **/proc/net/bonding**.

```
debian5:~# cat /proc/net/bonding/bond0
Ethernet Channel Bonding Driver: v3.2.5 (March 21, 2008)

Bonding Mode: fault-tolerance (active-backup)
Primary Slave: eth1
Currently Active Slave: eth1
MII Status: up
MII Polling Interval (ms): 0
Up Delay (ms): 0
Down Delay (ms): 0

Slave Interface: eth1
MII Status: up
Link Failure Count: 0
```

```
Permanent HW addr: 08:00:27:63:9a:95

Slave Interface: eth2
MII Status: up
Link Failure Count: 0
Permanent HW addr: 08:00:27:27:a4:92
```

24.5. practice: binding and bonding

1. Add an extra **ip address** to one of your network cards. Test that it works (have your neighbour ssh to it)!

2. Use **ifdown** to disable this extra **ip address**.

3. Make sure your neighbour also succeeded in **binding** an extra ip address before you continue.

4. Add an extra network card (or two) to your virtual machine and use the theory to **bond** two network cards.

24.6. solution: binding and bonding

1. Add an extra **ip address** to one of your network cards. Test that it works (have your neighbour ssh to it)!

```
Redhat/Fedora:
add an /etc/sysconfig/network-scripts/ifcfg-ethX:X file
as shown in the theory

Debian/Ubuntu:
expand the /etc/network/interfaces file
as shown in the theory
```

2. Use **ifdown** to disable this extra **ip address**.

```
ifdown eth0:0
```

3. Make sure your neighbour also succeeded in **binding** an extra ip address before you continue.

```
ping $extra_ip_neighbour
or
ssh $extra_ip_neighbour
```

4. Add an extra network card (or two) to your virtual machine and use the theory to **bond** two network cards.

```
Redhat/Fedora:
add ifcfg-ethX and ifcfg-bondX files in /etc/sysconfig/network-scripts
as shown in the theory
and don't forget the modprobe.conf

Debian/Ubuntu:
expand the /etc/network/interfaces file
as shown in the theory
and don't forget to install the ifenslave package
```

Chapter 25. ssh client and server

The **secure shell** or **ssh** is a collection of tools using a secure protocol for communications with remote Linux computers.

This chapter gives an overview of the most common commands related to the use of the **sshd** server and the **ssh** client.

25.1. about ssh

25.1.1. secure shell

Avoid using **telnet**, **rlogin** and **rsh** to remotely connect to your servers. These older protocols do not encrypt the login session, which means your user id and password can be sniffed by tools like **wireshark** or **tcpdump**. To securely connect to your servers, use **ssh**.

The **ssh protocol** is secure in two ways. Firstly the connection is **encrypted** and secondly the connection is **authenticated** both ways.

An ssh connection always starts with a cryptographic handshake, followed by **encryption** of the transport layer using a symmetric cypher. In other words, the tunnel is encrypted before you start typing anything.

Then **authentication** takes place (using user id/password or public/private keys) and communication can begin over the encrypted connection.

The **ssh protocol** will remember the servers it connected to (and warn you in case something suspicious happened).

The **openssh** package is maintained by the **OpenBSD** people and is distributed with a lot of operating systems (it may even be the most popular package in the world).

25.1.2. /etc/ssh/

Configuration of **ssh** client and server is done in the **/etc/ssh** directory. In the next sections we will discuss most of the files found in **/etc/ssh/**.

25.1.3. ssh protocol versions

The **ssh** protocol has two versions (1 and 2). Avoid using version 1 anywhere, since it contains some known vulnerabilities. You can control the protocol version via **/etc/ssh/ssh_config** for the client side and **/etc/ssh/sshd_config** for the openssh-server daemon.

```
paul@ubu1204:/etc/ssh$ grep Protocol ssh_config
#   Protocol 2,1
paul@ubu1204:/etc/ssh$ grep Protocol sshd_config
Protocol 2
```

25.1.4. public and private keys

The **ssh** protocol uses the well known system of **public and private keys**. The below explanation is succinct, more information can be found on wikipedia.

```
http://en.wikipedia.org/wiki/Public-key_cryptography
```

Imagine Alice and Bob, two people that like to communicate with each other. Using **public and private keys** they can communicate with **encryption** and with **authentication**.

When Alice wants to send an encrypted message to Bob, she uses the **public key** of Bob. Bob shares his **public key** with Alice, but keeps his **private key** private! Since Bob is the only one to have Bob's **private key**, Alice is sure that Bob is the only one that can read the encrypted message.

When Bob wants to verify that the message came from Alice, Bob uses the **public key** of Alice to verify that Alice signed the message with her **private key**. Since Alice is the only one to have Alice's **private key**, Bob is sure the message came from Alice.

25.1.5. rsa and dsa algorithms

This chapter does not explain the technical implementation of cryptographic algorithms, it only explains how to use the ssh tools with **rsa** and **dsa**. More information about these algorithms can be found here:

```
http://en.wikipedia.org/wiki/RSA_(algorithm)
http://en.wikipedia.org/wiki/Digital_Signature_Algorithm
```

25.2. log on to a remote server

The following screenshot shows how to use **ssh** to log on to a remote computer running Linux. The local user is named **paul** and he is logging on as user **admin42** on the remote system.

```
paul@ubu1204:~$ ssh admin42@192.168.1.30
The authenticity of host '192.168.1.30 (192.168.1.30)' can't be established.
RSA key fingerprint is b5:fb:3c:53:50:b4:ab:81:f3:cd:2e:bb:ba:44:d3:75.
Are you sure you want to continue connecting (yes/no)?
```

As you can see, the user **paul** is presented with an **rsa** authentication fingerprint from the remote system. The user can accepts this bu typing **yes**. We will see later that an entry will be added to the **~/.ssh/known_hosts** file.

```
paul@ubu1204:~$ ssh admin42@192.168.1.30
The authenticity of host '192.168.1.30 (192.168.1.30)' can't be established.
RSA key fingerprint is b5:fb:3c:53:50:b4:ab:81:f3:cd:2e:bb:ba:44:d3:75.
Are you sure you want to continue connecting (yes/no)? yes
Warning: Permanently added '192.168.1.30' (RSA) to the list of known hosts.
admin42@192.168.1.30's password:
Welcome to Ubuntu 12.04 LTS (GNU/Linux 3.2.0-26-generic-pae i686)

 * Documentation:  https://help.ubuntu.com/

1 package can be updated.
0 updates are security updates.

Last login: Wed Jun  6 19:25:57 2012 from 172.28.0.131
admin42@ubuserver:~$
```

The user can get log out of the remote server by typing **exit** or by using **Ctrl-d**.

```
admin42@ubuserver:~$ exit
logout
Connection to 192.168.1.30 closed.
paul@ubu1204:~$
```

25.3. executing a command in remote

This screenshot shows how to execute the **pwd** command on the remote server. There is no need to **exit** the server manually.

```
paul@ubu1204:~$ ssh admin42@192.168.1.30 pwd
admin42@192.168.1.30's password:
/home/admin42
paul@ubu1204:~$
```

25.4. scp

The **scp** command works just like **cp**, but allows the source and destination of the copy to be behind **ssh**. Here is an example where we copy the **/etc/hosts** file from the remote server to the home directory of user paul.

```
paul@ubu1204:~$ scp admin42@192.168.1.30:/etc/hosts /home/paul/serverhosts
admin42@192.168.1.30's password:
hosts                                          100%  809     0.8KB/s   00:00
```

Here is an example of the reverse, copying a local file to a remote server.

```
paul@ubu1204:~$ scp ~/serverhosts admin42@192.168.1.30:/etc/hosts.new
admin42@192.168.1.30's password:
serverhosts                                    100%  809     0.8KB/s   00:00
```

25.5. setting up passwordless ssh

To set up passwordless ssh authentication through public/private keys, use **ssh-keygen** to generate a key pair without a passphrase, and then copy your public key to the destination server. Let's do this step by step.

In the example that follows, we will set up ssh without password between Alice and Bob. Alice has an account on a Red Hat Enterprise Linux server, Bob is using Ubuntu on his laptop. Bob wants to give Alice access using ssh and the public and private key system. This means that even if Bob changes his password on his laptop, Alice will still have access.

25.5.1. ssh-keygen

The example below shows how Alice uses **ssh-keygen** to generate a key pair. Alice does not enter a passphrase.

```
[alice@RHEL5 ~]$ ssh-keygen -t rsa
Generating public/private rsa key pair.
Enter file in which to save the key (/home/alice/.ssh/id_rsa):
Created directory '/home/alice/.ssh'.
Enter passphrase (empty for no passphrase):
Enter same passphrase again:
Your identification has been saved in /home/alice/.ssh/id_rsa.
Your public key has been saved in /home/alice/.ssh/id_rsa.pub.
The key fingerprint is:
9b:ac:ac:56:c2:98:e5:d9:18:c4:2a:51:72:bb:45:eb alice@RHEL5
[alice@RHEL5 ~]$
```

You can use **ssh-keygen -t dsa** in the same way.

25.5.2. ~/.ssh

While **ssh-keygen** generates a public and a private key, it will also create a hidden **.ssh** directory with proper permissions. If you create the **.ssh** directory manually, then you need to chmod 700 it! Otherwise ssh will refuse to use the keys (world readable private keys are not secure!).

As you can see, the **.ssh** directory is secure in Alice's home directory.

```
[alice@RHEL5 ~]$ ls -ld .ssh
drwx------ 2 alice alice 4096 May  1 07:38 .ssh
[alice@RHEL5 ~]$
```

Bob is using Ubuntu at home. He decides to manually create the **.ssh** directory, so he needs to manually secure it.

```
bob@laika:~$ mkdir .ssh
bob@laika:~$ ls -ld .ssh
drwxr-xr-x 2 bob bob 4096 2008-05-14 16:53 .ssh
bob@laika:~$ chmod 700 .ssh/
bob@laika:~$
```

25.5.3. id_rsa and id_rsa.pub

The **ssh-keygen** command generate two keys in .ssh. The public key is named **~/.ssh/id_rsa.pub**. The private key is named **~/.ssh/id_rsa**.

```
[alice@RHEL5 ~]$ ls -l .ssh/
total 16
-rw------- 1 alice alice 1671 May  1 07:38 id_rsa
-rw-r--r-- 1 alice alice  393 May  1 07:38 id_rsa.pub
```

The files will be named **id_dsa** and **id_dsa.pub** when using **dsa** instead of **rsa**.

25.5.4. copy the public key to the other computer

To copy the public key from Alice's server tot Bob's laptop, Alice decides to use **scp**.

```
[alice@RHEL5 .ssh]$ scp id_rsa.pub bob@192.168.48.92:~/.ssh/authorized_keys
bob@192.168.48.92's password:
id_rsa.pub                                  100%  393     0.4KB/s   00:00
```

Be careful when copying a second key! Do not overwrite the first key, instead append the key to the same **~/.ssh/authorized_keys** file!

```
cat id_rsa.pub >> ~/.ssh/authorized_keys
```

Alice could also have used **ssh-copy-id** like in this example.

```
ssh-copy-id -i .ssh/id_rsa.pub bob@192.168.48.92
```

25.5.5. authorized_keys

In your ~/.ssh directory, you can create a file called **authorized_keys**. This file can contain one or more public keys from people you trust. Those trusted people can use their private keys to prove their identity and gain access to your account via ssh (without password). The example shows Bob's authorized_keys file containing the public key of Alice.

```
bob@laika:~$ cat .ssh/authorized_keys
ssh-rsa AAAAB3NzaC1yc2EAAAABIwAAAQEApCQ9xzyLzJes1sR+hPyqW2vyzt1D4zTLqk\
MDWBR4mMFuUZD/O583I3Lg/Q+JIq0RSksNzaL/BNLDou1jMpBe2Dmf/u22u4Kmq1JBfDhe\
yTmGSBzeNYCYRSMq78CT9l9a+y6x/shucwhaILsy8A2XfJ9VCggkVtu7X1WFDL2cum08/0\
mRFwVrfc/uPsAn5XkkTscl4g21mQbnp9wJC40pGSJXXMuFOk8MgCb5ieSnpKFniAKM+tEo\
/vjDGSi3F/bxu691jscrU0VUdIoOSo98HUfEf7jKBRikxGAC7I4HLa+/zX73OIvRFAb2hv\
tUhn6RHrBtUJUjbSGiYeFTLDfcTQ== alice@RHEL5
```

25.5.6. passwordless ssh

Alice can now use ssh to connect passwordless to Bob's laptop. In combination with **ssh**'s capability to execute commands on the remote host, this can be useful in pipes across different machines.

```
[alice@RHEL5 ~]$ ssh bob@192.168.48.92 "ls -l .ssh"
total 4
-rw-r--r-- 1 bob bob 393 2008-05-14 17:03 authorized_keys
[alice@RHEL5 ~]$
```

25.6. X forwarding via ssh

Another popular feature of **ssh** is called **X11 forwarding** and is implemented with **ssh -X**.

Below an example of X forwarding: user paul logs in as user greet on her computer to start the graphical application mozilla-thunderbird. Although the application will run on the remote computer from greet, it will be displayed on the screen attached locally to paul's computer.

```
paul@debian5:~/PDF$ ssh -X greet@greet.dyndns.org -p 55555
Warning: Permanently added the RSA host key for IP address \
'81.240.174.161' to the list of known hosts.
Password:
Linux raika 2.6.8-2-686 #1 Tue Aug 16 13:22:48 UTC 2005 i686 GNU/Linux

Last login: Thu Jan 18 12:35:56 2007
greet@raika:~$ ps fax | grep thun
greet@raika:~$ mozilla-thunderbird &
[1] 30336
```

25.7. troubleshooting ssh

Use **ssh -v** to get debug information about the ssh connection attempt.

```
paul@debian5:~$ ssh -v bert@192.168.1.192
OpenSSH_4.3p2 Debian-8ubuntu1, OpenSSL 0.9.8c 05 Sep 2006
debug1: Reading configuration data /home/paul/.ssh/config
debug1: Reading configuration data /etc/ssh/ssh_config
debug1: Applying options for *
debug1: Connecting to 192.168.1.192 [192.168.1.192] port 22.
debug1: Connection established.
debug1: identity file /home/paul/.ssh/identity type -1
debug1: identity file /home/paul/.ssh/id_rsa type 1
debug1: identity file /home/paul/.ssh/id_dsa type -1
debug1: Remote protocol version 1.99, remote software version OpenSSH_3
debug1: match: OpenSSH_3.9p1 pat OpenSSH_3.*
debug1: Enabling compatibility mode for protocol 2.0
...
```

25.8. sshd

The ssh server is called **sshd** and is provided by the **openssh-server** package.

```
root@ubu1204~# dpkg -l openssh-server | tail -1
ii  openssh-server   1:5.9p1-5ubuntu1    secure shell (SSH) server,...
```

25.9. sshd keys

The public keys used by the sshd server are located in **/etc/ssh** and are world readable. The private keys are only readable by root.

```
root@ubu1204~# ls -l /etc/ssh/ssh_host_*
-rw------- 1 root root  668 Jun  7  2011 /etc/ssh/ssh_host_dsa_key
-rw-r--r-- 1 root root  598 Jun  7  2011 /etc/ssh/ssh_host_dsa_key.pub
-rw------- 1 root root 1679 Jun  7  2011 /etc/ssh/ssh_host_rsa_key
-rw-r--r-- 1 root root  390 Jun  7  2011 /etc/ssh/ssh_host_rsa_key.pub
```

25.10. ssh-agent

When generating keys with **ssh-keygen**, you have the option to enter a passphrase to protect access to the keys. To avoid having to type this passphrase every time, you can add the key to **ssh-agent** using **ssh-add**.

Most Linux distributions will start the **ssh-agent** automatically when you log on.

```
root@ubu1204~# ps -ef | grep ssh-agent
paul      2405  2365  0 08:13 ?        00:00:00 /usr/bin/ssh-agent...
```

This clipped screenshot shows how to use **ssh-add** to list the keys that are currently added to the **ssh-agent**

```
paul@debian5:~$ ssh-add -L
ssh-rsa AAAAB3NzaC1yc2EAAAABIwAAAQEAvgI+Vx5UrIsusZPl8da8URHGsxG7yivv3/\
...
wMGqa48Kelwom8TGb4Sgcwpp/VO/1dA5m+BGCw== paul@deb503
```

25.11. practice: ssh

0. Make sure that you have access to **two Linux computers**, or work together with a partner for this exercise. For this practice, we will name one of the machines the server.

1. Install **sshd** on the server

2. Verify in the ssh configuration files that only protocol version 2 is allowed.

3. Use **ssh** to log on to the server, show your current directory and then exit the server.

4. Use **scp** to copy a file from your computer to the server.

5. Use **scp** to copy a file from the server to your computer.

6. (optional, only works when you have a graphical install of Linux) Install the xeyes package on the server and use ssh to run xeyes on the server, but display it on your client.

7. (optional, same as previous) Create a bookmark in firefox, then quit firefox on client and server. Use **ssh -X** to run firefox on your display, but on your neighbour's computer. Do you see your neighbour's bookmark ?

8. Use **ssh-keygen** to create a key pair without passphrase. Setup passwordless ssh between you and your neighbour. (or between your client and your server)

9. Verify that the permissions on the server key files are correct; world readable for the public keys and only root access for the private keys.

10. Verify that the **ssh-agent** is running.

11. (optional) Protect your keypair with a **passphrase**, then add this key to the **ssh-agent** and test your passwordless ssh to the server.

25.12. solution: ssh

0. Make sure that you have access to **two Linux computers**, or work together with a partner for this exercise. For this practice, we will name one of the machines the server.

1. Install **sshd** on the server

```
apt-get install openssh-server (on Ubuntu/Debian)
yum -y install openssh-server (on Centos/Fedora/Red Hat)
```

2. Verify in the ssh configuration files that only protocol version 2 is allowed.

```
grep Protocol /etc/ssh/ssh*_config
```

3. Use **ssh** to log on to the server, show your current directory and then exit the server.

```
user@client$ ssh user@server-ip-address
user@server$ pwd
/home/user
user@server$ exit
```

4. Use **scp** to copy a file from your computer to the server.

```
scp localfile user@server:~
```

5. Use **scp** to copy a file from the server to your computer.

```
scp user@server:~/serverfile .
```

6. (optional, only works when you have a graphical install of Linux) Install the xeyes package on the server and use ssh to run xeyes on the server, but display it on your client.

```
on the server:
apt-get install xeyes
on the client:
ssh -X user@server-ip
xeyes
```

7. (optional, same as previous) Create a bookmark in firefox, then quit firefox on client and server. Use **ssh -X** to run firefox on your display, but on your neighbour's computer. Do you see your neighbour's bookmark ?

8. Use **ssh-keygen** to create a key pair without passphrase. Setup passwordless ssh between you and your neighbour. (or between your client and your server)

```
See solution in book "setting up passwordless ssh"
```

9. Verify that the permissions on the server key files are correct; world readable for the public keys and only root access for the private keys.

```
ls -l /etc/ssh/ssh_host_*
```

10. Verify that the **ssh-agent** is running.

```
ps fax | grep ssh-agent
```

11. (optional) Protect your keypair with a **passphrase**, then add this key to the **ssh-agent** and test your passwordless ssh to the server.

```
man ssh-keygen
man ssh-agent
man ssh-add
```

Chapter 26. introduction to nfs

The **network file system** (or simply **nfs**) enables us since the Eighties to share a directory with other computers on the network.

In this chapter we see how to setup an **nfs** server and an **nfs** client computer.

26.1. nfs protocol versions

The older **nfs** versions 2 and 3 are stateless (**udp**) by default (but they can use **tcp**). The more recent **nfs version 4** brings a stateful protocol with better performance and stronger security.

NFS version 4 was defined in **rfc 3010** in 2000 and **rfc 3530** in 2003 and requires tcp (port 2049). It also supports **Kerberos** user authentication as an option when mounting a share. NFS versions 2 and 3 authenticate only the host.

26.2. rpcinfo

Clients connect to the server using **rpc** (on Linux this can be managed by the **portmap** daemon). Look at **rpcinfo** to verify that **nfs** and its related services are running.

```
root@RHELv4u2:~# /etc/init.d/portmap status
portmap (pid 1920) is running...
root@RHELv4u2:~# rpcinfo -p
program vers proto   port
100000    2   tcp    111  portmapper
100000    2   udp    111  portmapper
100024    1   udp  32768  status
100024    1   tcp  32769  status
root@RHELv4u2:~# service nfs start
Starting NFS services:                                     [  OK  ]
Starting NFS quotas:                                       [  OK  ]
Starting NFS daemon:                                       [  OK  ]
Starting NFS mountd:                                       [  OK  ]
```

The same **rpcinfo** command when **nfs** is started.

```
root@RHELv4u2:~# rpcinfo -p
program vers proto   port
100000    2   tcp    111  portmapper
100000    2   udp    111  portmapper
100024    1   udp  32768  status
100024    1   tcp  32769  status
100011    1   udp    985  rquotad
100011    2   udp    985  rquotad
100011    1   tcp    988  rquotad
100011    2   tcp    988  rquotad
100003    2   udp   2049  nfs
100003    3   udp   2049  nfs
100003    4   udp   2049  nfs
100003    2   tcp   2049  nfs
100003    3   tcp   2049  nfs
100003    4   tcp   2049  nfs
100021    1   udp  32770  nlockmgr
100021    3   udp  32770  nlockmgr
100021    4   udp  32770  nlockmgr
100021    1   tcp  32789  nlockmgr
100021    3   tcp  32789  nlockmgr
100021    4   tcp  32789  nlockmgr
100005    1   udp   1004  mountd
100005    1   tcp   1007  mountd
100005    2   udp   1004  mountd
100005    2   tcp   1007  mountd
100005    3   udp   1004  mountd
100005    3   tcp   1007  mountd
```

26.3. server configuration

nfs is configured in **/etc/exports**. You might want some way (**ldap**?) to synchronize userid's across computers when using **nfs** a lot.

The **rootsquash** option will change UID 0 to the UID of a **nobody** (or similar) user account. The **sync** option will write writes to disk before completing the client request.

26.4. /etc/exports

Here is a sample **/etc/exports** to explain the syntax:

```
paul@laika:~$ cat /etc/exports
# Everyone can read this share
/mnt/data/iso  *(ro)

# Only the computers named pasha and barry can readwrite this one
/var/www pasha(rw) barry(rw)

# same, but without root squashing for barry
/var/ftp pasha(rw) barry(rw,no_root_squash)

# everyone from the netsec.local domain gets access
/var/backup        *.netsec.local(rw)

# ro for one network, rw for the other
/var/upload   192.168.1.0/24(ro) 192.168.5.0/24(rw)
```

More recent incarnations of **nfs** require the **subtree_check** option to be explicitly set (or unset with **no_subtree_check**). The **/etc/exports** file then looks like this:

```
root@debian6 ~# cat /etc/exports
# Everyone can read this share
/srv/iso  *(ro,no_subtree_check)

# Only the computers named pasha and barry can readwrite this one
/var/www pasha(rw,no_subtree_check) barry(rw,no_subtree_check)

# same, but without root squashing for barry
/var/ftp pasha(rw,no_subtree_check) barry(rw,no_root_squash,no_subtree_check)
```

26.5. exportfs

You don't need to restart the nfs server to start exporting your newly created exports. You can use the **exportfs -va** command to do this. It will write the exported directories to **/var/lib/nfs/etab**, where they are immediately applied.

```
root@debian6 ~# exportfs -va
exporting pasha:/var/ftp
exporting barry:/var/ftp
exporting pasha:/var/www
exporting barry:/var/www
exporting *:/srv/iso
```

26.6. client configuration

We have seen the **mount** command and the **/etc/fstab** file before.

```
root@RHELv4u2:~# mount -t nfs barry:/mnt/data/iso /home/project55/
root@RHELv4u2:~# cat /etc/fstab | grep nfs
barry:/mnt/data/iso   /home/iso              nfs     defaults    0 0
root@RHELv4u2:~#
```

Here is another simple example. Suppose the project55 people tell you they only need a couple of CD-ROM images, and you already have them available on an **nfs** server. You could issue the following command to mount this storage on their **/home/project55** mount point.

```
root@RHELv4u2:~# mount -t nfs 192.168.1.40:/mnt/data/iso /home/project55/
root@RHELv4u2:~# ls -lh /home/project55/
total 3.6G
drwxr-xr-x  2 1000 1000 4.0K Jan 16 17:55 RHELv4u1
drwxr-xr-x  2 1000 1000 4.0K Jan 16 14:14 RHELv4u2
drwxr-xr-x  2 1000 1000 4.0K Jan 16 14:54 RHELv4u3
drwxr-xr-x  2 1000 1000 4.0K Jan 16 11:09 RHELv4u4
-rw-r--r--  1 root root 1.6G Oct 13 15:22 sled10-vmwarews5-vm.zip
root@RHELv4u2:~#
```

26.7. practice: introduction to nfs

1. Create two directories with some files. Use **nfs** to share one of them as read only, the other must be writable. Have your neighbour connect to them to test.

2. Investigate the user owner of the files created by your neighbour.

3. Protect a share by ip-address or hostname, so only your neighbour can connect.

Chapter 27. introduction to networking

27.1. introduction to iptables

27.1.1. iptables firewall

The Linux kernel has a built-in stateful firewall named **iptables**. To stop the **iptables** firewall on Red Hat, use the service command.

```
root@RHELv4u4:~# service iptables stop
Flushing firewall rules:                                  [  OK  ]
Setting chains to policy ACCEPT: filter                   [  OK  ]
Unloading iptables modules:                               [  OK  ]
root@RHELv4u4:~#
```

The easy way to configure iptables, is to use a graphical tool like KDE's **kmyfirewall** or **Security Level Configuration Tool**. You can find the latter in the graphical menu, somewhere in System Tools - Security, or you can start it by typing **system-config-securitylevel** in bash. These tools allow for some basic firewall configuration. You can decide whether to enable or disable the firewall, and what typical standard ports are allowed when the firewall is active. You can even add some custom ports. When you are done, the configuration is written to **/etc/sysconfig/iptables** on Red Hat.

```
root@RHELv4u4:~# cat /etc/sysconfig/iptables
# Firewall configuration written by system-config-securitylevel
# Manual customization of this file is not recommended.
*filter
:INPUT ACCEPT [0:0]
:FORWARD ACCEPT [0:0]
:OUTPUT ACCEPT [0:0]
:RH-Firewall-1-INPUT - [0:0]
-A INPUT -j RH-Firewall-1-INPUT
-A FORWARD -j RH-Firewall-1-INPUT
-A RH-Firewall-1-INPUT -i lo -j ACCEPT
-A RH-Firewall-1-INPUT -p icmp --icmp-type any -j ACCEPT
-A RH-Firewall-1-INPUT -p 50 -j ACCEPT
-A RH-Firewall-1-INPUT -p 51 -j ACCEPT
-A RH-Firewall-1-INPUT -p udp --dport 5353 -d 224.0.0.251 -j ACCEPT
-A RH-Firewall-1-INPUT -p udp -m udp --dport 631 -j ACCEPT
-A RH-Firewall-1-INPUT -m state --state ESTABLISHED,RELATED -j ACCEPT
-A RH-F...NPUT -m state --state NEW -m tcp -p tcp --dport 22 -j ACCEPT
-A RH-F...NPUT -m state --state NEW -m tcp -p tcp --dport 80 -j ACCEPT
-A RH-F...NPUT -m state --state NEW -m tcp -p tcp --dport 21 -j ACCEPT
-A RH-F...NPUT -m state --state NEW -m tcp -p tcp --dport 25 -j ACCEPT
-A RH-Firewall-1-INPUT -j REJECT --reject-with icmp-host-prohibited
COMMIT
root@RHELv4u4:~#
```

To start the service, issue the **service iptables start** command. You can configure iptables to start at boot time with chkconfig.

```
root@RHELv4u4:~# service iptables start
Applying iptables firewall rules:                         [  OK  ]
root@RHELv4u4:~# chkconfig iptables on
root@RHELv4u4:~#
```

One of the nice features of iptables is that it displays extensive **status** information when queried with the **service iptables status** command.

```
root@RHELv4u4:~# service iptables status
Table: filter
Chain INPUT (policy ACCEPT)
target     prot opt source               destination
RH-Firewall-1-INPUT  all  --  0.0.0.0/0            0.0.0.0/0

Chain FORWARD (policy ACCEPT)
target     prot opt source               destination
RH-Firewall-1-INPUT  all  --  0.0.0.0/0            0.0.0.0/0

Chain OUTPUT (policy ACCEPT)
target     prot opt source               destination

Chain RH-Firewall-1-INPUT (2 references)
target  prot opt source      destination
ACCEPT  all  --  0.0.0.0/0   0.0.0.0/0
ACCEPT  icmp --  0.0.0.0/0   0.0.0.0/0   icmp type 255
ACCEPT  esp  --  0.0.0.0/0   0.0.0.0/0
ACCEPT  ah   --  0.0.0.0/0   0.0.0.0/0
ACCEPT  udp  --  0.0.0.0/0   224.0.0.251 udp dpt:5353
ACCEPT  udp  --  0.0.0.0/0   0.0.0.0/0   udp dpt:631
ACCEPT  all  --  0.0.0.0/0   0.0.0.0/0   state RELATED,ESTABLISHED
ACCEPT  tcp  --  0.0.0.0/0   0.0.0.0/0   state NEW tcp dpt:22
ACCEPT  tcp  --  0.0.0.0/0   0.0.0.0/0   state NEW tcp dpt:80
ACCEPT  tcp  --  0.0.0.0/0   0.0.0.0/0   state NEW tcp dpt:21
ACCEPT  tcp  --  0.0.0.0/0   0.0.0.0/0   state NEW tcp dpt:25
REJECT  all  --  0.0.0.0/0   0.0.0.0/0   reject-with icmp-host-prohibited

root@RHELv4u4:~#
```

Mastering firewall configuration requires a decent knowledge of tcp/ip. Good iptables tutorials can be found online here http://iptables-tutorial.frozentux.net/iptables-tutorial.html and here http://tldp.org/HOWTO/IP-Masquerade-HOWTO/.

27.2. practice : iptables

1. Verify whether the firewall is running.

2. Stop the running firewall.

27.3. solution : iptables

1. Verify whether the firewall is running.

```
root@rhel55 ~# service iptables status | head
Table: filter
Chain INPUT (policy ACCEPT)
num  target     prot opt source               destination
1    RH-Firewall-1-INPUT  all  --  0.0.0.0/0            0.0.0.0/0

Chain FORWARD (policy ACCEPT)
num  target     prot opt source               destination
1    RH-Firewall-1-INPUT  all  --  0.0.0.0/0            0.0.0.0/0

Chain OUTPUT (policy ACCEPT)
```

2. Stop the running firewall.

```
root@rhel55 ~# service iptables stop
Flushing firewall rules:                                   [  OK  ]
Setting chains to policy ACCEPT: filter                    [  OK  ]
Unloading iptables modules:                                [  OK  ]
root@rhel55 ~# service iptables status
Firewall is stopped.
```

27.4. xinetd and inetd

27.4.1. the superdaemon

Back when resources like RAM memory were limited, a super-server was devised to listen to all sockets and start the appropriate daemon only when needed. Services like **swat**, **telnet** and **ftp** are typically served by such a super-server. The **xinetd** superdaemon is more recent than **inetd**. We will discuss the configuration both daemons.

Recent Linux distributions like RHEL5 and Ubuntu10.04 do not activate **inetd** or **xinetd** by default, unless an application requires it.

27.4.2. inetd or xinetd

First verify whether your computer is running **inetd** or **xinetd**. This Debian 4.0 Etch is running **inetd**.

```
root@barry:~# ps fax | grep inet
 3870 ?        Ss     0:00 /usr/sbin/inetd
```

This Red Hat Enterprise Linux 4 update 4 is running **xinetd**.

```
[root@RHEL4b ~]# ps fax | grep inet
 3003 ?        Ss     0:00 xinetd -stayalive -pidfile /var/run/xinetd.pid
```

Both daemons have the same functionality (listening to many ports, starting other daemons when they are needed), but they have different configuration files.

27.4.3. xinetd superdaemon

The **xinetd** daemon is often called a superdaemon because it listens to a lot of incoming connections, and starts other daemons when they are needed. When a connection request is received, **xinetd** will first check TCP wrappers (/etc/hosts.allow and /etc/hosts.deny) and then give control of the connection to the other daemon. This superdaemon is configured through **/etc/xinetd.conf** and the files in the directory **/etc/xinetd.d**. Let's first take a look at /etc/xinetd.conf.

```
paul@RHELv4u2:~$ cat /etc/xinetd.conf
#
# Simple configuration file for xinetd
#
# Some defaults, and include /etc/xinetd.d/

defaults
{
instances                = 60
log_type                 = SYSLOG authpriv
log_on_success           = HOST PID
log_on_failure           = HOST
cps                      = 25 30
```

```
}

includedir /etc/xinetd.d

paul@RHELv4u2:~$
```

According to the settings in this file, xinetd can handle 60 client requests at once. It uses the **authpriv** facility to log the host ip-address and pid of successful daemon spawns. When a service (aka protocol linked to daemon) gets more than 25 cps (connections per second), it holds subsequent requests for 30 seconds.

The directory **/etc/xinetd.d** contains more specific configuration files. Let's also take a look at one of them.

```
paul@RHELv4u2:~$ ls /etc/xinetd.d
amanda      chargen-udp  echo      klogin       rexec   talk
amandaidx   cups-lpd     echo-udp  krb5-telnet  rlogin  telnet
amidxtape   daytime      eklogin   kshell       rsh     tftp
auth        daytime-udp  finger    ktalk        rsync   time
chargen     dbskkd-cdb   gssftp    ntalk        swat    time-udp
paul@RHELv4u2:~$ cat /etc/xinetd.d/swat
# default: off
# description: SWAT is the Samba Web Admin Tool. Use swat \
#              to configure your Samba server. To use SWAT, \
#              connect to port 901 with your favorite web browser.
service swat
{
port            = 901
socket_type     = stream
wait            = no
only_from       = 127.0.0.1
user            = root
server          = /usr/sbin/swat
log_on_failure  += USERID
disable         = yes
}
paul@RHELv4u2:~$
```

The services should be listed in the **/etc/services** file. Port determines the service port, and must be the same as the port specified in /etc/services. The **socket_type** should be set to **stream** for tcp services (and to dgram for udp). The **log_on_failure** += concats the userid to the log message formatted in /etc/xinetd.conf. The last setting **disable** can be set to yes or no. Setting this to **no** means the service is enabled!

Check the xinetd and xinetd.conf manual pages for many more configuration options.

27.4.4. inetd superdaemon

This superdaemon has only one configuration file **/etc/inetd.conf**. Every protocol or daemon that it is listening for, gets one line in this file.

```
root@barry:~# grep ftp /etc/inetd.conf
tftp dgram udp wait nobody /usr/sbin/tcpd /usr/sbin/in.tftpd /boot/tftp
root@barry:~#
```

You can disable a service in inetd.conf above by putting a # at the start of that line. Here an example of the disabled vmware web interface (listening on tcp port 902).

```
paul@laika:~$ grep vmware /etc/inetd.conf
#902 stream tcp nowait root /usr/sbin/vmware-authd vmware-authd
```

27.5. practice : inetd and xinetd

1. Verify on all systems whether they are using xinetd or inetd.

2. Look at the configuration files.

3. (If telnet is installable, then replace swat in these questions with telnet) Is swat installed ? If not, then install swat and look at the changes in the (x)inetd configuration. Is swat enabled or disabled ?

4. Disable swat, test it. Enable swat, test it.

27.6. network file system

27.6.1. protocol versions

The older **nfs** versions 2 and 3 are stateless (udp) by default, but they can use tcp. Clients connect to the server using **rpc** (on Linux this is controlled by the **portmap** daemon. Look at **rpcinfo** to verify that **nfs** and its related services are running.

```
root@RHELv4u2:~# /etc/init.d/portmap status
portmap (pid 1920) is running...
root@RHELv4u2:~# rpcinfo -p
program vers proto   port
100000    2   tcp    111  portmapper
100000    2   udp    111  portmapper
100024    1   udp  32768  status
100024    1   tcp  32769  status
root@RHELv4u2:~# service nfs start
Starting NFS services:                                     [  OK  ]
Starting NFS quotas:                                       [  OK  ]
Starting NFS daemon:                                       [  OK  ]
Starting NFS mountd:                                       [  OK  ]
```

The same **rpcinfo** command when **nfs** is started.

```
root@RHELv4u2:~# rpcinfo -p
program vers proto   port
100000    2   tcp    111  portmapper
100000    2   udp    111  portmapper
100024    1   udp  32768  status
100024    1   tcp  32769  status
100011    1   udp    985  rquotad
100011    2   udp    985  rquotad
100011    1   tcp    988  rquotad
100011    2   tcp    988  rquotad
100003    2   udp   2049  nfs
100003    3   udp   2049  nfs
100003    4   udp   2049  nfs
100003    2   tcp   2049  nfs
100003    3   tcp   2049  nfs
100003    4   tcp   2049  nfs
100021    1   udp  32770  nlockmgr
100021    3   udp  32770  nlockmgr
100021    4   udp  32770  nlockmgr
100021    1   tcp  32789  nlockmgr
100021    3   tcp  32789  nlockmgr
100021    4   tcp  32789  nlockmgr
100005    1   udp   1004  mountd
100005    1   tcp   1007  mountd
100005    2   udp   1004  mountd
100005    2   tcp   1007  mountd
100005    3   udp   1004  mountd
100005    3   tcp   1007  mountd
root@RHELv4u2:~#
```

nfs version 4 requires tcp (port 2049) and supports **Kerberos** user authentication as an option. **nfs** authentication only takes place when mounting the share. **nfs** versions 2 and 3 authenticate only the host.

27.6.2. server configuration

nfs is configured in **/etc/exports**. Here is a sample **/etc/exports** to explain the syntax. You need some way (NIS domain or LDAP) to synchronize userid's across computers when using **nfs** a lot. The **rootsquash** option will change UID 0 to the UID of the nfsnobody user account. The **sync** option will write writes to disk before completing the client request.

```
paul@laika:~$ cat /etc/exports
# Everyone can read this share
/mnt/data/iso  *(ro)

# Only the computers barry and pasha can readwrite this one
/var/www pasha(rw) barry(rw)

# same, but without root squashing for barry
/var/ftp pasha(rw) barry(rw,no_root_squash)

# everyone from the netsec.lan domain gets access
/var/backup       *.netsec.lan(rw)

# ro for one network, rw for the other
/var/upload   192.168.1.0/24(ro) 192.168.5.0/24(rw)
```

You don't need to restart the nfs server to start exporting your newly created exports. You can use the **exportfs -va** command to do this. It will write the exported directories to **/var/lib/nfs/etab**, where they are immediately applied.

27.6.3. client configuration

We have seen the **mount** command and the **/etc/fstab** file before.

```
root@RHELv4u2:~# mount -t nfs barry:/mnt/data/iso /home/project55/
root@RHELv4u2:~# cat /etc/fstab | grep nfs
barry:/mnt/data/iso    /home/iso               nfs     defaults     0 0
root@RHELv4u2:~#
```

Here is another simple example. Suppose the project55 people tell you they only need a couple of CD-ROM images, and you already have them available on an **nfs** server. You could issue the following command to mount this storage on their **/home/project55** mount point.

```
root@RHELv4u2:~# mount -t nfs 192.168.1.40:/mnt/data/iso /home/project55/
root@RHELv4u2:~# ls -lh /home/project55/
total 3.6G
drwxr-xr-x  2 1000 1000 4.0K Jan 16 17:55 RHELv4u1
drwxr-xr-x  2 1000 1000 4.0K Jan 16 14:14 RHELv4u2
drwxr-xr-x  2 1000 1000 4.0K Jan 16 14:54 RHELv4u3
drwxr-xr-x  2 1000 1000 4.0K Jan 16 11:09 RHELv4u4
-rw-r--r--  1 root root 1.6G Oct 13 15:22 sled10-vmwarews5-vm.zip
root@RHELv4u2:~#
```

27.7. practice : network file system

1. Create two directories with some files. Use **nfs** to share one of them as read only, the other must be writable. Have your neighbour connect to them to test.

2. Investigate the user owner of the files created by your neighbour.

3. Protect a share by ip-address or hostname, so only your neighbour can connect.

Part VI. kernel management

Table of Contents

Chapter 28. the Linux kernel

28.1. about the Linux kernel

28.1.1. kernel versions

In 1991 Linux Torvalds wrote (the first version of) the Linux kernel. He put it online, and other people started contributing code. Over 4000 individuals contributed source code to the latest kernel release (version 2.6.27 in November 2008).

Major Linux kernel versions used to come in even and odd numbers. Versions **2.0**, **2.2**, **2.4** and **2.6** are considered stable kernel versions. Whereas **2.1**, **2.3** and **2.5** were unstable (read development) versions. Since the release of 2.6.0 in January 2004, all development has been done in the 2.6 tree. There is currently no v2.7.x and according to Linus the even/stable vs odd/development scheme is abandoned forever.

28.1.2. uname -r

To see your current Linux kernel version, issue the **uname -r** command as shown below.

This first example shows Linux major version **2.6** and minor version **24**. The rest **-22-generic** is specific to the distribution (Ubuntu in this case).

```
paul@laika:~$ uname -r
2.6.24-22-generic
```

The same command on Red Hat Enterprise Linux shows an older kernel (2.6.18) with **-92.1.17.el5** being specific to the distribution.

```
[paul@RHEL52 ~]$ uname -r
2.6.18-92.1.17.el5
```

28.1.3. /proc/cmdline

The parameters that were passed to the kernel at boot time are in **/proc/cmdline**.

```
paul@RHELv4u4:~$ cat /proc/cmdline
ro root=/dev/VolGroup00/LogVol00 rhgb quiet
```

28.1.4. single user mode

When booting the kernel with the **single** parameter, it starts in **single user mode**. Linux can start in a bash shell with the **root** user logged on (without password).

Some distributions prevent the use of this feature (at kernel compile time).

28.1.5. init=/bin/bash

Normally the kernel invokes **init** as the first daemon process. Adding **init=/bin/bash** to the kernel parameters will instead invoke bash (again with root logged on without providing a password).

28.1.6. /var/log/messages

The kernel reports during boot to **syslog** which writes a lot of kernel actions in **/var/log/messages**. Looking at this file reveals when the kernel was started, including all the devices that were detected at boot time.

```
[root@RHEL53 ~]# grep -A16 "syslogd 1.4.1:" /var/log/messages|cut -b24-
syslogd 1.4.1: restart.
kernel: klogd 1.4.1, log source = /proc/kmsg started.
kernel: Linux version 2.6.18-128.el5 (mockbuild@hs20-bc1-5.build.red...
kernel: BIOS-provided physical RAM map:
kernel:  BIOS-e820: 0000000000000000 - 000000000009f800 (usable)
kernel:  BIOS-e820: 000000000009f800 - 00000000000a0000 (reserved)
kernel:  BIOS-e820: 00000000000ca000 - 00000000000cc000 (reserved)
kernel:  BIOS-e820: 00000000000dc000 - 0000000000100000 (reserved)
kernel:  BIOS-e820: 0000000000100000 - 000000001fef0000 (usable)
kernel:  BIOS-e820: 000000001fef0000 - 000000001feff000 (ACPI data)
kernel:  BIOS-e820: 000000001feff000 - 000000001ff00000 (ACPI NVS)
kernel:  BIOS-e820: 000000001ff00000 - 0000000020000000 (usable)
kernel:  BIOS-e820: 00000000fec00000 - 00000000fec10000 (reserved)
kernel:  BIOS-e820: 00000000fee00000 - 00000000fee01000 (reserved)
kernel:  BIOS-e820: 00000000fffe0000 - 0000000100000000 (reserved)
kernel: 0MB HIGHMEM available.
kernel: 512MB LOWMEM available.
```

This example shows how to use **/var/log/messages** to see kernel information about **/dev/sda**.

```
[root@RHEL53 ~]# grep sda /var/log/messages | cut -b24-
kernel: SCSI device sda: 41943040 512-byte hdwr sectors (21475 MB)
kernel: sda: Write Protect is off
kernel: sda: cache data unavailable
kernel: sda: assuming drive cache: write through
kernel: SCSI device sda: 41943040 512-byte hdwr sectors (21475 MB)
kernel: sda: Write Protect is off
kernel: sda: cache data unavailable
kernel: sda: assuming drive cache: write through
kernel:  sda: sda1 sda2
kernel: sd 0:0:0:0: Attached scsi disk sda
kernel: EXT3 FS on sda1, internal journal
```

28.1.7. dmesg

The **dmesg** command prints out all the kernel bootup messages (from the last boot).

```
[root@RHEL53 ~]# dmesg | head
Linux version 2.6.18-128.el5 (mockbuild@hs20-bc1-5.build.redhat.com)
BIOS-provided physical RAM map:
 BIOS-e820: 0000000000000000 - 000000000009f800 (usable)
 BIOS-e820: 000000000009f800 - 00000000000a0000 (reserved)
 BIOS-e820: 00000000000ca000 - 00000000000cc000 (reserved)
 BIOS-e820: 00000000000dc000 - 0000000000100000 (reserved)
 BIOS-e820: 0000000000100000 - 000000001fef0000 (usable)
 BIOS-e820: 000000001fef0000 - 000000001feff000 (ACPI data)
 BIOS-e820: 000000001feff000 - 000000001ff00000 (ACPI NVS)
 BIOS-e820: 000000001ff00000 - 0000000020000000 (usable)
```

Thus to find information about /dev/sda, using **dmesg** will yield only kernel messages from the last boot.

```
[root@RHEL53 ~]# dmesg | grep sda
SCSI device sda: 41943040 512-byte hdwr sectors (21475 MB)
sda: Write Protect is off
sda: Mode Sense: 5d 00 00 00
sda: cache data unavailable
sda: assuming drive cache: write through
SCSI device sda: 41943040 512-byte hdwr sectors (21475 MB)
sda: Write Protect is off
sda: Mode Sense: 5d 00 00 00
sda: cache data unavailable
sda: assuming drive cache: write through
 sda: sda1 sda2
sd 0:0:0:0: Attached scsi disk sda
EXT3 FS on sda1, internal journal
```

28.2. Linux kernel source

28.2.1. ftp.kernel.org

The home of the Linux kernel source is **ftp.kernel.org**. It contains all official releases of the Linux kernel source code from 1991. It provides free downloads over http, ftp and rsync of all these releases, as well as changelogs and patches. More information can be otained on the website **www.kernel.org**.

Anyone can anonymously use an ftp client to access ftp.kernel.org

```
paul@laika:~$ ftp ftp.kernel.org
Connected to pub3.kernel.org.
220 Welcome to ftp.kernel.org.
Name (ftp.kernel.org:paul): anonymous
331 Please specify the password.
Password:
230-        Welcome to the
230-
230-    LINUX KERNEL ARCHIVES
230-        ftp.kernel.org
```

All the Linux kernel versions are located in the pub/linux/kernel/ directory.

```
ftp> ls pub/linux/kernel/v*
200 PORT command successful. Consider using PASV.
150 Here comes the directory listing.
drwxrwsr-x    2 536       536          4096 Mar 20  2003 v1.0
drwxrwsr-x    2 536       536         20480 Mar 20  2003 v1.1
drwxrwsr-x    2 536       536          8192 Mar 20  2003 v1.2
drwxrwsr-x    2 536       536         40960 Mar 20  2003 v1.3
drwxrwsr-x    3 536       536         16384 Feb 08  2004 v2.0
drwxrwsr-x    2 536       536         53248 Mar 20  2003 v2.1
drwxrwsr-x    3 536       536         12288 Mar 24  2004 v2.2
drwxrwsr-x    2 536       536         24576 Mar 20  2003 v2.3
drwxrwsr-x    5 536       536         28672 Dec 02 08:14 v2.4
drwxrwsr-x    4 536       536         32768 Jul 14  2003 v2.5
drwxrwsr-x    7 536       536        110592 Dec 05 22:36 v2.6
226 Directory send OK.
ftp>
```

28.2.2. /usr/src

On your local computer, the kernel source is located in **/usr/src**. Note though that the structure inside /usr/src might be different depending on the distribution that you are using.

First let's take a look at **/usr/src on Debian**. There appear to be two versions of the complete Linux source code there. Looking for a specific file (e1000_main.c) with find reveals it's exact location.

```
paul@barry:~$ ls -l /usr/src/
drwxr-xr-x 20 root root     4096 2006-04-04 22:12 linux-source-2.6.15
drwxr-xr-x 19 root root     4096 2006-07-15 17:32 linux-source-2.6.16
paul@barry:~$ find /usr/src -name e1000_main.c
/usr/src/linux-source-2.6.15/drivers/net/e1000/e1000_main.c
/usr/src/linux-source-2.6.16/drivers/net/e1000/e1000_main.c
```

This is very similar to **/usr/src on Ubuntu**, except there is only one kernel here (and it is newer).

```
paul@laika:~$ ls -l /usr/src/
drwxr-xr-x 23 root root     4096 2008-11-24 23:28 linux-source-2.6.24
paul@laika:~$ find /usr/src -name "e1000_main.c"
/usr/src/linux-source-2.6.24/drivers/net/e1000/e1000_main.c
```

Now take a look at **/usr/src on Red Hat Enterprise Linux.**

```
[paul@RHEL52 ~]$ ls -l /usr/src/
drwxr-xr-x 5 root root 4096 Dec  5 19:23 kernels
drwxr-xr-x 7 root root 4096 Oct 11 13:22 redhat
```

We will have to dig a little deeper to find the kernel source on Red Hat!

```
[paul@RHEL52 ~]$ cd /usr/src/redhat/BUILD/
[paul@RHEL52 BUILD]$ find . -name "e1000_main.c"
./kernel-2.6.18/linux-2.6.18.i686/drivers/net/e1000/e1000_main.c
```

28.2.3. downloading the kernel source

Debian

Installing the kernel source on Debian is really simple with **aptitude install linux-source**. You can do a search for all linux-source packeges first, like in this screenshot.

```
root@barry:~# aptitude search linux-source
v   linux-source            -
v   linux-source-2.6        -
id  linux-source-2.6.15     - Linux kernel source for version 2.6.15
i   linux-source-2.6.16     - Linux kernel source for version 2.6.16
p   linux-source-2.6.18     - Linux kernel source for version 2.6.18
p   linux-source-2.6.24     - Linux kernel source for version 2.6.24
```

And then use **aptitude install** to download and install the Debian Linux kernel source code.

```
root@barry:~# aptitude install linux-source-2.6.24
```

When the aptitude is finished, you will see a new file named **/usr/src/linux-source-<version>.tar.bz2**

```
root@barry:/usr/src# ls -lh
drwxr-xr-x 20 root root 4.0K 2006-04-04 22:12 linux-source-2.6.15
drwxr-xr-x 19 root root 4.0K 2006-07-15 17:32 linux-source-2.6.16
-rw-r--r--  1 root root  45M 2008-12-02 10:56 linux-source-2.6.24.tar.bz2
```

Ubuntu

Ubuntu is based on Debian and also uses **aptitude**, so the task is very similar.

```
root@laika:~# aptitude search linux-source
i   linux-source            - Linux kernel source with Ubuntu patches
v   linux-source-2.6        -
i A linux-source-2.6.24     - Linux kernel source for version 2.6.24
root@laika:~# aptitude install linux-source
```

And when aptitude finishes, we end up with a **/usr/src/linux-source-<version>.tar.bz** file.

```
oot@laika:~# ll /usr/src
total 45M
-rw-r--r--  1 root root  45M 2008-11-24 23:30 linux-source-2.6.24.tar.bz2
```

Red Hat Enterprise Linux

The Red Hat kernel source is located on the fourth source cdrom. The file is called **kernel-2.6.9-42.EL.src.rpm** (example for RHELv4u4). It is also available online at ftp://ftp.redhat.com/pub/redhat/linux/enterprise/5Server/en/os/SRPMS/ (example for RHEL5).

To download the kernel source on RHEL, use this long wget command (on one line, without the trailing \).

```
wget ftp://ftp.redhat.com/pub/redhat/linux/enterprise/5Server/en/os/\
SRPMS/kernel-`uname -r`.src.rpm
```

When the wget download is finished, you end up with a 60M .rpm file.

```
[root@RHEL52 src]# ll
total 60M
-rw-r--r-- 1 root root  60M Dec  5 20:54 kernel-2.6.18-92.1.17.el5.src.rpm
drwxr-xr-x 5 root root 4.0K Dec  5 19:23 kernels
drwxr-xr-x 7 root root 4.0K Oct 11 13:22 redhat
```

We will need to perform some more steps before this can be used as kernel source code.

First, we issue the **rpm -i kernel-2.6.9-42.EL.src.rpm** command to install this Red Hat package.

```
[root@RHEL52 src]# ll
total 60M
-rw-r--r-- 1 root root  60M Dec  5 20:54 kernel-2.6.18-92.1.17.el5.src.rpm
drwxr-xr-x 5 root root 4.0K Dec  5 19:23 kernels
drwxr-xr-x 7 root root 4.0K Oct 11 13:22 redhat
[root@RHEL52 src]# rpm -i kernel-2.6.18-92.1.17.el5.src.rpm
```

Then we move to the SPECS directory and perform an **rpmbuild**.

```
[root@RHEL52 ~]# cd /usr/src/redhat/SPECS
[root@RHEL52 SPECS]# rpmbuild -bp -vv --target=i686 kernel-2.6.spec
```

The rpmbuild command put the RHEL Linux kernel source code in **/usr/src/redhat/BUILD/kernel-<version>/**.

```
[root@RHEL52 kernel-2.6.18]# pwd
/usr/src/redhat/BUILD/kernel-2.6.18
[root@RHEL52 kernel-2.6.18]# ll
total 20K
drwxr-xr-x  2 root root 4.0K Dec  6  2007 config
-rw-r--r--  1 root root 3.1K Dec  5 20:58 Config.mk
drwxr-xr-x 20 root root 4.0K Dec  5 20:58 linux-2.6.18.i686
drwxr-xr-x 19 root root 4.0K Sep 20  2006 vanilla
drwxr-xr-x  8 root root 4.0K Dec  6  2007 xen
```

28.3. kernel boot files

28.3.1. vmlinuz

The **vmlinuz** file in /boot is the compressed kernel.

```
paul@barry:~$ ls -lh /boot | grep vmlinuz
-rw-r--r-- 1 root root 1.2M 2006-03-06 16:22 vmlinuz-2.6.15-1-486
-rw-r--r-- 1 root root 1.1M 2006-03-06 16:30 vmlinuz-2.6.15-1-686
-rw-r--r-- 1 root root 1.3M 2008-02-11 00:00 vmlinuz-2.6.18-6-686
paul@barry:~$
```

28.3.2. initrd

The kernel uses **initrd** (an initial RAM disk) at boot time. The initrd is mounted before the kernel loads, and can contain additional drivers and modules. It is a **compressed cpio archive**, so you can look at the contents in this way.

```
root@RHELv4u4:/boot# mkdir /mnt/initrd
root@RHELv4u4:/boot# cp initrd-2.6.9-42.0.3.EL.img TMPinitrd.gz
root@RHELv4u4:/boot# gunzip TMPinitrd.gz
root@RHELv4u4:/boot# file TMPinitrd
TMPinitrd: ASCII cpio archive (SVR4 with no CRC)
root@RHELv4u4:/boot# cd /mnt/initrd/
root@RHELv4u4:/mnt/initrd# cpio -i | /boot/TMPinitrd
4985 blocks
root@RHELv4u4:/mnt/initrd# ls -l
total 76
drwxr-xr-x  2 root root 4096 Feb  5 08:36 bin
drwxr-xr-x  2 root root 4096 Feb  5 08:36 dev
drwxr-xr-x  4 root root 4096 Feb  5 08:36 etc
-rwxr-xr-x  1 root root 1607 Feb  5 08:36 init
drwxr-xr-x  2 root root 4096 Feb  5 08:36 lib
drwxr-xr-x  2 root root 4096 Feb  5 08:36 loopfs
drwxr-xr-x  2 root root 4096 Feb  5 08:36 proc
lrwxrwxrwx  1 root root    3 Feb  5 08:36 sbin -> bin
drwxr-xr-x  2 root root 4096 Feb  5 08:36 sys
drwxr-xr-x  2 root root 4096 Feb  5 08:36 sysroot
root@RHELv4u4:/mnt/initrd#
```

28.3.3. System.map

The **System.map** contains the symbol table and changes with every kernel compile. The symbol table is also present in **/proc/kallsyms** (pre 2.6 kernels name this file /proc/ksyms).

```
root@RHELv4u4:/boot# head System.map-`uname -r`
00000400 A __kernel_vsyscall
0000041a A SYSENTER_RETURN_OFFSET
00000420 A __kernel_sigreturn
00000440 A __kernel_rt_sigreturn
c0100000 A _text
c0100000 T startup_32
c01000c6 t checkCPUtype
c0100147 t is486
c010014e t is386
c010019f t L6
root@RHELv4u4:/boot# head /proc/kallsyms
c0100228 t _stext
c0100228 t calibrate_delay_direct
c0100228 t stext
c0100337 t calibrate_delay
c01004db t rest_init
c0100580 t do_pre_smp_initcalls
c0100585 t run_init_process
c01005ac t init
c0100789 t early_param_test
c01007ad t early_setup_test
root@RHELv4u4:/boot#
```

28.3.4. .config

The last file copied to the /boot directory is the kernel configuration used for compilation. This file is not necessary in the /boot directory, but it is common practice to put a copy there. It allows you to recompile a kernel, starting from the same configuration as an existing working one.

28.4. Linux kernel modules

28.4.1. about kernel modules

The Linux kernel is a monolithic kernel with loadable modules. These modules contain parts of the kernel used typically for device drivers, file systems and network protocols. Most of the time the necessary kernel modules are loaded automatically and dynamically without administrator interaction.

28.4.2. /lib/modules

The modules are stored in the **/lib/modules/<kernel-version>** directory. There is a separate directory for each kernel that was compiled for your system.

```
paul@laika:~$ ll /lib/modules/
total 12K
drwxr-xr-x 7 root root 4.0K 2008-11-10 14:32 2.6.24-16-generic
drwxr-xr-x 8 root root 4.0K 2008-12-06 15:39 2.6.24-21-generic
drwxr-xr-x 8 root root 4.0K 2008-12-05 12:58 2.6.24-22-generic
```

28.4.3. <module>.ko

The file containing the modules usually ends in **.ko**. This screenshot shows the location of the isdn module files.

```
paul@laika:~$ find /lib/modules -name isdn.ko
/lib/modules/2.6.24-21-generic/kernel/drivers/isdn/i4l/isdn.ko
/lib/modules/2.6.24-22-generic/kernel/drivers/isdn/i4l/isdn.ko
/lib/modules/2.6.24-16-generic/kernel/drivers/isdn/i4l/isdn.ko
```

28.4.4. lsmod

To see a list of currently loaded modules, use **lsmod**. You see the name of each loaded module, the size, the use count, and the names of other modules using this one.

```
[root@RHEL52 ~]# lsmod | head -5
Module                  Size  Used by
autofs4                24517  2
hidp                   23105  2
rfcomm                 42457  0
l2cap                  29505  10 hidp,rfcomm
```

28.4.5. /proc/modules

/proc/modules lists all modules loaded by the kernel. The output would be too long to display here, so lets **grep** for the **vm** module.

We see that vmmon and vmnet are both loaded. You can display the same information with **lsmod**. Actually **lsmod** only reads and reformats the output of **/proc/modules**.

```
paul@laika:~$ cat /proc/modules | grep vm
vmnet 36896 13 - Live 0xffffffff88b21000 (P)
vmmon 194540 0 - Live 0xffffffff88af0000 (P)
paul@laika:~$ lsmod | grep vm
vmnet                  36896  13
vmmon                 194540  0
paul@laika:~$
```

28.4.6. module dependencies

Some modules depend on others. In the following example, you can see that the nfsd module is used by exportfs, lockd and sunrpc.

```
paul@laika:~$ cat /proc/modules | grep nfsd
nfsd 267432 17 - Live 0xffffffff88a40000
exportfs 7808 1 nfsd, Live 0xffffffff88a3d000
lockd 73520 3 nfs,nfsd, Live 0xffffffff88a2a000
sunrpc 185032 12 nfs,nfsd,lockd, Live 0xffffffff889fb000
paul@laika:~$ lsmod | grep nfsd
nfsd                  267432  17
exportfs                7808  1 nfsd
lockd                  73520  3 nfs,nfsd
sunrpc                185032  12 nfs,nfsd,lockd
paul@laika:~$
```

28.4.7. insmod

Kernel modules can be manually loaded with the **insmod** command. This is a very simple (and obsolete) way of loading modules. The screenshot shows **insmod** loading the fat module (for fat file system support).

```
root@barry:/lib/modules/2.6.17-2-686# lsmod | grep fat
root@barry:/lib/modules/2.6.17-2-686# insmod kernel/fs/fat/fat.ko
root@barry:/lib/modules/2.6.17-2-686# lsmod | grep fat
fat                    46588  0
```

insmod is not detecting dependencies, so it fails to load the isdn module (because the isdn module depends on the slhc module).

```
[root@RHEL52 drivers]# pwd
/lib/modules/2.6.18-92.1.18.el5/kernel/drivers
[root@RHEL52 kernel]# insmod isdn/i4l/isdn.ko
insmod: error inserting 'isdn/i4l/isdn.ko': -1 Unknown symbol in module
```

28.4.8. modinfo

As you can see in the screenshot of **modinfo** below, the isdn module depends in the slhc module.

```
[root@RHEL52 drivers]# modinfo isdn/i4l/isdn.ko | head -6
filename:       isdn/i4l/isdn.ko
license:        GPL
author:         Fritz Elfert
description:    ISDN4Linux: link layer
srcversion:     99650346E708173496F6739
depends:        slhc
```

28.4.9. modprobe

The big advantage of **modprobe** over **insmod** is that modprobe will load all necessary modules, whereas insmod requires manual loading of dependencies. Another advantage is that you don't need to point to the filename with full path.

This screenshot shows how modprobe loads the isdn module, automatically loading slhc in background.

```
[root@RHEL52 kernel]# lsmod | grep isdn
[root@RHEL52 kernel]# modprobe isdn
[root@RHEL52 kernel]# lsmod | grep isdn
isdn                  122433  0
slhc                   10561  1 isdn
[root@RHEL52 kernel]#
```

28.4.10. /lib/modules/<kernel>/modules.dep

Module dependencies are stored in **modules.dep**.

```
[root@RHEL52 2.6.18-92.1.18.el5]# pwd
/lib/modules/2.6.18-92.1.18.el5
[root@RHEL52 2.6.18-92.1.18.el5]# head -3 modules.dep
/lib/modules/2.6.18-92.1.18.el5/kernel/drivers/net/tokenring/3c359.ko:
/lib/modules/2.6.18-92.1.18.el5/kernel/drivers/net/pcmcia/3c574_cs.ko:
/lib/modules/2.6.18-92.1.18.el5/kernel/drivers/net/pcmcia/3c589_cs.ko:
```

28.4.11. depmod

The **modules.dep** file can be updated (recreated) with the **depmod** command. In this screenshot no modules were added, so **depmod** generates the same file.

```
root@barry:/lib/modules/2.6.17-2-686# ls -l modules.dep
-rw-r--r-- 1 root root 310676 2008-03-01 16:32 modules.dep
root@barry:/lib/modules/2.6.17-2-686# depmod
root@barry:/lib/modules/2.6.17-2-686# ls -l modules.dep
-rw-r--r-- 1 root root 310676 2008-12-07 13:54 modules.dep
```

28.4.12. rmmod

Similar to insmod, the **rmmod** command is rarely used anymore.

```
[root@RHELv4u3 ~]# modprobe isdn
[root@RHELv4u3 ~]# rmmod slhc
ERROR: Module slhc is in use by isdn
[root@RHELv4u3 ~]# rmmod isdn
[root@RHELv4u3 ~]# rmmod slhc
[root@RHELv4u3 ~]# lsmod | grep isdn
[root@RHELv4u3 ~]#
```

28.4.13. modprobe -r

Contrary to rmmod, **modprobe** will automatically remove unneeded modules.

```
[root@RHELv4u3 ~]# modprobe isdn
[root@RHELv4u3 ~]# lsmod | grep isdn
isdn                  133537  0
slhc                    7233  1 isdn
[root@RHELv4u3 ~]# modprobe -r isdn
[root@RHELv4u3 ~]# lsmod | grep isdn
[root@RHELv4u3 ~]# lsmod | grep slhc
[root@RHELv4u3 ~]#
```

28.4.14. /etc/modprobe.conf

The **/etc/modprobe.conf** file and the **/etc/modprobe.d** directory can contain aliases (used by humans) and options (for dependent modules) for modprobe.

```
[root@RHEL52 ~]# cat /etc/modprobe.conf
alias scsi_hostadapter mptbase
alias scsi_hostadapter1 mptspi
alias scsi_hostadapter2 ata_piix
alias eth0 pcnet32
alias eth2 pcnet32
```

```
alias eth1 pcnet32
```

28.5. compiling a kernel

28.5.1. extraversion

Enter into **/usr/src/redhat/BUILD/kernel-2.6.9/linux-2.6.9/** and change the **extraversion** in the Makefile.

```
[root@RHEL52 linux-2.6.18.i686]# pwd
/usr/src/redhat/BUILD/kernel-2.6.18/linux-2.6.18.i686
[root@RHEL52 linux-2.6.18.i686]# vi Makefile
[root@RHEL52 linux-2.6.18.i686]# head -4 Makefile
VERSION = 2
PATCHLEVEL = 6
SUBLEVEL = 18
EXTRAVERSION = -paul2008
```

28.5.2. make mrproper

Now clean up the source from any previous installs with **make mrproper**. If this is your first after downloading the source code, then this is not needed.

```
[root@RHEL52 linux-2.6.18.i686]# make mrproper
  CLEAN   scripts/basic
  CLEAN   scripts/kconfig
  CLEAN   include/config
  CLEAN   .config .config.old
```

28.5.3. .config

Now copy a working **.config** from /boot to our kernel directory. This file contains the configuration that was used for your current working kernel. It determines whether modules are included in compilation or not.

```
[root@RHEL52 linux-2.6.18.i686]# cp /boot/config-2.6.18-92.1.18.el5 .config
```

28.5.4. make menuconfig

Now run **make menuconfig** (or the graphical **make xconfig**). This tool allows you to select whether to compile stuff as a module (m), as part of the kernel (*), or not at all (smaller kernel size). If you remove too much, your kernel will not work. The configuration will be stored in the hidden **.config** file.

```
[root@RHEL52 linux-2.6.18.i686]# make menuconfig
```

28.5.5. make clean

Issue a **make clean** to prepare the kernel for compile. **make clean** will remove most generated files, but keeps your kernel configuration. Running a **make mrproper** at this point would destroy the .config file that you built with **make menuconfig**.

```
[root@RHEL52 linux-2.6.18.i686]# make clean
```

28.5.6. make bzImage

And then run **make bzImage**, sit back and relax while the kernel compiles. You can use **time make bzImage** to know how long it takes to compile, so next time you can go for a short walk.

```
[root@RHEL52 linux-2.6.18.i686]# time make bzImage
  HOSTCC  scripts/basic/fixdep
  HOSTCC  scripts/basic/docproc
  HOSTCC  scripts/kconfig/conf.o
  HOSTCC  scripts/kconfig/kxgettext.o
...
```

This command will end with telling you the location of the **bzImage** file (and with time info if you also specified the time command.

```
Kernel: arch/i386/boot/bzImage is ready  (#1)

real 13m59.573s
user 1m22.631s
sys 11m51.034s
[root@RHEL52 linux-2.6.18.i686]#
```

You can already copy this image to /boot with **cp arch/i386/boot/bzImage /boot/vmlinuz-<kernel-version>**.

28.5.7. make modules

Now run **make modules**. It can take 20 to 50 minutes to compile all the modules.

```
[root@RHEL52 linux-2.6.18.i686]# time make modules
  CHK     include/linux/version.h
  CHK     include/linux/utsrelease.h
  CC [M]  arch/i386/kernel/msr.o
  CC [M]  arch/i386/kernel/cpuid.o
  CC [M]  arch/i386/kernel/microcode.o
```

28.5.8. make modules_install

To copy all the compiled modules to **/lib/modules** just run **make modules_install** (takes about 20 seconds). Here's a screenshot from before the command.

```
[root@RHEL52 linux-2.6.18.i686]# ls -l /lib/modules/
total 20
drwxr-xr-x 6 root root 4096 Oct 15 13:09 2.6.18-92.1.13.el5
drwxr-xr-x 6 root root 4096 Nov 11 08:51 2.6.18-92.1.17.el5
drwxr-xr-x 6 root root 4096 Dec  6 07:11 2.6.18-92.1.18.el5
[root@RHEL52 linux-2.6.18.i686]# make modules_install
```

And here is the same directory after. Notice that **make modules_install** created a new directory for the new kernel.

```
[root@RHEL52 linux-2.6.18.i686]# ls -l /lib/modules/
total 24
drwxr-xr-x 6 root root 4096 Oct 15 13:09 2.6.18-92.1.13.el5
drwxr-xr-x 6 root root 4096 Nov 11 08:51 2.6.18-92.1.17.el5
drwxr-xr-x 6 root root 4096 Dec  6 07:11 2.6.18-92.1.18.el5
drwxr-xr-x 3 root root 4096 Dec  6 08:50 2.6.18-paul2008
```

28.5.9. /boot

We still need to copy the kernel, the System.map and our configuration file to /boot. Strictly speaking the .config file is not obligatory, but it might help you in future compilations of the kernel.

```
[root@RHEL52 ]# pwd
/usr/src/redhat/BUILD/kernel-2.6.18/linux-2.6.18.i686
[root@RHEL52 ]# cp System.map /boot/System.map-2.6.18-paul2008
[root@RHEL52 ]# cp .config /boot/config-2.6.18-paul2008
[root@RHEL52 ]# cp arch/i386/boot/bzImage /boot/vmlinuz-2.6.18-paul2008
```

28.5.10. mkinitrd

The kernel often uses an initrd file at bootup. We can use **mkinitrd** to generate this file. Make sure you use the correct kernel name!

```
[root@RHEL52 ]# pwd
/usr/src/redhat/BUILD/kernel-2.6.18/linux-2.6.18.i686
[root@RHEL52 ]# mkinitrd /boot/initrd-2.6.18-paul2008 2.6.18-paul2008
```

28.5.11. bootloader

Compilation is now finished, don't forget to create an additional stanza in grub or lilo.

28.6. compiling one module

28.6.1. hello.c

A little C program that will be our module.

```
[root@rhel4a kernel_module]# cat hello.c
#include <linux/module.h>
#include <section>

int init_module(void)
{
 printk(KERN_INFO "Start Hello World...\n");
 return 0;
}

void cleanup_module(void)
{
 printk(KERN_INFO "End Hello World... \n");
}
```

28.6.2. Makefile

The make file for this module.

```
[root@rhel4a kernel_module]# cat Makefile
obj-m += hello.o
all:
make -C /lib/modules/$(shell uname -r)/build M=$(PWD) modules
clean:
make -C /lib/modules/$(shell uname -r)/build M=$(PWD) clean
```

These are the only two files needed.

```
[root@rhel4a kernel_module]# ll
total 16
-rw-rw-r--  1 paul paul 250 Feb 15 19:14 hello.c
-rw-rw-r--  1 paul paul 153 Feb 15 19:15 Makefile
```

28.6.3. make

The running of the **make** command.

```
[root@rhel4a kernel_module]# make
make -C /lib/modules/2.6.9-paul-2/build M=~/kernel_module modules
make[1]: Entering dir... `/usr/src/redhat/BUILD/kernel-2.6.9/linux-2.6.9'
CC [M]  /home/paul/kernel_module/hello.o
Building modules, stage 2.
MODPOST
CC      /home/paul/kernel_module/hello.mod.o
LD [M]  /home/paul/kernel_module/hello.ko
make[1]: Leaving dir... `/usr/src/redhat/BUILD/kernel-2.6.9/linux-2.6.9'
[root@rhel4a kernel_module]#
```

Now we have more files.

```
[root@rhel4a kernel_module]# ll
total 172
-rw-rw-r--  1 paul paul   250 Feb 15 19:14 hello.c
-rw-r--r--  1 root root 64475 Feb 15 19:15 hello.ko
-rw-r--r--  1 root root   632 Feb 15 19:15 hello.mod.c
-rw-r--r--  1 root root 37036 Feb 15 19:15 hello.mod.o
-rw-r--r--  1 root root 28396 Feb 15 19:15 hello.o
-rw-rw-r--  1 paul paul   153 Feb 15 19:15 Makefile
[root@rhel4a kernel_module]#
```

28.6.4. hello.ko

Use **modinfo** to verify that it is really a module.

```
[root@rhel4a kernel_module]# modinfo hello.ko
filename:       hello.ko
vermagic:       2.6.9-paul-2 SMP 686 REGPARM 4KSTACKS gcc-3.4
depends:
[root@rhel4a kernel_module]#
```

Good, so now we can load our hello module.

```
[root@rhel4a kernel_module]# lsmod | grep hello
[root@rhel4a kernel_module]# insmod ./hello.ko
[root@rhel4a kernel_module]# lsmod | grep hello
hello                 5504  0
[root@rhel4a kernel_module]# tail -1 /var/log/messages
Feb 15 19:16:07 rhel4a kernel: Start Hello World...
[root@rhel4a kernel_module]# rmmod hello
[root@rhel4a kernel_module]#
```

Finally **/var/log/messages** has a little surprise.

```
[root@rhel4a kernel_module]# tail -2 /var/log/messages
Feb 15 19:16:07 rhel4a kernel: Start Hello World...
Feb 15 19:16:35 rhel4a kernel: End Hello World...
[root@rhel4a kernel_module]#
```

Chapter 29. library management

29.1. introduction

With **libraries** we are talking about dynamically linked libraries (aka shared objects). These are binaries that contain functions and are not started themselves as programs, but are called by other binaries.

Several programs can use the same library. The name of the library file usually starts with **lib**, followed by the actual name of the library, then the chracters **.so** and finally a version number.

29.2. /lib and /usr/lib

When you look at the **/lib** or the **/usr/lib** directory, you will see a lot of symbolic links. Most **libraries** have a detailed version number in their name, but receive a symbolic link from a filename which only contains the major version number.

```
root@rhel53 ~# ls -l /lib/libext*
lrwxrwxrwx 1 root root   16 Feb 18 16:36 /lib/libext2fs.so.2 -> libext2fs.so.2.4
-rwxr-xr-x 1 root root 113K Jun 30  2009 /lib/libext2fs.so.2.4
```

29.3. ldd

Many programs have dependencies on the installation of certain libraries. You can display these dependencies with **ldd**.

This example shows the dependencies of the **su** command.

```
paul@RHEL5 ~$ ldd /bin/su
 linux-gate.so.1 =>  (0x003f7000)
 libpam.so.0 => /lib/libpam.so.0 (0x00d5c000)
 libpam_misc.so.0 => /lib/libpam_misc.so.0 (0x0073c000)
 libcrypt.so.1 => /lib/libcrypt.so.1 (0x00aa4000)
 libdl.so.2 => /lib/libdl.so.2 (0x00800000)
 libc.so.6 => /lib/libc.so.6 (0x00ec1000)
 libaudit.so.0 => /lib/libaudit.so.0 (0x0049f000)
 /lib/ld-linux.so.2 (0x4769c000)
```

29.4. ltrace

The **ltrace** program allows to see all the calls made to library functions by a program. The example below uses the -c option to get only a summary count (there can be many calls), and the -l option to only show calls in one library file. All this to see what calls are made when executing **su - serena** as root.

```
root@deb503:~# ltrace -c -l /lib/libpam.so.0 su - serena
serena@deb503:~$ exit
logout
% time     seconds  usecs/call     calls      function
------ ----------- ----------- --------- --------------------
 70.31    0.014117       14117         1 pam_start
 12.36    0.002482        2482         1 pam_open_session
  5.17    0.001039        1039         1 pam_acct_mgmt
  4.36    0.000876         876         1 pam_end
  3.36    0.000675         675         1 pam_close_session
  3.22    0.000646         646         1 pam_authenticate
  0.48    0.000096          48         2 pam_set_item
  0.27    0.000054          54         1 pam_setcred
  0.25    0.000050          50         1 pam_getenvlist
  0.22    0.000044          44         1 pam_get_item
------ ----------- ----------- --------- --------------------
100.00    0.020079                    11 total
```

29.5. dpkg -S and debsums

Find out on Debian/Ubuntu to which package a library belongs.

```
paul@deb503:/lib$ dpkg -S libext2fs.so.2.4
e2fslibs: /lib/libext2fs.so.2.4
```

You can then verify the integrity of all files in this package using **debsums**.

```
paul@deb503:~$ debsums e2fslibs
/usr/share/doc/e2fslibs/changelog.Debian.gz                             OK
/usr/share/doc/e2fslibs/copyright                                       OK
/lib/libe2p.so.2.3                                                      OK
/lib/libext2fs.so.2.4                                                   OK
```

Should a library be broken, then reinstall it with **aptitude reinstall $package**.

```
root@deb503:~# aptitude reinstall e2fslibs
Reading package lists... Done
Building dependency tree
Reading state information... Done
Reading extended state information
Initializing package states... Done
Reading task descriptions... Done
The following packages will be REINSTALLED:
  e2fslibs
...
```

29.6. rpm -qf and rpm -V

Find out on Red Hat/Fedora to which package a library belongs.

```
paul@RHEL5 ~$ rpm -qf /lib/libext2fs.so.2.4
e2fsprogs-libs-1.39-8.el5
```

You can then use **rpm -V** to verify all files in this package. In the example below the output shows that the **S**ize and the **T**ime stamp of the file have changed since installation.

```
root@rhel53 ~# rpm -V e2fsprogs-libs
prelink: /lib/libext2fs.so.2.4: prelinked file size differs
S.?....T    /lib/libext2fs.so.2.4
```

You can then use **yum reinstall $package** to overwrite the existing library with an original version.

```
root@rhel53 lib# yum reinstall e2fsprogs-libs
Loaded plugins: rhnplugin, security
Setting up Reinstall Process
Resolving Dependencies
--> Running transaction check
---> Package e2fsprogs-libs.i386 0:1.39-23.el5 set to be erased
---> Package e2fsprogs-libs.i386 0:1.39-23.el5 set to be updated
--> Finished Dependency Resolution
...
```

The package verification now reports no problems with the library.

```
root@rhel53 lib# rpm -V e2fsprogs-libs
root@rhel53 lib#
```

29.7. tracing with strace

More detailed tracing of all function calls can be done with **strace**. We start by creating a read only file.

```
root@deb503:~# echo hello > 42.txt
root@deb503:~# chmod 400 42.txt
root@deb503:~# ls -l 42.txt
-r-------- 1 root root 6 2011-09-26 12:03 42.txt
```

We open the file with **vi**, but include the **strace** command with an output file for the trace before **vi**. This will create a file with all the function calls done by **vi**.

```
root@deb503:~# strace -o strace.txt vi 42.txt
```

The file is read only, but we still change the contents, and use the **:w!** directive to write to this file. Then we close **vi** and take a look at the trace log.

```
root@deb503:~# grep chmod strace.txt
chmod("42.txt", 0100600)                = -1 ENOENT (No such file or directory)
chmod("42.txt", 0100400)                = 0
root@deb503:~# ls -l 42.txt
-r-------- 1 root root 12 2011-09-26 12:04 42.txt
```

Notice that **vi** changed the permissions on the file twice. The trace log is too long to show a complete screenshot in this book.

```
root@deb503:~# wc -l strace.txt
941 strace.txt
```

Part VII. backup management

Table of Contents

Chapter 30. backup

30.1. About tape devices

Don't forget that the name of a device strictly speaking has no meaning since the kernel will use the major and minor number to find the hardware! See the man page of **mknod** and the devices.txt file in the Linux kernel source for more info.

30.1.1. SCSI tapes

On the official Linux device list (http://www.lanana.org/docs/device-list/) we find the names for SCSI tapes (major 9 char). SCSI tape devices are located underneath **/dev/st** and are numbered starting with 0 for the first tape device.

```
/dev/st0    First tape device
/dev/st1    Second tape device
/dev/st2    Third tape device
```

To prevent **automatic rewinding of tapes**, prefix them with the letter n.

```
/dev/nst0    First no rewind tape device
/dev/nst1    Second no rewind tape device
/dev/nst2    Third no rewind tape device
```

By default, SCSI tapes on Linux will use the highest hardware compression that is supported by the tape device. To lower the compression level, append one of the letters l (low), m (medium) or a (auto) to the tape name.

```
/dev/st0l    First low compression tape device
/dev/st0m    First medium compression tape device
/dev/nst2m   Third no rewind medium compression tape device
```

30.1.2. IDE tapes

On the official Linux device list (http://www.lanana.org/docs/device-list/) we find the names for IDE tapes (major 37 char). IDE tape devices are located underneath **/dev/ht** and are numbered starting with 0 for the first tape device. No rewind and compression is similar to SCSI tapes.

```
/dev/ht0    First IDE tape device
/dev/nht0   Second no rewind IDE tape device
/dev/ht0m   First medium compression IDE tape device
```

30.1.3. mt

To manage your tapes, use **mt** (Magnetic Tape). Some examples.

To receive information about the status of the tape.

```
mt -f /dev/st0 status
```

To rewind a tape...

```
mt -f /dev/st0 rewind
```

To rewind and eject a tape...

```
mt -f /dev/st0 eject
```

To erase a tape...

```
mt -f /dev/st0 erase
```

30.2. Compression

It can be beneficial to compress files before backup. The two most popular tools for compression of regular files on Linux are **gzip/gunzip** and **bzip2/bunzip2**. Below you can see gzip in action, notice that it adds the **.gz** extension to the file.

```
paul@RHELv4u4:~/test$ ls -l allfiles.tx*
-rw-rw-r--  1 paul paul 8813553 Feb 27 05:38 allfiles.txt
paul@RHELv4u4:~/test$ gzip allfiles.txt
paul@RHELv4u4:~/test$ ls -l allfiles.tx*
-rw-rw-r--  1 paul paul 931863 Feb 27 05:38 allfiles.txt.gz
paul@RHELv4u4:~/test$ gunzip allfiles.txt.gz
paul@RHELv4u4:~/test$ ls -l allfiles.tx*
-rw-rw-r--  1 paul paul 8813553 Feb 27 05:38 allfiles.txt
paul@RHELv4u4:~/test$
```

In general, gzip is much faster than bzip2, but the latter one compresses a lot better. Let us compare the two.

```
paul@RHELv4u4:~/test$ cp allfiles.txt bllfiles.txt
paul@RHELv4u4:~/test$ time gzip allfiles.txt

real    0m0.050s
user    0m0.041s
sys     0m0.009s
paul@RHELv4u4:~/test$ time bzip2 bllfiles.txt

real    0m5.968s
user    0m5.794s
sys     0m0.076s
paul@RHELv4u4:~/test$ ls -l ?llfiles.tx*
-rw-rw-r--  1 paul paul 931863 Feb 27 05:38 allfiles.txt.gz
-rw-rw-r--  1 paul paul 708871 May 12 10:52 bllfiles.txt.bz2
paul@RHELv4u4:~/test$
```

30.3. tar

The **tar** utility gets its name from **Tape ARchive**. This tool will receive and send files to a destination (typically a tape or a regular file). The c option is used to create a tar archive (or tarfile), the f option to name/create the **tarfile**. The example below takes a backup of / etc into the file /backup/etc.tar .

```
root@RHELv4u4:~# tar cf /backup/etc.tar /etc
root@RHELv4u4:~# ls -l /backup/etc.tar
-rw-r--r--  1 root root 47800320 May 12 11:47 /backup/etc.tar
root@RHELv4u4:~#
```

Compression can be achieved without pipes since tar uses the z flag to compress with gzip, and the j flag to compress with bzip2.

```
root@RHELv4u4:~# tar czf /backup/etc.tar.gz /etc
root@RHELv4u4:~# tar cjf /backup/etc.tar.bz2 /etc
root@RHELv4u4:~# ls -l /backup/etc.ta*
-rw-r--r--  1 root root 47800320 May 12 11:47 /backup/etc.tar
-rw-r--r--  1 root root  6077340 May 12 11:48 /backup/etc.tar.bz2
-rw-r--r--  1 root root  8496607 May 12 11:47 /backup/etc.tar.gz
root@RHELv4u4:~#
```

The t option is used to **list the contents of a tar file**. Verbose mode is enabled with v (also useful when you want to see the files being archived during archiving).

```
root@RHELv4u4:~# tar tvf /backup/etc.tar
drwxr-xr-x root/root         0 2007-05-12 09:38:21 etc/
-rw-r--r-- root/root      2657 2004-09-27 10:15:03 etc/warnquota.conf
-rw-r--r-- root/root     13136 2006-11-03 17:34:50 etc/mime.types
drwxr-xr-x root/root         0 2004-11-03 13:35:50 etc/sound/
...
```

To **list a specific file in a tar archive**, use the t option, added with the filename (without leading /).

```
root@RHELv4u4:~# tar tvf /backup/etc.tar etc/resolv.conf
-rw-r--r-- root/root        77 2007-05-12 08:31:32 etc/resolv.conf
root@RHELv4u4:~#
```

Use the x flag to **restore a tar archive**, or a single file from the archive. Remember that by default tar will restore the file in the current directory.

```
root@RHELv4u4:~# tar xvf /backup/etc.tar etc/resolv.conf
etc/resolv.conf
root@RHELv4u4:~# ls -l /etc/resolv.conf
-rw-r--r--  2 root root 40 May 12 12:05 /etc/resolv.conf
root@RHELv4u4:~# ls -l etc/resolv.conf
-rw-r--r--  1 root root 77 May 12 08:31 etc/resolv.conf
root@RHELv4u4:~#
```

You can **preserve file permissions** with the p flag. And you can exclude directories or file with **--exclude**.

```
root ~# tar cpzf /backup/etc_with_perms.tgz /etc
```

```
root ~# tar cpzf /backup/etc_no_sysconf.tgz /etc --exclude /etc/sysconfig
root ~# ls -l /backup/etc_*
-rw-r--r--  1 root root 8434293 May 12 12:48 /backup/etc_no_sysconf.tgz
-rw-r--r--  1 root root 8496591 May 12 12:48 /backup/etc_with_perms.tgz
root ~#
```

You can also create a text file with names of files and directories to archive, and then supply this file to tar with the -T flag.

```
root@RHELv4u4:~# find /etc -name *.conf > files_to_archive.txt
root@RHELv4u4:~# find /home -name *.pdf >> files_to_archive.txt
root@RHELv4u4:~# tar cpzf /backup/backup.tgz -T files_to_archive.txt
```

The tar utility can receive filenames from the find command, with the help of xargs.

```
find /etc -type f -name "*.conf" | xargs tar czf /backup/confs.tar.gz
```

You can also use tar to copy a directory, this is more efficient than using cp -r.

```
(cd /etc; tar -cf - . ) | (cd /backup/copy_of_etc/; tar -xpf - )
```

Another example of tar, this copies a directory securely over the network.

```
(cd /etc;tar -cf - . )|(ssh user@srv 'cd /backup/cp_of_etc/; tar -xf - ')
```

tar can be used together with gzip and copy a file to a remote server through ssh

```
cat backup.tar | gzip | ssh bashuser@192.168.1.105 "cat - > backup.tgz"
```

Compress the tar backup when it is on the network, but leave it uncompressed at the destination.

```
cat backup.tar | gzip | ssh user@192.168.1.105 "gunzip|cat - > backup.tar"
```

Same as the previous, but let ssh handle the compression

```
cat backup.tar | ssh -C bashuser@192.168.1.105 "cat - > backup.tar"
```

30.4. Backup Types

Linux uses **multilevel incremental** backups using distinct levels. A full backup is a backup at level 0. A higher level x backup will include all changes since the last level x-1 backup.

Suppose you take a full backup on Monday (level 0) and a level 1 backup on Tuesday, then the Tuesday backup will contain all changes since Monday. Taking a level 2 on Wednesday will contain all changes since Tuesday (the last level 2-1). A level 3 backup on Thursday will contain all changes since Wednesday (the last level 3-1). Another level 3 on Friday will also contain all changes since Wednesday. A level 2 backup on Saturday would take all changes since the last level 1 from Tuesday.

30.5. dump and restore

While **dump** is similar to tar, it is also very different because it looks at the file system. Where tar receives a lists of files to backup, dump will find files to backup by itself by examining ext2. Files found by dump will be copied to a tape or regular file. In case the target is not big enough to hold the dump (end-of-media), it is broken into multiple volumes.

Restoring files that were backed up with dump is done with the **restore** command. In the example below we take a full level 0 backup of two partitions to a SCSI tape. The no rewind is mandatory to put the volumes behind each other on the tape.

```
dump 0f /dev/nst0 /boot
dump 0f /dev/nst0 /
```

Listing files in a dump archive is done with **dump -t**, and you can compare files with **dump -C**.

You can omit files from a dump by changing the dump attribute with the **chattr** command. The d attribute on ext will tell dump to skip the file, even during a full backup. In the following example, /etc/hosts is excluded from dump archives.

```
chattr +d /etc/hosts
```

To restore the complete file system with **restore**, use the -r option. This can be useful to change the size or block size of a file system. You should have a clean file system mounted and cd'd into it. Like this example shows.

```
mke2fs /dev/hda3
mount /dev/hda3 /mnt/data
cd /mnt/data
restore rf /dev/nst0
```

To extract only one file or directory from a dump, use the -x option.

```
restore -xf /dev/st0 /etc
```

30.6. cpio

Different from tar and dump is **cpio** (Copy Input and Output). It can be used to receive filenames, but copies the actual files. This makes it an easy companion with find! Some examples below.

find sends filenames to cpio, which puts the files in an archive.

```
find /etc -depth -print | cpio -oaV -O archive.cpio
```

The same, but compressed with gzip

```
find /etc -depth -print | cpio -oaV | gzip -c > archive.cpio.gz
```

Now pipe it through ssh (backup files to a compressed file on another machine)

```
find /etc -depth -print|cpio -oaV|gzip -c|ssh server "cat - > etc.cpio.gz"
```

find sends filenames to cpio | cpio sends files to ssh | ssh sends files to cpio 'cpio extracts files'

```
find /etc -depth -print | cpio -oaV | ssh user@host 'cpio -imVd'
```

the same but reversed: copy a dir from the remote host to the local machine

```
ssh user@host "find path -depth -print | cpio -oaV" | cpio -imVd
```

30.7. dd

30.7.1. About dd

Some people use **dd** to create backups. This can be very powerful, but dd backups can only be restored to very similar partitions or devices. There are however a lot of useful things possible with dd. Some examples.

30.7.2. Create a CDROM image

The easiest way to create a **.ISO file** from any CD. The if switch means Input File, of is the Output File. Any good tool can burn a copy of the CD with this .ISO file.

```
dd if=/dev/cdrom of=/path/to/cdrom.ISO
```

30.7.3. Create a floppy image

A little outdated maybe, but just in case : make an image file from a 1.44MB floppy. Blocksize is defined by bs, and count contains the number of blocks to copy.

```
dd if=/dev/floppy of=/path/to/floppy.img bs=1024 count=1440
```

30.7.4. Copy the master boot record

Use dd to copy the **MBR** (Master Boot Record) of hard disk /dev/hda to a file.

```
dd if=/dev/hda of=/MBR.img bs=512 count=1
```

30.7.5. Copy files

This example shows how dd can copy files. Copy the file summer.txt to copy_of_summer.txt .

```
dd if=~/summer.txt of=~/copy_of_summer.txt
```

30.7.6. Image disks or partitions

And who needs ghost when dd can create a (compressed) image of a partition.

```
dd if=/dev/hdb2 of=/image_of_hdb2.IMG
dd if=/dev/hdb2 | gzip > /image_of_hdb2.IMG.gz
```

30.7.7. Create files of a certain size

dd can be used to create a file of any size. The first example creates a one MEBIbyte file, the second a one MEGAbyte file.

```
dd if=/dev/zero of=file1MB count=1024 bs=1024
dd if=/dev/zero of=file1MB count=1000 bs=1024
```

30.7.8. CDROM server example

And there are of course endless combinations with ssh and bzip2. This example puts a bzip2 backup of a cdrom on a remote server.

```
dd if=/dev/cdrom |bzip2|ssh user@host "cat - > /backups/cd/cdrom.iso.bz2"
```

30.8. split

The **split** command is useful to split files into smaller files. This can be useful to fit the file onto multiple instances of a medium too small to contain the complete file. In the example below, a file of size 5000 bytes is split into three smaller files, with maximum 2000 bytes each.

```
paul@laika:~/test$ ls -l
total 8
-rw-r--r-- 1 paul paul 5000 2007-09-09 20:46 bigfile1
paul@laika:~/test$ split -b 2000 bigfile1 splitfile.
paul@laika:~/test$ ls -l
total 20
-rw-r--r-- 1 paul paul 5000 2007-09-09 20:46 bigfile1
-rw-r--r-- 1 paul paul 2000 2007-09-09 20:47 splitfile.aa
-rw-r--r-- 1 paul paul 2000 2007-09-09 20:47 splitfile.ab
-rw-r--r-- 1 paul paul 1000 2007-09-09 20:47 splitfile.ac
```

30.9. practice: backup

!! Careful with tar options and the position of the backup file, mistakes can destroy your system!!

1. Create a directory (or partition if you like) for backups. Link (or mount) it under /mnt/backup.

2a. Use tar to backup /etc in /mnt/backup/etc_date.tgz, the backup must be gzipped. (Replace date with the current date)

2b. Use tar to backup /bin to /mnt/backup/bin_date.tar.bz2, the backup must be bzip2'd.

2c. Choose a file in /etc and /bin and verify with tar that the file is indeed backed up.

2d. Extract those two files to your home directory.

3a. Create a backup directory for your neighbour, make it accessible under /mnt/neighbourName

3b. Combine ssh and tar to put a backup of your /boot on your neighbours computer in /mnt/YourName

4a. Combine find and cpio to create a cpio archive of /etc.

4b. Choose a file in /etc and restore it from the cpio archive into your home directory.

5. Use dd and ssh to put a backup of the master boot record on your neighbours computer.

6. (On the real computer) Create and mount an ISO image of the ubuntu cdrom.

7. Combine dd and gzip to create a 'ghost' image of one of your partitions on another partition.

8. Use dd to create a five megabyte file in ~/testsplit and name it biggest. Then split this file in smaller two megabyte parts.

```
mkdir testsplit

dd if=/dev/zero of=~/testsplit/biggest count=5000 bs=1024

split -b 2000000 biggest parts
```

Part VIII. Appendices

Table of Contents

Appendix A. disk quotas

A.1. About Disk Quotas

To limit the disk space used by user, you can set up **disk quotas**. This requires adding **usrquota** and/or **grpquota** to one or more of the file systems in **/etc/fstab**.

```
root@RHELv4u4:~# cat /etc/fstab | grep usrquota
/dev/VolGroup00/LogVol02      /home       ext3       usrquota,grpquota    0 0
```

Next you need to remount the file system.

```
root@RHELv4u4:~# mount -o remount /home
```

The next step is to build the **quota.user** and/or **quota.group** files. These files (called the **quota files**) contain the table of the disk usage on that file system. Use the **quotacheck** command to accomplish this.

```
root@RHELv4u4:~# quotacheck -cug /home
root@RHELv4u4:~# quotacheck -avug
```

The **-c** is for create, **u** for user quota, **g** for group, **a** for checking all quota enabled file systems in /etc/fstab and **v** for verbose information. The next step is to edit individual user quotas with **edquota** or set a general quota on the file system with **edquota -t**. The tool will enable you to put **hard** (this is the real limit) and **soft** (allows a grace period) limits on **blocks** and **inodes**. The **quota** command will verify that quota for a user is set. You can have a nice overview with **repquota**.

The final step (before your users start complaining about lack of disk space) is to enable quotas with **quotaon(1)**.

```
root@RHELv4u4:~# quotaon -vaug
```

Issue the **quotaoff** command to stop all complaints.

```
root@RHELv4u4:~# quotaoff -vaug
```

A.2. Practice Disk quotas

1. Implement disk quotas on one of your new partitions. Limit one of your users to 10 megabyte.

2. Test that they work by copying many files to the quota'd partition.

Appendix B. introduction to vnc

B.1. About VNC

VNC can be configured in gnome or KDE using the **Remote Desktop Preferences.** **VNC** can be used to run your desktop on another computer, and you can also use it to see and take over the Desktop of another user. The last part can be useful for help desks to show users how to do things. VNC has the added advantage of being operating system independent, a lot of products (realvnc, tightvnc, xvnc, ...) use the same protocol on Solaris, Linux, BSD and more.

B.2. VNC Server

Starting the vnc server for the first time.

```
[root@RHELv4u3 conf]# rpm -qa | grep -i vnc
vnc-server-4.0-8.1
vnc-4.0-8.1
[root@RHELv4u3 conf]# vncserver :2

You will require a password to access your desktops.

Password:
Verify:
xauth:  creating new authority file /root/.Xauthority

New 'RHELv4u3.localdomain:2 (root)' desktop is RHELv4u3.localdomain:2

Creating default startup script /root/.vnc/xstartup
Starting applications specified in /root/.vnc/xstartup
Log file is /root/.vnc/RHELv4u3.localdomain:2.log

[root@RHELv4u3 conf]#
```

B.3. VNC Client

You can now use the **vncviewer** from another machine to connect to your vnc server. It will default to a very simple graphical interface...

```
paul@laika:~$ vncviewer 192.168.1.49:2
VNC viewer version 3.3.7 - built Nov 20 2006 13:05:04
Copyright (C) 2002-2003 RealVNC Ltd.
Copyright (C) 1994-2000 AT&T Laboratories Cambridge.
See http://www.realvnc.com for information on VNC.
VNC server supports protocol version 3.8 (viewer 3.3)
Password:
VNC authentication succeeded
Desktop name "RHELv4u3.localdomain:2 (root)"
Connected to VNC server, using protocol version 3.3
...
```

If you don't like the simple twm window manager, you can comment out the last two lines of **~/.vnc/xstartup** and add a **gnome-session &** line to have vnc default to gnome instead.

```
[root@RHELv4u3 ~]# cat .vnc/xstartup
#!/bin/sh

# Uncomment the following two lines for normal desktop:
# unset SESSION_MANAGER
# exec /etc/X11/xinit/xinitrc

[ -x /etc/vnc/xstartup ] && exec /etc/vnc/xstartup
[ -r $HOME/.Xresources ] && xrdb $HOME/.Xresources
xsetroot -solid grey
vncconfig -iconic &
# xterm -geometry 80x24+10+10 -ls -title "$VNCDESKTOP Desktop" &
# twm &
gnome-session &
[root@RHELv4u3 ~]#
```

Don't forget to restart your vnc server after changing this file.

```
[root@RHELv4u3 ~]# vncserver -kill :2
Killing Xvnc process ID 5785
[root@RHELv4u3 ~]# vncserver :2

New 'RHELv4u3.localdomain:2 (root)' desktop is RHELv4u3.localdomain:2

Starting applications specified in /root/.vnc/xstartup
Log file is /root/.vnc/RHELv4u3.localdomain:2.log
```

B.4. Practice VNC

1. Use VNC to connect from one machine to another.

Appendix C. License

GNU Free Documentation License

Version 1.3, 3 November 2008

Copyright © 2000, 2001, 2002, 2007, 2008 Free Software Foundation, Inc.

Everyone is permitted to copy and distribute verbatim copies of this license document, but changing it is not allowed.

0. PREAMBLE

The purpose of this License is to make a manual, textbook, or other functional and useful document "free" in the sense of freedom: to assure everyone the effective freedom to copy and redistribute it, with or without modifying it, either commercially or noncommercially. Secondarily, this License preserves for the author and publisher a way to get credit for their work, while not being considered responsible for modifications made by others.

This License is a kind of "copyleft", which means that derivative works of the document must themselves be free in the same sense. It complements the GNU General Public License, which is a copyleft license designed for free software.

We have designed this License in order to use it for manuals for free software, because free software needs free documentation: a free program should come with manuals providing the same freedoms that the software does. But this License is not limited to software manuals; it can be used for any textual work, regardless of subject matter or whether it is published as a printed book. We recommend this License principally for works whose purpose is instruction or reference.

1. APPLICABILITY AND DEFINITIONS

This License applies to any manual or other work, in any medium, that contains a notice placed by the copyright holder saying it can be distributed under the terms of this License. Such a notice grants a world-wide, royalty-free license, unlimited in duration, to use that work under the conditions stated herein. The "Document", below, refers to any such manual or work. Any member of the public is a licensee, and is addressed as "you". You accept the license if you copy, modify or distribute the work in a way requiring permission under copyright law.

A "Modified Version" of the Document means any work containing the Document or a portion of it, either copied verbatim, or with modifications and/or translated into another language.

A "Secondary Section" is a named appendix or a front-matter section of the Document that deals exclusively with the relationship of the publishers or authors of the Document to the Document's overall subject (or to related matters) and contains nothing that could fall directly within that overall subject. (Thus, if the Document is in part a textbook of mathematics, a Secondary Section may not explain any mathematics.) The relationship could be a matter of historical connection with the subject or with related matters, or of legal, commercial, philosophical, ethical or political position regarding them.

The "Invariant Sections" are certain Secondary Sections whose titles are designated, as being those of Invariant Sections, in the notice that says that the Document is released under this License. If a section does not fit the above definition of Secondary then it is not allowed to be designated as Invariant. The Document may contain zero Invariant Sections. If the Document does not identify any Invariant Sections then there are none.

The "Cover Texts" are certain short passages of text that are listed, as Front-Cover Texts or Back-Cover Texts, in the notice that says that the Document is released under this License. A Front-Cover Text may be at most 5 words, and a Back-Cover Text may be at most 25 words.

A "Transparent" copy of the Document means a machine-readable copy, represented in a format whose specification is available to the general public, that is suitable for revising the document straightforwardly with generic text editors or (for images composed of pixels) generic paint programs or (for drawings) some widely available drawing editor, and that is suitable for input to text formatters or for automatic translation to a variety of formats suitable for input to text formatters. A copy made in an otherwise Transparent file format whose markup, or absence of markup, has been arranged to thwart or discourage subsequent modification by readers is not Transparent. An image format is not Transparent if used for any substantial amount of text. A copy that is not "Transparent" is called "Opaque".

Examples of suitable formats for Transparent copies include plain ASCII without markup, Texinfo input format, LaTeX input format, SGML or XML using a publicly available DTD, and standard-conforming simple HTML, PostScript or PDF designed for human modification. Examples of transparent image formats include PNG, XCF and JPG. Opaque formats include proprietary formats that can be read and edited only by proprietary word processors, SGML or XML for which the DTD and/or processing tools are not generally available, and the machine-generated HTML, PostScript or PDF produced by some word processors for output purposes only.

The "Title Page" means, for a printed book, the title page itself, plus such following pages as are needed to hold, legibly, the material this License requires to appear in the title page. For works in formats which do not have any title page as such, "Title Page" means the text near the most prominent appearance of the work's title, preceding the beginning of the body of the text.

The "publisher" means any person or entity that distributes copies of the Document to the public.

A section "Entitled XYZ" means a named subunit of the Document whose title either is precisely XYZ or contains XYZ in parentheses following text that translates XYZ in another language. (Here XYZ stands for a specific section name mentioned below, such as "Acknowledgements", "Dedications", "Endorsements", or "History".) To "Preserve the Title" of such a section when you modify the Document means that it remains a section "Entitled XYZ" according to this definition.

The Document may include Warranty Disclaimers next to the notice which states that this License applies to the Document. These Warranty Disclaimers are considered to be included by reference in this License, but only as regards disclaiming warranties: any other implication that these Warranty Disclaimers may have is void and has no effect on the meaning of this License.

2. VERBATIM COPYING

You may copy and distribute the Document in any medium, either commercially or noncommercially, provided that this License, the copyright notices, and the license notice saying this License applies to the Document are reproduced in all copies, and that you add no other conditions whatsoever to those of this License. You may not use technical measures to obstruct or control the reading or further copying of the copies you make or distribute. However, you may accept compensation in exchange for copies. If you distribute a large enough number of copies you must also follow the conditions in section 3.

You may also lend copies, under the same conditions stated above, and you may publicly display copies.

3. COPYING IN QUANTITY

If you publish printed copies (or copies in media that commonly have printed covers) of the Document, numbering more than 100, and the Document's license notice requires Cover Texts, you must enclose the copies in covers that carry, clearly and legibly, all these Cover Texts: Front-Cover Texts on the front cover, and Back-Cover Texts on the back cover. Both covers must also clearly and legibly identify you as the publisher of these copies. The front cover must present the full title with all words of the title equally prominent and visible. You may add other material on the covers in addition. Copying with changes limited to the covers, as long as they preserve the title of the Document and satisfy these conditions, can be treated as verbatim copying in other respects.

If the required texts for either cover are too voluminous to fit legibly, you should put the first ones listed (as many as fit reasonably) on the actual cover, and continue the rest onto adjacent pages.

If you publish or distribute Opaque copies of the Document numbering more than 100, you must either include a machine-readable Transparent copy along with each Opaque copy, or state in or with each Opaque copy a computer-network location from which the general network-using public has access to download using public-standard network protocols a complete Transparent copy of the Document, free of added material. If you use the latter option, you must take reasonably prudent steps, when you begin distribution of Opaque copies in quantity, to ensure that this Transparent copy will remain thus accessible at the stated location until at least one year after the last time you distribute an Opaque copy (directly or through your agents or retailers) of that edition to the public.

It is requested, but not required, that you contact the authors of the Document well before redistributing any large number of copies, to give them a chance to provide you with an updated version of the Document.

4. MODIFICATIONS

You may copy and distribute a Modified Version of the Document under the conditions of sections 2 and 3 above, provided that you release the Modified Version under precisely this License, with the Modified Version filling the role of the Document, thus licensing distribution and modification of the Modified Version to whoever possesses a copy of it. In addition, you must do these things in the Modified Version:

* A. Use in the Title Page (and on the covers, if any) a title distinct from that of the Document, and from those of previous versions (which should, if there were any, be listed in the History section of the Document). You may use the same title as a previous version if the original publisher of that version gives permission.

* B. List on the Title Page, as authors, one or more persons or entities responsible for authorship of the modifications in the Modified Version, together with at least five of the principal authors of the Document (all of its principal authors, if it has fewer than five), unless they release you from this requirement.
* C. State on the Title page the name of the publisher of the Modified Version, as the publisher.
* D. Preserve all the copyright notices of the Document.
* E. Add an appropriate copyright notice for your modifications adjacent to the other copyright notices.
* F. Include, immediately after the copyright notices, a license notice giving the public permission to use the Modified Version under the terms of this License, in the form shown in the Addendum below.
* G. Preserve in that license notice the full lists of Invariant Sections and required Cover Texts given in the Document's license notice.
* H. Include an unaltered copy of this License.
* I. Preserve the section Entitled "History", Preserve its Title, and add to it an item stating at least the title, year, new authors, and publisher of the Modified Version as given on the Title Page. If there is no section Entitled "History" in the Document, create one stating the title, year, authors, and publisher of the Document as given on its Title Page, then add an item describing the Modified Version as stated in the previous sentence.
* J. Preserve the network location, if any, given in the Document for public access to a Transparent copy of the Document, and likewise the network locations given in the Document for previous versions it was based on. These may be placed in the "History" section. You may omit a network location for a work that was published at least four years before the Document itself, or if the original publisher of the version it refers to gives permission.
* K. For any section Entitled "Acknowledgements" or "Dedications", Preserve the Title of the section, and preserve in the section all the substance and tone of each of the contributor acknowledgements and/or dedications given therein.
* L. Preserve all the Invariant Sections of the Document, unaltered in their text and in their titles. Section numbers or the equivalent are not considered part of the section titles.
* M. Delete any section Entitled "Endorsements". Such a section may not be included in the Modified Version.
* N. Do not retitle any existing section to be Entitled "Endorsements" or to conflict in title with any Invariant Section.
* O. Preserve any Warranty Disclaimers.

If the Modified Version includes new front-matter sections or appendices that qualify as Secondary Sections and contain no material copied from the Document, you may at your option designate some or all of these sections as invariant. To do this, add their titles to the list of Invariant Sections in the Modified Version's license notice. These titles must be distinct from any other section titles.

You may add a section Entitled "Endorsements", provided it contains nothing but endorsements of your Modified Version by various parties—for example, statements of peer review or that the text has been approved by an organization as the authoritative definition of a standard.

You may add a passage of up to five words as a Front-Cover Text, and a passage of up to 25 words as a Back-Cover Text, to the end of the list of Cover Texts in the Modified Version. Only one passage of Front-Cover Text and one of Back-Cover Text may be added by (or through arrangements made by) any one entity. If the Document already includes a cover text for the same cover, previously added by you or by arrangement made by the same entity you are acting on behalf of, you may not add another; but you may replace the old one, on explicit permission from the previous publisher that added the old one.

The author(s) and publisher(s) of the Document do not by this License give permission to use their names for publicity for or to assert or imply endorsement of any Modified Version.

5. COMBINING DOCUMENTS

You may combine the Document with other documents released under this License, under the terms defined in section 4 above for modified versions, provided that you include in the combination all of the Invariant Sections of all of the original documents, unmodified, and list them all as Invariant Sections of your combined work in its license notice, and that you preserve all their Warranty Disclaimers.

The combined work need only contain one copy of this License, and multiple identical Invariant Sections may be replaced with a single copy. If there are multiple Invariant Sections with the same name but different contents, make the title of each such section unique by adding at the end of it, in parentheses, the name of the original author or publisher of that section if known, or else a unique number. Make the same adjustment to the section titles in the list of Invariant Sections in the license notice of the combined work.

In the combination, you must combine any sections Entitled "History" in the various original documents, forming one section Entitled "History"; likewise combine any sections Entitled "Acknowledgements", and any sections Entitled "Dedications". You must delete all sections Entitled "Endorsements".

6. COLLECTIONS OF DOCUMENTS

You may make a collection consisting of the Document and other documents released under this License, and replace the individual copies of this License in the various documents with a single copy that is included in the collection, provided that you follow the rules of this License for verbatim copying of each of the documents in all other respects.

You may extract a single document from such a collection, and distribute it individually under this License, provided you insert a copy of this License into the extracted document, and follow this License in all other respects regarding verbatim copying of that document.

7. AGGREGATION WITH INDEPENDENT WORKS

A compilation of the Document or its derivatives with other separate and independent documents or works, in or on a volume of a storage or distribution medium, is called an "aggregate" if the copyright resulting from the compilation is not used to limit the legal rights of the compilation's users beyond what the individual works permit. When the Document is included in an aggregate, this License does not apply to the other works in the aggregate which are not themselves derivative works of the Document.

If the Cover Text requirement of section 3 is applicable to these copies of the Document, then if the Document is less than one half of the entire aggregate, the Document's Cover Texts may be placed on covers that bracket the Document within the aggregate, or the electronic equivalent of covers if the Document is in electronic form. Otherwise they must appear on printed covers that bracket the whole aggregate.

8. TRANSLATION

Translation is considered a kind of modification, so you may distribute translations of the Document under the terms of section 4. Replacing Invariant Sections with translations requires special permission from their copyright holders, but you may include translations of some or all Invariant Sections in addition to the original versions of these Invariant Sections. You may include a translation of this License, and all the license notices in the Document, and any Warranty Disclaimers, provided that you also include the original English version of this License and the original versions of those notices and disclaimers. In case of a disagreement between the translation and the original version of this License or a notice or disclaimer, the original version will prevail.

If a section in the Document is Entitled "Acknowledgements", "Dedications", or "History", the requirement (section 4) to Preserve its Title (section 1) will typically require changing the actual title.

9. TERMINATION

You may not copy, modify, sublicense, or distribute the Document except as expressly provided under this License. Any attempt otherwise to copy, modify, sublicense, or distribute it is void, and will automatically terminate your rights under this License.

However, if you cease all violation of this License, then your license from a particular copyright holder is reinstated (a) provisionally, unless and until the copyright holder explicitly and finally terminates your license, and (b) permanently, if the copyright holder fails to notify you of the violation by some reasonable means prior to 60 days after the cessation.

Moreover, your license from a particular copyright holder is reinstated permanently if the copyright holder notifies you of the violation by some reasonable means, this is the first time you have received notice of violation of this License (for any work) from that copyright holder, and you cure the violation prior to 30 days after your receipt of the notice.

Termination of your rights under this section does not terminate the licenses of parties who have received copies or rights from you under this License. If your rights have been terminated and not permanently reinstated, receipt of a copy of some or all of the same material does not give you any rights to use it.

10. FUTURE REVISIONS OF THIS LICENSE

The Free Software Foundation may publish new, revised versions of the GNU Free Documentation License from time to time. Such new versions will be similar in spirit to the present version, but may differ in detail to address new problems or concerns. See http://www.gnu.org/copyleft/.

Each version of the License is given a distinguishing version number. If the Document specifies that a particular numbered version of this License "or any later version" applies to it, you have the option of following the terms and conditions either of that specified version or of any later version that has been published (not as a draft) by the Free Software Foundation. If the Document does not specify a version number of this License, you may choose any version ever published (not as a draft) by the Free Software Foundation. If the Document specifies that a proxy can decide which future versions of this License can be used, that proxy's public statement of acceptance of a version permanently authorizes you to choose that version for the Document.

11. RELICENSING

"Massive Multiauthor Collaboration Site" (or "MMC Site") means any World Wide Web server that publishes copyrightable works and also provides prominent facilities for anybody to edit those works. A public wiki that anybody can edit is an example of such a server. A "Massive Multiauthor Collaboration" (or "MMC") contained in the site means any set of copyrightable works thus published on the MMC site.

"CC-BY-SA" means the Creative Commons Attribution-Share Alike 3.0 license published by Creative Commons Corporation, a not-for-profit corporation with a principal place of business in San Francisco, California, as well as future copyleft versions of that license published by that same organization.

"Incorporate" means to publish or republish a Document, in whole or in part, as part of another Document.

An MMC is "eligible for relicensing" if it is licensed under this License, and if all works that were first published under this License somewhere other than this MMC, and subsequently incorporated in whole or in part into the MMC, (1) had no cover texts or invariant sections, and (2) were thus incorporated prior to November 1, 2008.

The operator of an MMC Site may republish an MMC contained in the site under CC-BY-SA on the same site at any time before August 1, 2009, provided the MMC is eligible for relicensing.

Index

Symbols

A

G

H

I

J

K

L

M

W

X

Y

Z

www.ingramcontent.com/pod-product-compliance
Lightning Source LLC
LaVergne TN
LVHW060134070326
832902LV00018B/2790
* 9 7 8 9 8 8 8 4 0 6 1 7 3 *